ACE G... ...ook

wkc
Kent College

...on or before the date last
CONTENT... ...time is granted

Fifth edition

© 2001 Published by the
Advisory Centre for Education
1C Aberdeen Studios, 22 Highbury Grove,
London N5 2DQ

Designed by Sally and Richard Doust.
Printed by Albert Gait, Castle Press, Grimsby.

ISBN: 1 870672 90 9

Abbreviations and legal references

References to Acts are abbreviated so S4 EA96
refers to Section 4 of the Education Act 1996;
Para.9 Sched.2 EA97 refers to Paragraph 9 of
Schedule 2 to the Education Act 1997.
SSFA = School Standards and Framework Act
Reg/SI = Regulation or Statutory Instrument
COP= Code of Practice
LEA = local education authority
DfEE = Department for Education and
Employment
NAW = National Assembly of Wales

This reference book covers the law in England
and Wales; while the statute for England and
Wales is the same, Welsh guidance and
Regulations may differ from those in Engla...
and we give separate references where po...

CONTENTS

The evolution of governing bodies

The school governor's role is as old as schools themselves. Long before there was a system of public education, when schooling for all was a dream still centuries away, people accepted that education was important in a special way to the whole community. Schools would produce professionally qualified people to teach our children, heal our diseases, solemnise our marriages, and write our wills. Above all they would shape people's values and opinions, and influence how they behaved towards each other. School governors were always lay people, representing the public in a service whose quality was of public concern, bringing common sense, everyday experience, and the light of ordinariness to bear on expert decisions. When schooling became a public service spending public money, this was another compelling reason for community representation.

Early days of public education

At the beginning of Queen Victoria's reign, there was a variety of schools for older pupils established by individuals, private concerns, guilds and charities. They all had trustees of some kind. Elementary education, as it was then called, was provided mainly by the churches, who were finding it increasingly difficult to meet the growing demand from their limited financial resources. Thus in 1830 the first government grants were voted by Parliament to assist the provision of schools by religious bodies. It was a condition of this aid that the schools were open to inspection and had local managing boards to oversee their use of public funds.

The provision made by the churches remained patchy. As the century wore on, the development of industry and commerce and the shifts of population created a demand for more organised provision of schooling. The new employers wanted workers who were literate, while universal suffrage also demanded a literate electorate.

In 1870, the **Forster Education Act** established a nationwide system of public elementary education, with locally elected boards charged to build schools and raise local rates for the purpose where church provision was insufficient. These public elementary schools also had to have boards of managers.

The next milestone was 1902. The Education Act of that year established Local Education Authorities (LEAs) which took over the running costs of the schools provided by the churches as well as those built since 1870 by the school boards. These new authorities were responsible for both elementary and secondary education; there was no universal entitlement to education and it was not free, though secondary schools established by county councils under that Act awarded scholarships to a proportion of pupils. The law provided that secondary schools should have governors and primary schools managers. This difference in nomenclature remained until 1980, though the functions were virtually the same.

The Education Act 1944

Towards the end of the Second World War, there was a long and widespread consultation about a new framework for public education and the **Education Act 1944** (the Butler Act) was introduced with the support of all parties and the churches. It gave all children the right to free primary and secondary schooling to 15 (later 16), and gave LEAs not only the duty but also the power to provide education and ancillary services for all age groups. The voluntary (mainly church) schools were integrated into this system, though they retained the right to offer education of a denominational character. Unless they chose to become 'controlled' schools (which many without adequate independent funds opted for), they also had responsibility for keeping the external fabric of the buildings in good repair, a duty matched by a degree of independence.

Again the law required primary schools to have managers and secondary schools to have governors, appointed by the LEA in county schools and by the foundation in voluntary-aided schools. No real guidance was given about what sort of people should be appointed; functions were left to be set out in local Instruments and Articles with the help of a model issued by the Ministry of Education in 1945. This model, followed in most areas, gave managers and governors the care of the premises, a share in budgeting for the school and appointing its head and staff (in voluntary-aided schools the governors employ all staff), and the 'general direction' of its conduct and curriculum. Schools were allowed to be grouped for the purpose.

1945-65: Twenty years of unclaimed responsibility

With honourable exceptions, the system of school governance did not represent a very lively force in the schooling system. In voluntary-aided schools, the managers and governors had more responsibility and probably more direct concern, but in county schools as a whole the reality of the 1944 vision of local oversight ranged from the remote to the perfunctory. The provision for grouping was widely abused: many primary schools were managed in large groups and in extreme cases all the schools in an LEA area were governed by one group of people, a sub-committee of the local council. Party political influence was dominant in many areas. Most important decisions about resources and organisation were made at town or county hall. Increasingly, professionals enjoyed considerable independence in forming and delivering the curriculum.

It was a time of rapid growth in the service to repair the ravages and neglect of the war years. Large numbers of new teachers were trained. There was, relatively speaking, plenty of money, and a good deal of innovation and experiment in the classroom. Much of this was exciting and well-directed, but towards the end of the period there was concern about the perceived freedom of teachers to depart from familiar and well-understood methods and about the lack of accountability of schools. This concern reflected the fact that many parents were unable to relate what went on in the classroom to the learning experience of their own schooldays, and few schools at the time saw any reason to explain and demonstrate what they were doing. School governors on the whole, because of the way they were organised and the kind of people who were appointed to the task, were not equipped to bridge the gap in public understanding or to influence the policies of schools towards better communication. It is important to understand these trends as background to the changes which have now come about.

1965-77: Stirrings of change

There were few visible changes during these years but under the surface there were many indications of changing perceptions, growing concern, and new thinking which were to form the basis of a totally different structure of school government.

Research was increasingly stressing the importance of home support to pupils and community support for schools. The parent teacher association (PTA) movement was developing, and new organisations like the Advisory Centre for Education (ACE) and the Campaign for the Advancement of State Education (CASE) were beginning to campaign for a system more responsive to parents and community and, increasingly, a reform of school government. Under these influences some LEAs began to introduce, at least on a token scale, representation of parents and teachers on school governing bodies. By 1975, a majority had moved in this direction. Some also provided for co-opted governors from the local community and a handful had even voluntarily renounced their own majority.

A Labour Government in 1975 appointed a committee under the chairmanship of Tom (later Lord) Taylor to look into the government of schools – and indeed the whole question of schools' relations with parents and the community. Labour Prime Minister James Callaghan, in a speech in 1976, urged a national debate on the accountability of schools. He stressed particularly the relevance of education and its relation to the world of work; a series of regional conferences took up this theme in the so-called 'Great Debate'. In 1977, the Taylor Committee published its report *A New Partnership for our Schools*, which recommended that governing bodies be liberated from LEA domination and constructed on the basis of equal partnership of LEA, parents, teachers, and community, sharing in all aspects of school life and work. Governors were to determine curriculum policy; have an equal say in the appointment of heads in county schools and retain total responsibility in voluntary-aided schools; assume overall responsibility for staff appointments even if they chose to delegate it; share in budget decisions; and ensure that the school communicated effectively with parents and others in the school community. Governors were also to be trained. It was nearly ten years before these recommendations found their way onto the statute book in the form of the **Education Act 1986**, a fact which probably owed something to the strong opposition of some teachers' unions to any interference by lay people in the school curriculum.

Governors from the community

As well as containing provisions on parental choice of school and the information to be given by schools to parents, the **Education Act 1980** tentatively edged towards community-based governing bodies. It required all schools to have at least two governors representing parents and one or two (depending on the size of the school) representing teachers. It did not prescribe how other governors were to be chosen, continuing to allow LEAs to retain a majority in county schools; most did so.

The **Education Act 1986**, however, implemented almost in its entirety the recommendations of the 1977 Taylor Report. In county schools, parents were to have equal representations with LEAs (two to five members each); between three and six members were to be co-opted from the community; and teachers, as before, were to have one or two representatives. In voluntary-aided schools there was no advance on the 1980 provisions, with two parents as governors in all sizes of school, with the majority of governors appointed by the foundation. The 1986 Act established a sharing role for governors in all aspects of school policy, made them accountable to parents through an annual report and an annual meeting, and provided for them to have training. Meanwhile, the **Education Act 1981** on special education gave governors a specific responsibility to see that special needs were identified and met in their school.

Schools in the market-place

The **Education Reform Act 1988** cannot be seen simply as a continuation of the series. It went far beyond the representation of different interests in school decision-making and the accountability of schools to parents. It was the outcome of a quite separate process of political thought, was more contentious, and amounted to the creation of an 'education market' in which schools competed for parental custom. They were required to offer a more standard product (in the form of a centrally determined National Curriculum) against which pupils were to be regularly tested. Test results enabled parents to judge schools' performance. Open enrolment up to nationally determined standard numbers encouraged parental choice, while formula funding related budgets directly to the number of pupils which schools recruited. Meanwhile, new forms of competition within state education were provided by the creation of city technology colleges (CTCs), supported by central government and industry, and grant-maintained (GM) schools, funded direct by government.

Changing the balance of power

Although the 1988 Act amended and repealed very little of the legislation which preceded it, that Act and its 1992 and 1993 sequels, altered in fundamental ways the balance of power in education in favour of central government on the one hand and individual schools on the other, significantly reducing local authority involvement. The National Curriculum, delivered and custom-finished by the school, largely removed the LEA's direct responsibility for pupils' learning, though the LEA retained an overall responsibility for the effectiveness of its schools as a whole. Open enrolment and the grant-maintained option combined to undermine its strategic role. Local management of schools (LMS) removed from the LEA much of the discretion it once had to direct resources according to need, and its control over staffing levels, spending priorities and the nuts-and-bolts of curriculum delivery. Its role in the inspection of schools was changed radically by the **Education (Schools) Act 1992**, which established private inspection teams able to bid to the Office for Standards in Education (Ofsted) for regular inspections of schools. Increasingly, most LEA services instead of being routinely provided to schools, would be offered for schools to buy.

The creation of Ofsted and the introduction of regular school inspections under its auspices paved the way for severe measures to be introduced to take over and, if necessary, close schools which fail to come up to standard. These were contained in the **Education Act 1993**, which also set up the Funding Agency for Schools appointed by central government to administer the grant-maintained sector. The Agency shared with, and the Government hoped, would take over, strategic powers of the LEA, if and when the number of grant-maintained schools in an area reached stipulated proportions of the total. The agencies would then be able to bring about changes of character in grant-maintained schools and establish new ones. The total effect could have been to divide the control of education in completely new ways.

Pause for breath

The **Education Act of 1996** consolidated all the education law still in force up to and including 1993. This mammoth work will be very helpful to governors, since the outburst of legislation in the 'eighties and 'nineties has left many uncertain about what if any earlier law remained in force.

The Education Act 1997

This was the last legislation to be introduced by the fourth Conservative administration, and its more controversial elements were somewhat reduced in horse-trading with the opposition parties to get it passed before the election. (Some of its provisions were repeated with variations in the 1998 Act.) It provided for LEAs, as well as schools, to be Ofsted-inspected. It established base-line assessments for all children entering primary school. It replaced SCAA and the NCVQ with a new body called the Qualifications and Curriculum Authority. Finally it allowed a school to exchange home-school agreements with parents on admission (since overtaken by the 1998 Act). The Act's main significance for governors was that it required them to establish, after consulting parents, general principles of behaviour to guide headteachers in maintaining discipline (Ss1 – 3). It also gave teachers the right to restrain a pupil in a preventive sense, stopping short of corporal punishment (S4), allowed detention without parental consent on 24 hours' notice and subject to safeguards (S5), and changed some of the provisions on exclusion. The Act also provided for governors to set school performance targets (S19).

Legislation under Labour

The **School Standards and Framework Act 1998**, (SSFA) the first of a Labour Government, established a new framework for schools in which county schools became community schools and grant-maintained schools became foundation schools. It also brought in some changes in the composition of governing bodies with additional parent governors, LEA governors in all types of school, representation of support staff, and some flexibility on governing body size (S36 and Sched.10). It gave the Secretary of State power to limit infant class sizes (Ss1 – 4); and provided for education action zones to be established in areas with entrenched education problems (Ss10 – 13) with a local forum in each such zone to work co-operatively for improvement. Teachers' pay and conditions could be varied in these areas and the National Curriculum disapplied.

Some of the status lost to LEAs in previous legislation was restored, in that they were given a clear duty to promote high standards, and were required to produce educational development plans, to make adequate provision for pre-school children and establish early years partnerships. They were given various powers of intervention in schools causing concern (like the DfEE they may appoint additional governors and may also remove local management powers).

The Act abolished Articles of Government (but not Instruments which deal with membership), leaving governing bodies' powers and procedures to be included in legislation or statutory regulations. Regulations and Codes of Practice brought out following the Act now determine the business of governing bodies and try to set some boundaries between the role of head, governing bodies and LEAs. As well as the **School Government Regulations** which detail the rules for how meetings are run and committees set up, the **Education (School Government) (Terms of Reference) Regulations** have clarified the boundaries between governing bodies and headteachers. They state that the governing body should take a strategic role in the running of the school. The concept of the governing body as a "critical friend" to the headteacher is also introduced into the regulations.

The SSFA spelled out governors' powers and duties including a new responsibility for promoting high standards and educational achievement (S38) - activities such as target setting and performance management are now routine duties for governing bodies. Nutritional standards were reintroduced for school lunches and, where a school contracts the meals, the governing body became responsible for compliance.

As well as reinforcing the duty to draw up a discipline statement after consultation with parents, this Act imposed a new duty to establish a complaints procedure although regulations which would have set out standard procedures were abandoned following complaints of too much bureaucracy from heads. Among other new powers introduced was the right (with permission) for community schools to buy, invest, and enter into contracts, though not with teachers.

The Act repeated most of the provisions in the 1997 Act on exclusion but among the more significant changes was the right for parents to make oral representations to a governors' meeting. Governors were no longer able to sit on the independent appeal committee hearing appeals against exclusions from their own school, as was the case for grant-maintained and voluntary aided schools. However, LEAs lost the power to reinstate pupils permanently excluded from community and controlled schools.

School admissions became the subject of local consultation with an adjudicator to settle disputes but voluntary schools retained their right to give preference to families of their faith. Selection by ability, even partial selection, was only allowed in existing selective schools and the adjudicator was given powers to end such selection. But selection of up to ten per cent by aptitude was permitted. In existing wholly selective schools a change of status may be brought about by parental ballot although the rules governing this have made it almost impossible for parents to achieve a ballot in many areas.

It is clear that the legislation of the 1990s, far from diminishing the responsibilities given to governors in 1986 and 1988, has reinforced their central strategic role, and in particular, has brought their duties closer to many areas of professional sensitivity.

Changes affecting the wider world also affect governors' responsibilities. New equal opportunities legislation in particular will mean new duties: the **Race Relations Amendment Act 2000** requires governing bodies to promote good race relations; provision of education is to be brought under disability discrimination law; and the **Human Rights Act 1998** is beginning to affect education practice and policies. While the full implications of the HRA are as yet uncertain, it is clear that schools will need to review their policies and practices to comply with the principles of the Act.

The **Local Government Act 2000** gave parent governors the right to elect from among their number, representatives (PGRs) to represent the views of parents on LEA education committees. To date some 326 PGRs have been elected for terms of up to four years.

Devolution has meant that different rules and good practice are now being introduced in Wales. While many areas of education law still rely on regulations and guidance applying to both England and Wales, this handbook includes those which have been introduced by the National Assembly since its inception.

School governors: past, present and future

School government has moved rapidly from the viewing platform somewhere above the action, poised to play a more active part only in moments of crisis. The first move was to a central place in the formulation of school policy but still within a cohesive and, in the last resort, protective and directive local service. All too rapidly for most governors, this role has again changed. Much of the local infra-structure has been dismantled and schools are left to find their position in the market place, managing their own money, appointing their own staff, looking after their premises, determining in detail their learning programmes, formulating action plans after inspections, and deciding what services they need to buy in. They also have many detailed obligations to inform (but not necessarily consult) parents and some big choices to make about status and character.

Governors of all types of schools clearly need much guidance and support in playing their part in this new system. They need to have precise information about their duties. They need to be shown good ways of getting to know their schools and establishing friendly relationships with teachers especially as the duties of governors increasingly bring them up against areas of great teacher sensitivity. They often want help in working out clear guidelines to ensure that they share genuinely in decision-making, yet avoid conflict with headteachers. They must have assistance in team-building, sharing out the work so that they can operate efficiently, with space for everyone to contribute with mutual trust. Finally, they need the stimulation of debate within their school and with other schools about the values, principles and good practices if, amid all the talk of promotion and marketing individual schools, education is to remain a public service based on justice for children.

We hope this handbook will help in all these ways.

Joan Sallis

School Government

School governors are not new: they have existed for about 600 years and their role has not changed as much as people might imagine. Long before there was schooling for all children, people accepted that the community had some responsibility for a service whose quality nevertheless affected everybody. What is new is the higher profile of governing bodies resulting from the demand for more accountability within the education service. To help governing bodies meet these greater expectations, we begin this governors' guide with the framework for school government.

The Framework – Part 1

The Instrument of Government

The **School Standards and Framework Act 1998** introduced changes to the categories of schools and their governing bodies. The composition of governing bodies changed to give more parent governors in most types of school and introduce LEA governors on foundation (former grant-maintained schools). The make-up of the governing body is set out in the school's Instrument of Government(S37 SSFA).

Articles of Government which set out the powers and duties of the governing body have been replaced by statute and regulations (**Education (School Government) (England) Regulations 1999 SI 2163** (as amended) and **Education(School Government) (Wales) Regulations 1999 SI 2242)** (similar amendments in the pipeline for Wales).

Here we set out the rules governing membership of governing bodies and the way the governing body conducts its business.

Membership of governing bodies

Since September 1999 all schools have had separate governing bodies and in all schools the headteacher is a governor unless at any time s/he decides otherwise. In all primary schools where there is a minor authority (district or parish council) one co-option must go to a nominee of that authority. In cases where there is more than one such authority the governors choose which should be represented. Extra co-options are allowed in certain special cases.

Types of governor

Parent governors: elected by and from the parents of the school by secret ballot. Candidates may nominate themselves or be nominated by another parent. The 'first past the post' rule applies. Parent governors may serve their full term if they wish even if their last child leaves the school before the four years have expired.

Teacher governors: also elected by secret ballot from and by the whole teaching staff. They have to stop being governors when they cease to be employed at the school. Teachers and other staff cannot be co-opted to the governing body in their own school.

Staff governors: all but the smallest schools will have a staff governor representing and elected by support staff.

LEA governors: appointed by LEA councillors. These governors may be selected on political grounds with political parties nominating people, possibly local councillors, in proportion to their strength on the council. In other areas the LEA will advertise for interested local people to put themselves forward for these positions.

Foundation governors: are appointed to help preserve and develop the religious character of schools which have such a character or, where the school has a trust deed, they are appointed to secure that the school is conducted in accordance with the deed.

Co-opted governors: chosen by other governors from the wider community, including business. In Wales, the governing body must appoint a governor who is a member of the local community if the community is under-represented among co-opted governors on the governing body.

Additional co-opted governors: covers those governors nominated by minor authorities and those nominated by and from any one or more of a school's sponsors. Where a school is participating in an education action zone, the governing body may decide to include an additional co-opted governor nominated by the zone's education action forum.

Partnership governors: exist only at foundation and foundation special schools which do not have a foundation or trustees. They must be members of the community served by the school who are committed to the good government and success of the school. Appointed by the governing body which seeks nominations for them through advertising, they cannot be parents of pupils at the school, staff or teachers at the school or LEA. (Sched.9 SSFA)

Elections

Teacher governors, staff governors and parent governors are elected to the governing body. Any election which is contested is held by secret ballot. For community, community special or voluntary controlled schools, the LEA is responsible for the election although this may be delegated to the headteacher of the school; the governing body is responsible for elections in voluntary aided, foundation or foundation special schools but may delegate authority to the LEA if it agrees.

In some situations, parent governors may be appointed by the governing body rather than elected - for example where there are fewer parents standing for election than there are vacancies.

The LEA or governors have overall responsibility for elections although they may delegate certain matters to the headteacher. They must, however, determine for the purposes of the election if someone is a parent of a registered pupil and so eligible to be a parent governor, and if someone is eligible to be elected as a teacher governor or staff governor.(**Sched. 4 Education (School Government) England Regs 1999 and Sched. 5 Education (School Government) Wales Regs 1999**).

Who can vote?

Every parent must be given the opportunity to vote. Parents may vote by post or, if they prefer, return the ballot paper via a registered pupil at the school. In cases where a school does not know the address of a parent with whom the pupil does not live, it should make the resident parent aware that the non-resident parent is entitled to be involved in the child's education.

The LEA (community and VC schools) or governing body (VA and foundation) must ensure that every person who is known to them to be a parent of a registered pupil at the school is informed of the vacancy and of their right both to stand as a candidate and to vote in the election. **S576 EA96** defines a parent as:

- All natural parents, whether they are married or not
- Any person who, although not a natural parent, has parental responsibility* for a child or young person
- Any person who, although not a natural parent, has care of a child or young person.

* Parental responsibility is defined by the **Children Act 1989** and includes relatives or friends, such as step-parents, who have obtained from the courts a residence order, been appointed a guardian, named in an emergency protection order or have adopted a child. Parents who have divorced keep parental responsibility, even when their child does not live with them.

Term of Office

Governors may hold office for a term of not more than four years, unless they hold office ex officio, such as the headteacher. They may resign office at any time, or be disqualified during their period of office or may be elected or appointed for a further term. Disqualifications prevent people holding or continuing to hold office in a range of circumstances including those relating to bankruptcy, mental health disorder, and criminal convictions. (*See para 4* **non attendance** *below.*)

Composition of governing bodies

The following sets out the composition of governing bodies as set out by **Sched.9 SSFA**:

Primary Schools

A. COMMUNITY SCHOOL*
4 or 5 parent governors
3 or 4 LEA governors
1 or 2 teacher governors
1 support staff governor
3 or 4 co-opted governors

B. COMMUNITY SCHOOL UNDER 100 PUPILS
3 parent governors
2 LEA governors
1 teacher governor
1 support staff governor (optional)
2 co-opted governors
(these smaller schools can choose between models A and B)

C. COMMUNITY SPECIAL SCHOOL
May choose between A and B regardless of size. One co-opted governor to be replaced in a hospital school by a representative of the Health Authority or Trust and in any other school by a representative of the appropriate voluntary organisation.

D. FOUNDATION SCHOOL*
5 or 6 parent governors
2 LEA governors
1 teacher governor
1 staff governor
3 or 4 foundation governors
1 co-opted governor

E. FOUNDATION SCHOOL UNDER 100 PUPILS
4 parent governors
2 LEA governors
1 teacher governor
1 staff governor (optional)
2 foundation governors
1 co-opted governor
(can choose between models D and E)

F. VOLUNTARY CONTROLLED SCHOOL*
4 or 5 parent governors
3 LEA governors
1 teacher governor
1 staff governor
3 or 4 foundation governors
1 co-opted governor

G. VOLUNTARY CONTROLLED SCHOOL UNDER 100 PUPILS
3 parent governors
2 LEA governors
1 teacher governor
1 staff governor (optional)
2 foundation governors
1 co-opted governor
(can choose between models F and G)

H. VOLUNTARY AIDED SCHOOL*

1 or 2 parent governors
1 or 2 LEA governors
1 teacher governor
1 staff governor
Sufficient foundation governors to give a majority of 2 overall, at least 2 of them current parents.

I. VOLUNTARY AIDED PRIMARY SCHOOL UNDER 100 PUPILS

1 parent governor
1 LEA governor
1 teacher governor
1 staff governor (optional)
Sufficient foundation governors to give a majority of 2 overall, at least 2 of them current parents.

Secondary Schools

J. COMMUNITY SCHOOL

6 parent governors
5 LEA governors
2 teacher governors
1 staff governor
5 co-opted governors

K. COMMUNITY SCHOOL UNDER 600 PUPILS

5 parent governors
4 LEA governors
2 teacher governors
1 staff governor
4 co-opted governors
(can choose between models J and K)

L. FOUNDATION SCHOOL

7 parent governors
2 LEA governors
2 teacher governors
1 staff governor
5 foundation governors
2 co-opted governors

M. FOUNDATION SCHOOL UNDER 600 PUPILS

6 parent governors
2 LEA governors
2 teacher governors
1 staff governor
4 foundation governors
2 co-opted governors
(can choose between models L and M)

N. VOLUNTARY CONTROLLED SCHOOL

6 parent governors
4 LEA governors
2 teacher governors
1 staff governor
5 foundation governors
2 co-opted governors

O. VOLUNTARY CONTROLLED SCHOOL UNDER 600 PUPILS

5 parent governors
3 LEA governors
2 teacher governors
1 staff governor
4 foundation governors
2 co-opted governors
(can choose between models N and O)

P. VOLUNTARY AIDED SCHOOL

3 parent governors
2 LEA governors
2 teacher governors
1 staff governor
Sufficient foundation governors to give a majority of 3 overall, at least 3 of them current parents.

Q. VOLUNTARY AIDED SCHOOL UNDER 600 PUPILS

2 parent governors
1 LEA governor
2 teacher governors
1 staff governor
Sufficient foundation governors to give a majority of two overall, at least 2 of them current parents.
(can choose between models P and Q)

*Where in any category there is a choice of numbers for more than one kind of governor, eg in a voluntary aided primary school 1 or 2 parent governors and 1 or 2 LEA governors, a governing body must choose the higher or lower option wholesale, ie no mixing and matching.

Rules and good practice for working together

1. Corporate responsibility All the responsibilities belong to the governing body working together. An individual governor has no authority, except the chair in certain special circumstances.

2. Meetings Governors of all but new schools must meet at least once a term. Notice of meetings must be given with the agenda, at least seven days in advance. Where an urgent matter arises which cannot await the next meeting the chair may call a special meeting at shorter notice. Any three governors may also request a special meeting and this request must be granted.

3. Chair and vice-chair Nominations for chair should be made in advance and included in the agenda. If no names are listed on the agenda, governors can put themselves forward for election at the meeting. Governors elect a chair and vice-chair annually by secret ballot at the first meeting of the school year. No employee or pupil of the school is eligible. If the chair resigns in mid-year a new chair must be elected. There is provision for removing a chair from office (*see 16 below*).

4. Non-attendance Apart from the head, those governors who, without permission, fail to attend meetings for six months may be disqualified. LEA governors or co-opted governors who have been disqualified may not be a governor of that school in the same category for 12 months following the disqualification. Any apologies from governors must be recorded in the minutes which must also state whether the governing body consented to an absence. A copy of the minutes must be sent to governors who send apologies.

5. The headteacher may be a full voting governor but has the option to decline membership by giving written notice. All headteachers, whether governors or not, have the right to attend meetings of the governing body and its committees *(but see 17 below)*.

6. Chair's power in emergency The chair may act on behalf of the governing body only in urgent matters where there is no time even to call a special meeting, and where the matter concerned is one which can legally be delegated *(see 10 below)*. An emergency would be a situation where delay would be seriously detrimental to the school or to a teacher, pupil or parent. He or she must report that action to the governing body.

7. Voting Governors make decisions by consensus or majority vote. They themselves normally decide whether on any matter a secret ballot is desirable, except that in the election of chair a secret ballot is required. Where on any matter voting is equal, the chair has a second or casting vote.

8. Quorum For a governing body to be able to make decisions, one third of the total membership, the latter calculated to include any vacancies, must be present. For certain decisions a higher quorum of two thirds of governors in post and eligible to vote is required (note the different basis of calculation). The most common circumstances are when any new governors are being selected (eg co-options), when the chair or a co-opted governor is being removed *(see 16 below)* or when power is being delegated to committees.

9. Committees Governors are required to set up a committee of at least three members to deal with staff dismissal* and either three or five members for pupil discipline. These are statutory committees and must be clerked. Neither a member of the governing body, nor the headteacher may be clerk. Committees, but not individuals, are allowed to appoint the clerk to a committee.

For staff dismissal there should also be a second or appeal committee of governors who are not on the first committee and who have had no prior involvement, and this should have no fewer members than the first committee. On pupil exclusions, governors may establish a pool of governors on whom they may call for individual exclusion panels.
*There is a concession on the size of first committees - intended especially for small schools - whereby the requirement on numbers is waived if fewer than six governors in all are eligible to serve, thus making it impossible to have two committees of three each. In these cases the governors decide on numbers, subject to the appeal committee having no fewer members than the first committee. In England amendment regulations (**SI 2000/1848**) make clear that a staff dismissal or dismissal appeal committee set up with two governor members cannot consider cases unless both members are present. (Similar amendment regulations are currently in draft form in Wales.)

Governors may set up such other committees as they think fit. Members of committees must be elected by the whole governing body, and membership, terms of reference and procedures must be reviewed annually.

10. Delegation Governors are allowed to delegate some functions to committees, but there are many exceptions which are given in full in your DfEE *Guide to the Law*. Among those which cannot be delegated are:
* alteration, discontinuance or change of category of the school;
* appointment of the chair and vice-chair and removing the chair;
* setting up committees, their members and delegating functions;
* formally submitting the budget to the LEA;
* co-opting or appointing new governors and removing governors;
* ratifying the appointment of new head and deputy;
* arranging dismissal appeals;
* approving the prospectus and annual report to parents and adopting and reviewing the home-school agreement;
* admission policies, collective worship, school discipline policies, sex education policies; charging policies, and the fixing of school terms, holidays and daily sessions;
* ceding functions to an Education Action Forum or reclaiming those functions.

The **Terms of Reference Regulations 2000** (**SI 2122 England; SI 195 Wales**) state that governing bodies may delegate some of their functions to the head while having regard for their strategic role and the head's role for internal school organisation.

11. Co-option to committees Non-governors may be co-opted to committees provided (a) that governors are always in a majority and (b) that no non-governor chairs a committee, and (c) that any co-option of a non-governor has been agreed by a vote of the whole governing body.

12. Chairing committees In general governors may elect chairs when they set up committees or leave the committee to choose its own. No employee of the school may chair a committee with delegated power.

13. Committee proceedings In general a committee meeting is conducted in the same way and under the same rules as a full governors' meeting though in a non-statutory committee the governing body may appoint one of its number as a clerk. Minutes must be kept and minutes and other papers made available to any interested party (excluding confidential items). Governors who are employed by the school may not take part in the discussion of the appraisal or pay of an individual, though they may participate in the establishment of policies on these matters.

14. Rescinding a resolution If a governing body rescinds a resolution they have made at a previous meeting, the item must have been on the circulated agenda as a specific item of business.

15. Co-options Teachers and other staff are no longer eligible to be co-opted to their own governing bodies. Co-opted members may not vote in new co-options.

16. Removal of governors Elected (ie parent, teacher and staff) governors cannot be removed, and LEA and foundation governors can only be removed (for good reason) by the appointing body. Co-opted governors can, however, be removed by resolution of the governing body to which they were co-opted or, in the case of additional co-opted governors, at the instigation of the appointing body (though in this case the removal must also have the support of the governing body). The procedure has to be spread over two meetings, with 14 days at least between. In each case the removal must be clearly included on the agenda as an item of business and a resolution must be passed. The governor or governors proposing the removal must give reasons, and the governor concerned must be given an opportunity to respond. If then a resolution to remove is confirmed (two-thirds quorum required), the governor is removed. Exactly the same procedure applies to the removal from office (but not in this case from the governing body) of the chair of governors.

In the case of chairs nominated by the Secretary of State for the governing body of a school in special measures, the duty of a governing body to elect a chair does not apply and the governing body cannot remove the Secretary of State's appointee (**School Government Amendment Regulations 2000** (England)). (Similar amendments in draft form in Wales)

17. Declaring an interest A governor may play no part in a discussion, or vote, if he or she has a conflict of interest or there is reasonable doubt about his or her ability to be impartial. This does not prevent anyone who is in a position to give evidence on a matter under discussion eg a witness to a disciplinary incident, being heard by the relevant committee, but if the circumstances are such that that person could not be impartial (eg in the case of a pupil, the parents of a victim) s/he takes no part in the decision. By the same token, the headteacher would not be present when the governors decide the outcome of an exclusion, though s/he would normally present the school's case beforehand.

Under finance regulations all schools must keep a register of any business interests of the governors and the headteacher. In these days of delegated budgets, schools wield much greater power to choose between providers of bought-in services from major capital projects to day-to-day services. It is important, therefore, that governors disclose any interest in matters under discussion as soon as possible and withdraw from the meeting during the discussion and should not vote on any question. Schedules to the school government regulations (**Sched.6** England; **Sched.7** Wales) detail the pecuniary interests which would restrict a governor's involvement in decision making.

Regulations prevent a member of the school staff being present at meetings considering the appointment of his or her successor (**School Government Amendment Regulations 2000** (England)) (Similar amendments in draft form in Wales).

18. Visitors to meetings The governing body decides which, if any, visitors it invites to its meetings, either on a regular basis or for a particular occasion.

19. Minutes and papers The governing body's agenda and related papers, and their minutes, once they have been approved in draft by the chair, may be seen on request by any member of the public as well as staff and parents. Excluded items will be those which the governing body itself has classified as confidential. Only the governing body can classify an item as confidential: this classification is intended primarily to protect the privacy of any individuals who are mentioned by name or can be easily identified. It should not be used excessively. **The Terms of Reference Regulations 2000** (England and Wales) require governors to be open about their decisions and actions; they should ensure that parents, in particular, know the issues which the governing body is considering and how they can see the minutes with the minimum of formality

LEAs have a right to inspect copies of governing body minutes, including those in draft (**Sched.11 SSFA** and **School Government Regulations** (England and Wales)).

20. Clerking The governing body appoints and if necessary dismisses its clerk. Neither the headteacher nor any member of the governing body may be clerk. This restriction does not apply to non-statutory committees.

Expenses and time off work

Governing bodies may reimburse governors for expenses (eg transport and subsistence) but not for loss of earnings or attendance allowances. The DfEE gives the following examples which allowances may be made for: childcare; care arrangements for dependent relatives; support for governors with special needs or English as a second language and telephone, photocopying and stationery charges. The law includes governors among those groups entitled to take reasonable time off work to carry out their duties. Employees have to agree with employers what is reasonable but they can complain to an industrial tribunal if the employer unreasonable refuses them time off. Employers do not have to pay governors for time off although some do.

Governor training

LEAs provide free training in some authorities; in others the governing body will have to buy in training from their LEA or other providers. Concern that governors are reluctant to use school budgets for their own expenses or training has led to calls for earmarked funding and, for the 1999/2000 financial year, the Government ring fenced five per cent of the Standards Fund School Improvement Grant specifically for training school governors.

Election to LEA committees

All local authorities must have held elections and appoint parent governor representatives to their committees dealing with education (**S9 SSFA**). Changes to local government means that parent governor representatives are appointed to education overview and scrutiny committees established under the **Local Government Act 2000**.

All parent governors in schools maintained by the relevant LEA are eligible to vote by secret ballot in the elections for parent governor representatives in that area. Parent governors are eligible to stand as long as they have a child being educated by the LEA at the date of the election and they are not employees of the local authority or its schools, councillors of any local authority or already parent governor representatives in this or another authority so that their term of office would overlap with that of the vacancy. (The rules are different in the two smallest authorities: City of London and Isles of Scilly where parents vote and are eligible to stand even if their children are educated by other authorities.)

Candidates are responsible for preparing their own election addresses although the local authority will pay for printing and distribution. Campaigns should be non-political and local authorities may remove party political references in candidates' addresses.

Local authorities are responsible for making sure arrangements for an election are made whether it is contested or not. They are given some discretion on how many parent governor representatives to have; the method of voting; what to include on the ballot paper; how to publicise the election to those who can vote and stand, and on the term of office - although this must be between two and four years. Local authorities may organise elections so that different categories or type of school or different geographical areas are represented. The local authority must publish the results of the elections within one week.
Education (Parent Governor Representatives Regulations) (England) 2001 (SI 478); Education (Parent Governor Representatives(Wales) Regulations 1999 (SI 1900).

Role of the parent governor representative

The Government believes that giving a bigger say to parents on LEA committees will help raise standards. They ask parent governor representatives "to represent all parents on education policy formation and monitoring". Parent governor representatives will have the right to vote on any decision coming up in relevant committees which relate either to schools maintained by the local authority and/or pupils who attend LEA maintained schools or are educated by the local authority in some other way. They will also be allowed to vote on matters which affect how earmarked education funds are to be spent, deciding issues such as how much of the education budget should be devolved and the amount to be allocated to each of the four main areas which are centrally funded: school improvement, pupil access, special educational provision and strategic management. There are voting constraints - parent governors should not vote on any matter which would require the council to raise the council tax, or any matter which had a direct impact on the school at which they are parent governors or where their children are taught.

Local authorities must appoint at least two and no more than five parent governor representatives to each relevant committee.

Guidance says that parent governors should not sit on the executive or on committees or panels dealing solely with individual cases, appeals or complaints such as an admission or exclusion appeals panel. They may sit on a school organisation committee as long as they satisfy the requirements for membership.

The law does not require local authorities to include parent governor representatives on subcommittees but a local authority has the discretion to invite a parent governor representative to sit on any such committees dealing with education.
(DfEE Statutory Guidance (87/2001) Parent governor representatives on local authority committees dealing with education); NAW Circular 15/99 Parent governor representatives on local authority committees dealing with education).

Further Information

A Guide to the Law for School Governors, produced in different versions for voluntary aided, foundation, community and community special schools, free DfEE: 0845 6022260

A Manual for Governing Bodies and their Clerks, 1999, ISCG, Avondale Park School, Sirdar Road, London W11 4EE, £10.

School Governors: a plain guide for people like you, 1999, by Joan Sallis, ACE, price £5.00 plus £1 p&p.

Managing Better with Governors: a practical guide to working together for school success, 1999, Financial Times Management, 128 Long Acre, London WC2E 9AN, £69.

Heads in Partnership: working with your governors for a successful school, 2001 by Joan Sallis, Pearson Education,£16.

Governors' Liability – Part 2

This is a complex subject because there are various kinds of liability, both under statute and at common law. It is important, therefore, to understand the main areas in which liability might arise, and to ensure that liability is not incurred in the first place, and that adequate insurance cover is arranged for those occasions when liability does arise.

Personal Liability

Governors are protected against personal liability by S36(2) and Sched.10 SSFA which give corporate status to the governing bodies of maintained schools. The effect of incorporation is that the governing body as a legal entity is generally held liable for any wrongdoing rather than individual governors being held personally liable. However individual governors will need to show that they acted honestly, reasonably and within their powers when carrying out their functions. Governors have no powers as individuals (except the chair on rare occasions) and should not act without the authority of the governing body.

Liability as charity trustees

Some money raised by schools through fundraising and other activities is held in charitable trusts, thus making the governors' charity trustees subject to charity law. In schools which have charitable status, the governors may be the charity trustees as well or, alternatively, each role may be carried out by different personnel. Ideally, the charity trustees and the school governors should not be the same people because conflicts of duty and interest may arise. Charity trustees must understand their status and legal responsibilities. Failure to comply with the law can result in personal liability for governors, even though their governing body is a corporate body. Governing bodies may therefore wish to consider the possibility of trustee indemnity insurance. Further information about fundraising and the responsibility of charity trustees is available from the Directory of Social Change. *(See further information.)*

Insurance

Insurance is a serious issue for governors, particularly in relation to their responsibilities as managers of premises and as employers. While this is normally arranged by the LEA, in some areas it may be included instead in schools' delegated budgets. Arrangements for voluntary aided and foundation schools, whose premises are owned by trustees, will differ from those of community schools. Governing bodies will need to check what insurance the LEA has arranged and decide whether to buy extra cover, for example, personal liability insurance *(see also page 88 - governors' legal duties in* **Governors and Staffing***)*.

Insurance is needed to cover claims from third parties and employees. Third party claims could come from personal injury such as from a slate falling off the roof or faulty sports equipment. Products liability would cover claims over food poisoning. Policies often include school activities outside school hours but not events run by the PTA, where separate policies are available through PTA organisations. Standard third party liability policies often do not cover damage to teachers' cars in the school grounds by pupils or vandals, or the theft of pupils' belongings. Personal accidents are not covered by public liability policies so governors might want to consider whether to cover volunteers, including themselves. A group personal accident policy can be offered to parents to insure pupils against accidents at school.

Employers' liability insurance is required to cover accidents and injuries to employees in the workplace although this may not include staff involved in extra-curricular activities. LEA policies often cover schools for fraud, theft of large sums of money from school, and offer indemnity to officials (including governors) for loss of income to third parties. This provision might cover governors against a claim that a child was not properly educated and was thus unable to get a job. Policies for libel are an option to cover written comments by governors.

Property insurance is often divided into two sections. A major part, usually supplied by the LEA, covers the buildings and all contents and risks such as fire, lightening, explosion and terrorism, and provides for reinstatement if the whole building is destroyed. Some LEAs insure equipment such as lifts through an engineering policy that provides regular maintenance. On top of this further cover is required for malicious damage, theft, flood etc, as well as risks to do with hiring out premises, such as

loss of income if there is a disaster or hirers not taking care of the building. This kind of policy, often called 'balance of risks', can also cover money such as unofficial funds. When school buildings are let outside school hours for an activity which is neither wholly nor partly sponsored by the school or LEA, the governing body should ensure that the lessees themselves are insured against any liability which might arise from their occupancy of the premises and that they understand their responsibility.

Negligence

Governors may fail in their duties and so become liable, because of their negligence, to pay damages to whoever has suffered loss or injury as a result. Some governors may also be liable as employers if teachers or others they employ are negligent.

Negligence arises when it can be proven on a balance of probabilities that:
- a legal duty of care exists;
- the standard of care reasonably expected is breached and
- damage (injury or loss) is suffered as a direct result.

The person who has suffered injury or loss can claim compensation for that. Claims for damages can be made in civil proceedings in the County Court or High Court. However, court action is usually avoided because compensation is paid under insurance policies taken out for the purpose. This was the case when a former Richmond schoolboy accepted £30,000 damages in 1996 from the insurers of his former school, which he claimed had failed to protect him from violence.

When children are at school, teachers act in place of their parents. A teacher's duty while *in loco parentis* is measured by the standard of a reasonably prudent parent. This applies in the context of the school setting rather than the home – clearly teachers have the care of far more children in school than parents usually have at home. The duty is to take reasonable care. Accidents sometimes happen that could not have been avoided. In such cases there will be no liability in negligence if reasonable care has been taken. What is 'reasonable' depends on the age and capabilities of the child concerned, the nature of the activity, and the dangers which should reasonably be foreseen.

In a case involving a bullied schoolboy from Greater Manchester, the court ruled that he should be awarded damages because the school had fallen down in its procedures and had not, therefore, taken "reasonable steps to minimise bullying". However, the judge concluded that teachers could not have foreseen that this would lead to a serious assault during a school trip so damages were limited to £1,500 for the verbal bullying.

Vicarious liability

Where an employee is negligent during the course of his or her employment, the employer will be vicariously liable for that negligence. So, for example, if a teacher is negligent in the classroom and this causes injury to a child, then either the teacher or the employer could be sued, or both jointly. Usually the employer would be sued because the employer, or the employer's insurers, are more likely to be able to afford to pay damages. The LEA is responsible as the employer for the purposes of vicarious liability except in voluntary aided and foundation schools where the governors are the employers and should ensure that adequate insurance is taken out to cover them for any liability that might arise.

The House of Lords' judgment, **Phelps v Hillingdon 2000**, in which it was determined that an LEA educational psychologist had a duty of care to pupils as well as to her employer, has opened the door to claims for negligent provision of education. The plaintiff won damages after arguing that the psychologist's failure to diagnose her dyslexia reduced her job prospects.

An LEA or governing body might also be liable for the action of pupils. In one case a seven-year-old child was awarded £13,000 in damages after an accident involving sharp scissors. The court judged that the injury would not have happened if blunt scissors had been used.

Liability for premises

The New Deal for School grants programme is addressing much of the backlog of repairs to school buildings and health and safety criteria are among those used to prioritise the work. But schools which have not benefited need to remember that under-investment in school buildings provides no defence when considering liability.

The governing body needs to work closely with the LEA to ensure the authority's Asset Management Plan reflects any potential risk caused by sub-standard buildings (*see page 34*).

The pattern of ownership of school premises is complex. In broad terms, the LEA owns the premises and assets of community and controlled schools. In voluntary aided schools, the foundation holds the main premises, but the LEA generally owns the playing fields, while the governing body of a foundation school (with its foundation in the case of a former voluntary school) owns all the school's assets. (*See* **Capital: Governors and spending** *page 33*)

Where responsibility for premises is shared, confusion might arise over who has legal responsibility for the safety of premises. Either the governors or the LEA, or both, might be liable under relevant statute and case law. They may feel it helpful to co-opt outside expertise to their premises committees to help with technical matters, for example.

Health and Safety *(see also page 83)*

Governing bodies are responsible for ensuring that health and safety is maintained in their school. In community and controlled schools they will follow the LEA's health and safety policy although they may also have a similar policy setting out school procedures of their own. Foundation and voluntary aided schools must have their own policy which they must follow. Many governing bodies feel ill-prepared for carrying out health and safety assessments and complain that this is a responsibility for professionals with the relevant expertise. Making practical checks are not intended to be the responsibility of governors – health and safety expertise which the head and school staff cannot provide

must be sought from the LEA or from outside agencies such as the fire brigade. Governors should ask for regular reports of any accidents. Ensuring that all the legal requirements are met, that the health and safety policy and procedures are followed, and that monitoring informs future policy and practice is all part of governors' strategic role.

An outline of the relevant statute follows:

The Health and Safety at Work Act 1974
This provides the general requirement that buildings be maintained in a condition that is safe and without risk to health with safe means of access and exit.

Management of Health and Safety at Work Regulations 1999 (SI 3242) require employers to assess the risks to which their employees and other might be exposed.
(*See also* **Health and Safety**, *page 83.*)

The Education (School Premises) Regulations 1999 (SI 199/2) (*see box*)These regulations which apply to all maintained schools, set out minimum standards relating to the health, safety and welfare of pupils in schools; boarding accommodation; and playing fields. Deregulation removed minimum space standards for teaching accommodation. Where the LEA owns the school premises or employs the staff (community, community special and voluntary controlled schools), it can issue directions to the governing body and head concerning health and safety either on school premises or elsewhere where school activities are taking place. The governing body and head must comply with any such direction.

Environmental Protection Act 1990 A complaint can be made to the magistrates court under S82 of the Act about the state of school buildings if the premises are in such a state as to be 'prejudicial to health or a nuisance'. An LEA was successfully prosecuted by two pupils using this Act in 1997. The council was required to answer four charges of causing statutory nuisance contrary to that Act. The complaint concerned leaking roofs. The magistrates court can impose an immediate fine when the complaint is brought by an individual. In addi-

---

The **Education School Premises Regulations 1999** (for England and Wales) cover:

- Washrooms, washbasins and sinks
- changing room facilities
- cloakroom facilities
- facilities for preparing food and drinks and washing up
- medical accommodation
- staff accommodation
- requirements for boarding schools
- structural requirements including weather protection, health, safety and welfare, acoustics, lighting, heating, ventilation, water supplies and drainage
- minimum requirements for size of playing fields suitable for team games for pupils of eight and over

tion, the court is also required to make an order to require the defendant to carry out works to stop the nuisance and/ or to prevent a recurrence of it. Time limits are imposed in both cases. Lack of finance will not be a defence to a complaint although it may be mitigation. Governors should be alert to the possible legal consequences of a complaint couched in terms of 'nuisance' or 'prejudice to health'. It would be advisable to immediately notify the LEA in the case of community schools, and in the case of foundation schools to take all reasonable steps to remedy the situation.

Occupiers' Liability Acts 1957 and 1984 The 1957 Act imposes a duty of care on the 'occupier' of premises – that is, on who is in control of the premises – the governors, the LEA, or most likely both of them. In the case of foundation schools, the governors are the occupiers. Under the Act, a common duty of care is owed to lawful visitors to the premises. This includes pupils, parents, teachers and others with permission to come on to the premises. The duty is "to take such care as in all the circumstances of the case is reasonable to see that the visitor will be reasonably safe in using the premises for the purpose for which he is invited or permitted by the occupier to be there" (S2(2)). Liability could be incurred if, for example, a child or teacher slipped on a wet polished floor, where reasonable care had not been taken to prevent an accident. In certain circumstances under the **Occupiers' Liability Act 1984** a duty of care is also owed by occupiers to trespassers on their property.

Premises Checklist

✔ check the standards of your premises against the Disability Discrimination Act (see below), health and safety law including school premises regulations, and the policy on health and safety (LEA policy in community and voluntary controlled schools; school policy in voluntary aided and foundation schools).

✔ ensure regular risk assessments on premises are carried out and that the LEA is aware of any problems which should be reflected in the Asset Management Plan.

✔ draw up a maintenance plan which should include an audit of facilities and maintenance requirements, with repairs and improvements costed and prioritised.

✔ prioritise school repairs and building improvements in the School Development Plan.

✔ oversee the drawing up of contracts and ensure that health and safety standards are specified in any contracts awarded for work such as cleaning and building.

✔ oversee implementation of contracts.

✔ take up the idea from the Campaign for State Education (CASE) to make a video of any poor conditions in your school and show it to the education committee, your MP and the Press. (See also The Occupiers' Liability Acts, and the Environmental Protection Act, above.)

✔ draw up and review lettings policy (see page 33)

Further Information

Charity Law A-Z, 1998, Jordans, £19.50.
Managing Health and Safety in Schools, 1995, Health and Safety Commission, HSE Books, £5.95.

Equal opportunities and human rights legislation – Part 3

Under anti-discrimination laws, LEAs are responsible for ensuring that pupils and employees, and anyone else who comes into contact with the education service, do not encounter discrimination on the grounds of gender, race or disability. Governing bodies have a similar duty and should promote equality of opportunity for pupils and staff in school. An equal opportunities policy is an important way schools can show they are committed to equality of opportunity for all pupils. In Wales, under **The School Government (Terms of Reference) (Wales) Regulations 2000**, there is a duty on governing bodies to promote equal opportunities and good relations. The **Race Relations Amendment Act 2000** also means schools will need to introduce an equal opportunities policy if they do not already have one in place.

An equal opportunities policy should link with other policies, in particular those covering admissions, employment, curriculum, behaviour, special needs and sex education and with any mission statement expressing commitment to equal opportunities. It should also be a factor underpinning monitoring of all aspects of the school's work from pupil attainment and attendance to membership of the governing body. Schools should monitor the impact of their policies and procedures on different groups by race, gender and disability (*DfEE Circular 10/99 Social Inclusion: Pupil Support*). Governors should assess the effectiveness of policies at their meetings. The duties under anti-discrimination legislation are extremely wide. Breach of the law can result in civil proceedings in the County Court or, in employment cases, in a claim being made to an Employment Tribunal. Disability discrimination cases brought against schools and LEAs on education grounds by parents of disabled pupils will be heard by the Special Educational Needs Tribunal when new SEN and Disability legislation is implemented.

Sex discrimination

The **Sex Discrimination Act (SDA)1975** prohibits discrimination on the basis of marital status or gender and applies to both men and women, boys and girls. Governing bodies need to ensure no discrimination in their policies and practice on recruitment, selection, promotion and dismissal of school staff as well as access to training and all 'benefits, facilities and services'.

The Act makes it unlawful for schools to discriminate on the grounds of gender a) in the terms in which they admit students; b) by refusing to admit a student (although single-sex schools are exempted); c) by refusing access to any courses, facilities or other benefits provided by the school; d) by excluding them or in any other way subjecting them to unfavourable treatment. Exemptions are allowed in some circumstances, for example if a school welfare assistant has to take a teenager to the toilet, it is reasonable that the post should be filled by a person of the same sex as the pupil.

In the context of sex discrimination, rules about uniform must not discriminate by treating one sex less favourably than the other. The SDA does not prevent schools from having rules about the standard of dress of its pupils but it would clearly be unlawful for a school to allow boys to wear whatever they liked but have a strict dress code for girls. A more usual situation is where a school's uniform rules differ according to sex and it may not be obvious how to decide whether different rules constitute less favourable treatment.

A case involving a school girl from Gateshead who claimed that it was unlawful sex discrimination for her school to prevent her wearing trousers was settled when the school backed down. It still remains, therefore, for the courts to rule on this question in relation to schools. Dress codes at work may give some guidance and in one case, the Professional Golf Association was held to have discriminated unlawfully against an employee when they instructed her to go home and change from a smart trouser suit into a skirt.

From a practical point of view, teachers and governors need to be aware of ways in which the law can be broken unintentionally, such as when boys or girls are not given an equal chance to enjoy every part of the school curriculum, or when pupils are discriminated against because they are segregated or taught in different ways on the basis of their sex.

Racial discrimination

Section 17 of the **Race Relations Act (RRA) 1976** makes it unlawful for schools and LEAs to discriminate racially in the provision of any of their services. This includes discrimination in the admission of pupils to schools, the treatment they are accorded as pupils, and their exclusion from school. Like the SDA, the Act makes a distinction between direct and indirect discrimination. Direct discrimination occurs where a pupil is treated less favourably on racial grounds. Indirect discrimination can occur when a school imposes a condition or requirement which some racial groups cannot comply with. The classic example of indirect discrimination determined by the House of Lords in **Mandla v Dowell Lee (1983)** are school uniform rules that exclude particular racial groups who cannot comply with them for cultural reasons. In the law the term race includes colour, nationality, citizenship and ethnic or national origins.

Though it is often claimed that racism is widespread in education, there have been very few cases where discrimination, in the narrow legal sense, has been proven. Unlawful discrimination has been found in university admissions, school uniform requirements, the employment of teachers and the separate provision for English as a second language pupils.

Following the Macpherson Report into the death of Stephen Lawrence the **Race Relations (Amendment) Act 2000** was introduced to ensure that all public bodies promote racial equality. From 2 April 2001 there has been a positive legal duty on public bodies, including schools and local education authorities, to promote good race relations and equality of opportunity. This is likely to involve more monitoring of ethnicity and will impact on governors as employers as well as in their duties for pupils. *Circular 10/99 Social Inclusion: Pupil Support* advises that schools should record all racial incidents and that parents and governors should be informed of them and the action to deal with them. Governors should also report the pattern and frequency of incidents to the LEA each year.

The Government is proposing that governing bodies should have specific duties to:
* prepare a written policy on race equality
* assess the impact of their policies on ethnic minority pupils, staff and parents, with the emphasis on the attainment of ethnic minority pupils
* monitor the levels of attainment of ethnic minority pupils, and the impact of their race equality policy on pupils, staff and parents.

Schools should ensure that racism is monitored in relation to pupil achievement, exclusions, bullying incidents, and staffing issues. LEAs and/or governing bodies may have to assess and consult on possible racial dimensions to school admissions policies. A new circular on ethnic minority monitoring, Home Office guidance and a CRE Code of Practice for schools are all expected later in 2001.

There has been much concern over the years with the disproportionately high rate of African Caribbean boys excluded from school. Governing bodies are expected to monitor the use of sanctions against pupils of ethnic minority background to ensure that the school's behaviour policy against racial prejudice and harassment is being fully enforced. ACE's experience of advising parents whose children have been excluded from school includes a relatively high number of cases involving bullying including racial harassment; some of these were victims who were excluded after hitting back. A recent Ofsted report based on special inspection of schools with high levels of exclusion *(Improving Attendance and Behaviour in Secondary Schools, 2001)* found that the lengths of fixed period exclusions varied considerably in some schools between black and white pupils for what were described as the same or similar incidents – black pupils experiencing longer exclusions in the main. Few of the schools were aware of this because they had not analysed the characteristics, both social and educational, of pupils excluded or most often in trouble.

Circular 10/99: Social Inclusion Pupil Support says in relation to exclusion that "where there is unjustified over-representation of Black Caribbean pupils, a strategy should be implemented to address this". It goes on to warn of the risks of stereotyping and misunderstanding cultural differences such as body language. Similar guidance is issued in Wales *(NAW Circular 3.99 Pupil Support and Social Inclusion)* which advises particular care in dealing with incidents provoked by alleged racial harassment.

The underachievement of Black pupils has long been a matter of concern but fewer than one in 200 schools has effective policies in this area according to a report for the teachers' union NASUWT.

Ofsted (October 2000) has revealed a large gap between the GCSE performance of African-Caribbean and Pakistani pupils and their white and Indian counterparts. Ofsted has also found that although African Caribbean boys were often the lowest performing group in GCSE exams they often made a good start in primary schools. A number of reasons from peer pressure, youth culture and materialism, poverty, institutional racism and racial harassment have been identified. The causes are clearly complex and Circular 10/99 warns that 'colour-blind' policies can lead to the persistence of inequalities. It recommends ethnic monitoring of achievement, community mentoring schemes, high quality home-school liaison, development of a Black perspective in the school curriculum, focus on minority pupil achievers; and effective links between mainstream and supplementary schools.

Training for governors and staff in race awareness should be a priority even in areas with low minority ethnic communities. Race issues can often be overlooked in rural areas, for example, resulting in pupils and staff from ethnic backgrounds facing worse prejudice and discrimination than in more mixed communities.

Disability discrimination

The Disability Discrimination Act (DDA) 1995 does not apply to the provision of education but does have some implications for schools. For disability provisions affecting education, governing bodies will need to prepare for the SEN and Disability legislation, passing through Parliament at the time of writing. This will introduce new duties on LEAs and schools (see page57).

The DDA was introduced in 1995 but some provisions concerning rights of access to goods and services came on stream only in October 1999. The three main areas which affect LEAs and governing bodies are employment, rights of access to non-educational goods and services and the provision of information on admissions, access etc.

Rights of access to goods and services

The DDA covers the provision of non-educational services and this includes areas such as childcare, governing body's annual meetings, meetings to hear parents' appeals, PTA fundraising events, leisure activities not involving educational development, use of sports facilities and hiring of school accommodation to the public. Service providers - for example the LEA, PTA, governing body or local club which has hired premises - are responsible for complying with the rights of access. They must take reasonable steps to change policies, practices or procedures which make it impossible or unreasonably difficult for disabled people to use a service. Unlike the duties associated with employment where reasonable adjustments are made once a disabled person is to join the school staff, the duty to make reasonable adjustments to allow access is an anticipatory duty. This means that providers should not wait until a disabled person wants to use a service before considering adjustments but should take positive steps to make their services accessible to disabled people.

The duties do not carry obligations to adapt premises but governing bodies should consider phasing in access improvements over time. By 2004 service providers will be required to make alterations to provide reasonable access for disabled people.

The SEN and Disability Bill – when it becomes law - will require governing bodies to produce an accessibility plan for improving, over a prescribed period, the physical environment of their school to improve inclusion (see page 59).

A legal case being brought by a diabetic pupil against his school which had banned him from a water sports holiday may test the extent of existing legislation. The boy's lawyers will argue that the holiday is extra curricular and comes under the provision of goods and services.

Employment

Governing bodies must not discriminate against members of staff or people applying for jobs because of disability. This now applies to employers of more than 15 people and includes part-timers, temporary casual and contract staff and agency supply teachers. Governing bodies or LEAs may have to make reasonable adjustments to premises or to employment arrangements. There is a right to complain to an Employment Tribunal where employees or job applicants feel they have been unlawfully discriminated against or the employer refused to make reasonable adjustments.

Governing bodies must not discriminate against existing disabled employees eg in their terms and conditions; opportunities for promotion; career development or training or dismissal proceedings. Reasonable adjustments may need to be made for an employee with a progressive condition. Circular 20/99 What the Disability Discrimination Act means for Schools and LEAs recommends that among the issues governing bodies should consider when recruiting staff are job advertisements, the application process, selection criteria, interview procedure and terms of employment.

Information

Governors' annual reports to parents for all maintained schools except special schools must include a description of the admission arrangements for pupils with disabilities; details of the steps taken to prevent pupils with disabilities from being treated less favourably than other pupils; and details of facilities provided to assist access by pupils with disabilities (S317(6) EA96). These provisions relate to disabled pupils as defined by the DDA. Governing bodies are not required to make changes to their arrangements for disabled pupils but they should note that having published their arrangements for admitting disabled pupils in their annual report that a dissatisfied parent could make the school's non-compliance with the stated policy a central issue at a local admission appeal or at the Special Educational Needs Tribunal.

Human Rights Act 1998

The Act came fully into force from October 2, 2000 when the rights and freedoms guaranteed under the European Convention for the Protection of Human Rights and Fundamental Freedoms was incorporated into domestic UK law. In the past a case had to be taken to the Strasbourg court to rely on Convention rights; now cases are dealt with directly by our courts. Both pupils and staff will be protected by the Convention.

Governing bodies, when acting as public bodies carrying out a public function, are subject to the requirements of the Act and it is unlawful for them to act in a way which infringes a person's rights and freedoms under the Convention. It is too early to give clear cut advice on how governors should avoid actions but by following the law and guidance and the rules of natural justice (*see box below*), there will be less likelihood of cases being brought. The DfEE is to review education law and guidance to ensure they are compatible with the Act. It recommends that LEAs and governing bodies check their policies and procedures, ensure they follow best practice, keep records of action taken and check they are covered in their insurance policy for legal challenges under the HRA. Articles of the Convention which have particular relevance to schools are:

Article 2 of Protocol 1 which states that no person shall be denied the right to education. This does not mean that a pupil has the right to attend a particular school or to a particular type or level of education; it is more a right of access to pre-existing facilities and to gain benefit from the education received. The article also states that parents' right to ensure their child's education conforms with their own "religious and philosophical aims" must be respected. The UK has entered a proviso stating that this should be compatible with the provision of efficient education and use of resources. This article may have an impact on pupils' rights to have work set and marked during an exclusion and on the provision which is made for permanently excluded pupils pending readmission.

Article 3, prohibition of torture and inhuman or degrading treatment - governing bodies need to ensure that discipline policies and sanctions used by the school do not infringe this in any way. The issues of bullying and sexual and racial harassment and how schools deal with them could be affected by this article. The use of reasonable force to control or restrain a disruptive or violent pupil would probably be safe unless the force was used to punish or humiliate the pupil.

Article 5, right to liberty - after-school disciplinary procedures could be affected by this unless adequate notice is given (*see* **S550B EA96**).

Article 6, right to a fair trial – governing bodies need to ensure they follow law, guidance and procedures to avoid possible challenges over procedures at admission, exclusion or disciplinary hearings.

Article 8, right to respect for private and family life – governing bodies need to bear this in mind in relation to policies involving the appointment or dismissal of staff; random searches of students could result in challenges.

Article 9, freedom of thought, conscience and religion - might be raised in challenges involving time off for staff or students who wish to observe religious festivals or in connection with school uniforms (*see Article 10 below*).

Article 10, freedom of expression – this could apply to uniform disputes. Schools can have a dress code, but they must make sure it is clearly known and understood by all staff and pupils and does not discriminate against pupils of different sexes, religion, race etc (*see also Article 14 below*).

Article 13, right to effective remedy - governing bodies should consider setting up or reviewing complaints procedures and remedies.

Article 14, prohibits any person being denied their Convention rights because of discrimination.

It applies to any situation where another article is breached. It cannot be used by itself as an anti-discrimination article. It could have implications for admission and exclusion policies.

Principles of natural justice

- No member of the panel should have a vested interest in the outcome of the proceedings or any involvement in an earlier stage of the proceedings; if you were consulted by the head at an earlier stage, you should not take part in a discipline committee meeting; governors who sit on a committee dealing with staff dismissal should not sit on a second or appeal committee.

- Each side should be given an opportunity to state their case without unreasonable interruption

- Written material must have been seen by all parties. If a new issue arises during proceedings, parties should be offered an opportunity to consider and comment on it.

If these principles are not observed when they should be, a court could quash the decision and send the appeal back to the committee to be heard properly.

Further Information

Raising the attainment of minority ethnic pupils – school and LEA responses, 1999, Ofsted, free from Ofsted Publications (07002 637833).

Improving Attendance and Behaviour in Secondary Schools, 2001, Ofsted (phone number above) free.

The Human Rights Act and your school, DfEE 0194/2000, DfEE Publications 0845 6022260, free.

What the Disability Discrimination Act 1995 means for Schools and LEAs, DfEE Circular 3/97 (phone number above) free.

Sex Discrimination in Schools - ACE guide, ACE, 1C Aberdeen Studios, 22 Highbury Grove, London N5 2DQ, £2.

Governors and Admissions

Governors of all maintained schools should be aware of their own school's admissions policies and arrangements: how many places, who gets a place if there are too many applicants; induction of new pupils and so on. But no school is an island and what is going on at local and national level will also affect your school. Local factors which affect the demand for school places can range from a change in the birth rate to parental sensitivity to local league tables. At national level, policies such as the greater inclusion of children with special educational needs into mainstream and the proposed expansion of the specialist schools programme are factors governors will need to bear in mind whether they or the LEA are responsible for their school's admissions.

Changes to the law

Admissions is an area of education law and guidance that has seen considerable change since the **School Standards and Framework Act 1998**, with its accompanying regulations and two Codes of Practice, came fully into force from April 1999.

The major changes are:

- that infant classes are restricted to 30 pupils when they are being taught in an ordinary session with a single qualified teacher;
- a new appeal test is now used when the child has been refused a place on class size grounds;
- the requirement for local consultation and collaboration over admission arrangements has been strengthened;
- local disputes about school organisation come under the jurisdiction of the adjudicator
- all admissions appeals are now independent of the admissions authority and consist of no more than five panel members.

Governors' role

The changes in the law and guidance will not, however, address all the concerns of governors and parents. Parents by law have a right to state a preference for a school and their reasons for that preference. In many cases parents interpret that as having a choice and are therefore bitterly disappointed when the child is refused a place at their preferred school. It can be very difficult for governors when they know that children who attended the nursery school will not be given a place in reception or where a secondary school is so oversubscribed that nine out of ten applicants will be refused a place. Conversely, it is frustrating for governors when they see that the arrangements locally are not best serving the interests of local children or see that their school is missing out on applications.

A sound knowledge of the law and guidance will ensure that governors are aware of their right to be consulted on local admissions arrangements and when and how to make an objection. It will help governors, especially of foundation and voluntary aided schools, to ensure that their admissions policy and arrangements are lawful. It will also enable governors to respond in an informed way to parents' inquiries about admissions and if necessary answer any questions posed by the Ombudsman if they are subject to investigation. Like LEAs, the actions of the governing body of a foundation or voluntary aided school are subject to the scrutiny of the Local Government Ombudsman when they are acting as the admissions authority, as are all appeal panels.

The law and guidance

The law and guidance on admissions can be found in **Ss 84–109** and **Schedules 23,24, 25** of **The School Standards and Framework Act 1998**, accompanying Regulations and Codes of Practice - (in England) the Code of Practice on School Admissions (CPSA) and the School Admissions Appeals Code of Practice (SAACP); (in Wales) the School Admissions - Welsh Office Code of Practice and School Admissions Appeals -The National Assembly for Wales Code of Practice). The provisions of the Act and Regulations state what 'must' happen and guidance states what 'should' happen. The Codes of Practice are statutory meaning that, although they are guidance and not law, governors, local education authorities and independent appeal panels have a legal duty to have regard to the provisions of the Codes **(S84 (3) SSFA)**. To ignore the provisions of the guidance would potentially lay governors open to an allegation that they had acted unreasonably.

A letter from the DfEE dated the 23 March 1999 complete with annexes provides a useful summary of the regulations that underpin the new framework for admissions.

Admissions arrangements

These are the arrangements, including drawing up of an admissions policy, that are put in place by the admissions authority to govern how children are admitted to a school. The admissions authority for community and voluntary controlled schools is the local education authority (LEA). For foundation and voluntary aided schools the admissions authority is the governing body (**S88 SSFA**). When the school is the admissions authority, the power to determine who shall or shall not be admitted cannot be delegated to an individual but can be delegated to a committee, known as the admissions committee. The committee consists of the headteacher and at least two other governors. Nobody who is a non-governor (apart from the head) may be a member of the admissions committee and decisions about admitting pupils must not be passed onto an individual (**Education (School Government) (England) Regulations 1999 (SI 1999-2163)** and the **Education (School Government) (Wales) Regulations 1999 (SI2242 (W2))**.

Consultation

School Admissions: Timetable of Events

The SSFA established a new statutory framework for consultations on admissions.

By end July	LEA consultation on and determination of the relevant area(s) (*see below*).
Autumn - end Feb	consultation on proposed admission arrangements.
March - mid-April	determination of admission arrangements.
April - July	adjudication if necessary
September	publication of admission arrangements for following September.

Determining the relevant area

The first step in the procedures is that the LEA has to establish the extent of the area within which the consultation for each local school must take place. This procedure is called determining the relevant area(s) and is set out in **The Education (Relevant Areas for Consultation on Admission Arrangements) Regulations 1999 (SI 124)**. The LEA consults locally on its proposals, and after allowing time for objections, makes a decision and notifies all those consulted. Relevant areas must be reviewed within two years of their determination.

Determining admission arrangements

The second step is to determine the admissions arrangements for each school. This is governed by the **Education (Determination of Admissions Arrangements) Regulations 1999 (SI 126)**. This process has four stages: consultation, determination, notification and publication.

Consultation has to be completed before the 1st March for admissions in the September, 18 months later. All admissions authorities in the relevant area must be consulted. If the school is a primary school only other primaries need be consulted. Where the admissions authority is the LEA, it must consult, amongst others, the governing body.

Where the admissions authority is the governing body, the following must be consulted:
- the LEA.
- the admissions authority for all maintained schools in the relevant area. In the case of a pri-

mary school the admissions authority need only consult the admissions authority of other primaries.
- any education authority within the relevant area or within a specified distance from the school concerned. The distance is 3.2 km (just under two miles) for a primary or 8 km (just under five miles) for a secondary school.

(**S89(2) SSFA and Reg.4, 5.**)

Consultation must relate to all of the proposed admissions arrangements for the particular school except the arrangements for grammar schools in relation to keeping or ceasing selection.

A written copy shall be sent or e-mailed to all bodies with an invitation for comment. (**Reg.7**) Once arrangements have been determined they shall be sent or e-mailed to all those consulted within 14 days (**Reg.8**).

Additional publication requirements

Where admissions arrangements provide for selection of pupils there are additional publication requirements. **Reg.9** requires the admissions authority to publish the following information in a local newspaper:

Name of the admissions authority
Name of school
The selection arrangements
The right of parents to refer the arrangements to the adjudicator or National Assembly in Wales
Address and date by which objections must be made
A contact name for parents to obtain more information.

Variation of admissions arrangements

Once admissions arrangements have been determined they can be varied only as permitted by **S89(4)** of the Act. Any proposed variation based on a major change of circumstances, such as a serious fire, must be referred to the adjudicator and all bodies previously consulted must be notified. Where there is no major change in circumstances, variations may be made only in the case of genuine error or in the light of a decision of the adjudicator or Secretary of State. Again all bodies consulted must be notified (**S89(5)SSFA, CPSA.Annex.A.14**).

Information

The publication of admissions arrangements are covered by **S92 SSFA** and the **Education (School Information) Regulations 1998 (SI 2526)** as amended in **1999 SI 251**) and their Welsh equivalent (**1999 SI 1812**) of the same name.

School prospectus

The governing body of all schools are required to publish particulars of the school's admissions policy as part of their school prospectus (**Reg.11 and Sched.2.**). The details must include: 1) particulars of the admissions policy adopted for the school 2) arrangements, if any, for visiting the school 3) (for secondary schools) the number of places available at the normal year of entry and the number of applications received the preceding year. The prospectus must be published not later than six weeks before the date when parents must apply or state a preference for the school (**Reg.11(3)**). Copies shall be made available at the school free of charge for distribution to parents and for reference (**Reg.11(2)**).

Admission authority duties

All admissions authorities have a duty to publish details of their admissions arrangements. Where the governing body of a foundation or voluntary aided school agrees, the LEA may publish the information on its behalf. The governing body shall otherwise publish the following information:1) the admissions arrangements for the school 2) the arrangements for appealing and 3) any other matters of interest to parents of pupils seeking admission (**S92(2)**).

LEA duties

From the admission school year 2000/2001 the regulations have required LEAs to publish for each school year a composite prospectus of admission information for schools in their LEA area or in the consultative area for a maintained school (**Reg.7A and Sched.1A**). The LEA may publish a single composite prospectus covering all these schools, or may produce separate prospectuses each covering part of the total area. Separate prospectuses for primary and secondary sector schools are permitted. Composite prospectuses must be available six weeks before parents must express a preference for a school and should be available on request at LEA offices, local schools and libraries.

Information which must be included in LEA composite prospectus

1. Name, address and telephone number of each school and the name of a person to whom inquiries should be addressed together with the expected number of pupils at the school and their age range.
2. The classification of each such school eg community, primary, comprehensive, co-educational.
3. A summary of each school's admissions policy.
4. Any religious affiliations.
5. For secondary schools: the number of places for pupils at the normal age of entry and the number of applications for those places in the previous year (Sched.1A SSFA).

The Code warns that the admissions policy should be set out clearly and unambiguously. It also recommends that such information should be written in plain English, and translated into commonly-used community languages where appropriate. It also stresses the importance of including information giving:

- timescales for each stage of the admission process, particularly the deadline for receipt of applications
- details of each school's admission policy and oversubscription criteria and how they are applied
- the number of applicants who were successful in previous years and the criteria under which they were accepted. The Code also suggests LEAs

consider publishing information on whether and to what extent schools have been oversubscribed
- what is expected from parents and what the parent can expect from the school and the LEA at each stage
- the date when parents will know whether or not their applications have been successful and how to appeal
- name and details of a contact point for further information.

(CPSA3.4)

Objections

If any of the bodies consulted about admissions arrangements objects, it can do so to an adjudicator or in Wales to the National Assembly (NAW) (**S90 SSFA**). There is a time limit of six weeks to object which runs from the date of being notified of the arrangements. Parents too may object to the adjudicator about certain types of pre-existing selection. (**S89(4) SSFA**). The relevant regulations are the **Education (Objections to Admission Arrangements) Regulations 1999**. In England, if agreement cannot be made locally, adjudicators rule on objections which an admissions authority makes about admissions arrangements determined by another admissions authority. The adjudicator, appointed by, but independent of, the Secretary of State must decide whether and to what extent any objection should be upheld. S/he will need to consider whether the arrangements act in the best interests of local children, including those with special educational needs, and parents, or work against those interests; whether they disrupt the sensible and efficient provision of education locally; and whether they have a detrimental effect on parental choice. The adjudicator must also have regard to the effect of any decision taken on the obligations on admissions authorities under the **Sex Discrimination Act 1975 (SDA)** and the **Race Relations Act 1976 (RRA)**. For example, an admissions criteria that gave preference to the children of staff employed on a permanent basis was considered to be a potential breach of the **RRA**. Decisions of the adjudicator can be found on their website (www.schoolsadjudicator.gov.uk). Certain types of objections, namely objections based on admissions criteria relating to a person's religious denomination or religious practice, must be referred to the Secretary of State (**Reg.7**).

Local admission forums

LEAs, together with other school admission authorities, should set up local admissions forums on which the governing bodies of schools may be represented. Forums are not statutory bodies, but the *School Admission Code of Practice* strongly recommends they be established. The Government intends them to solve differences between admission authorities and discuss contentious proposals, such as proposals to change planned admission numbers or introduce partial selection. Governors may wish to find out from the headteacher and parents the difficulties that arise locally around admissions and to consider what improvements may be possible, both to their own admission arrangements and to those of other schools in the vicinity. The forums will offer the opportunity to discuss solutions, such as co-ordinated admissions, to admission problems. Foundation schools may ask their LEAs to act as a clearing house for applications to their schools, for example. The Government also hopes that admission authorities will agree policies on admission of excluded children or children with challenging behaviour so that some schools do not have to take a disproportionate number of children with such difficulties. The Code anticipates that forums will enable all admission authorities in an area to consider how to best meet the needs of parents as well as discuss other issues such as admission of children with special needs.

School organisation committee

The Act provides a framework for decisions on school organisation to be taken at local level by a school organisation committee which brings together the key partners in the provision of education.

Its role is to agree a school organisation plan drawn up by the LEA covering the supply of school places and the addition or removal of school places. The plan, which takes a five-year view, should set out strategies for identifying and providing support for these pupils with special educational needs. Over time it will reflect any regional arrangements which LEAs may make for pupils with SEN, including those with low incidence learning difficulties. The plan will include a statement of policies or principles specifically relating the provision of school places to the securing of improved standards of achievement by pupils.

Once a draft plan is drawn up copies must be deposited in public libraries and sent to neighbouring LEAs and all maintained schools in the area. There are no restrictions on who may object to the draft plan but objections must be in within two months of a notice being placed in a local newspaper stating that the plan has been published.

If the committee cannot agree on the final plan, it will subsequently be referred to the adjudicator or (in the case of Wales) the National Assembly.

Membership of the new organisations

Membership of School Organisation Committees (SOC) includes elected members of the LEA, Church representatives, members nominated by the Learning and Skills Council and governors of different categories of schools. DfEE guidance says there should be a range of type of governor and, if possible, one with expertise in SEN provision in mainstream schools. People who represent a specific section of the local community may also be members of the committee.

Membership of a Local Admissions Forum is not prescribed but typically will include LEAs, headteachers, governors, local parents, diocesan authorities, and representatives of Early Years Development Partnerships, special educational needs, and ethnic minority organisations.

Standard numbers

All maintained schools have a fixed entry number, or standard number, which applies to the age group in which pupils are normally admitted into the school eg year 7. Standard numbers represent the minimum number of pupils schools must admit if sufficient applications are received. Admission authorities must keep standard numbers under review. An admission authority may set a higher number for a particular year, a published admission number. Parents must be informed of this in the annual prospectus. All schools must admit pupils up to their standard number or published admission number before applicants can be turned away on the grounds that the school is full, except in the circumstances described below (*see* **Parental Preference** *below*). Schools should not admit above the standard number or published admission number unless exceptional circumstances apply.

Under **Sched.23** of the **SSFA**, the mechanism for changing standard number has changed. If the LEA or governing body wishes to increase the standard number it must consult the LEA or governing body, publish its proposals and apply to the National Assembly in Wales, the school organisation committee in England. The procedures which must be followed are set out in *Circular 9/99: Organisation of School Places*, and in the **Education (School Organisation Proposals) (England) Regulations 1999 (SI 701)** and in Wales **(SI 1671)**. If the committee feels that the standard number should be greater or less than the number proposed, it will consult the LEA and the governing body of the school. The committee must agree to a reduction to allow the limit on infant class sizes to be met. Where the committee cannot come to a decision they must refer the matter to the adjudicator.

Admission criteria

Admissions authorities should draw up admissions criteria and make clear the order of the priority that they will apply when allocating places in the event of a school being oversubscribed.

Authorities have a fairly wide discretion to determine their own oversubscription criteria but should bear in mind the *Code of Practice* on admissions which states that criteria should be "objective, clear, fair, compatible with admissions and equal opportunities legislation..."(**5.2** and **5.3**) For example, criteria such as family links should not be used without careful consideration of the possible impact on specific groups in the local community. Commonly used criteria include sibling links, distance from school, access by public transport and attendance at feeder schools. How any tie-break decisions will be made should also be made clear.

Parents living near the LEA boundaries may wish to apply for places in a neighbouring authority. Their applications must be treated equally with in-borough applications since the **Greenwich judgment of 1989** established that LEA-maintained schools may not give priority to children living in the LEA area. The **Rotherham judgment (1998)** established that there is nothing unlawful in operating catchment areas as part of an oversub-scription criteria.

Interviewing of parents and pupils is a contentious area. Parents sometimes claim that the interview is a mask for social selection with inappropriate questions covering parents' occupations and holiday destinations. The Code makes clear that the content and conduct of the interview could be used as evidence in any appeal against an unsuccessful application. It also says that schools or admission authorities should not interview parents as any part of the application or admission process. Church schools may interview to "assess religious or denominational commitment". The school's published admission arrangements should indicate the additional factors to the application which will be assessed at the interview.

Admission authorities for schools that are consistently oversubscribed need to be scrupulous in applying the admissions criteria, and in specifying exactly how those criteria apply. For example - 'distance from school' may not be specific enough because it does not say how that distance is measured - is it 'as the crow flies' or is it according to the safest walking route? Popular small primary schools in urban areas may even need to specify from which entrance measurements will be taken. The front or back gate could mean the difference between entry or refusal to a local family.

The annual consultations over admissions provides governors with an opportunity to consider how well the admission criteria are operating, to discuss any pressure on places or problems of under-subscription, and keep under review the standard number for their school.

Types of admissions arrangements

Selective schools

A community, foundation, or voluntary school can have selective arrangements. Primary schools are not allowed to select.

There are two types of selection:

1) **Partial selection where schools can admit a proportion of children on the grounds of ability or aptitude.**

Partial selection by ability has been restricted by the SSFA and is restricted to sixth forms, banding (*see below*) and schools which have pre-existing arrangements for selection that have been in place since the beginning of the 1997-98 school year (CPSA5.11) The school must not increase the proportion or the basis of the selection.

Banding: Fair banding is permitted by **S101 SSFA** (*see also* **CPSA 5.13**). Banding is adopted by schools to ensure that their intake includes a proportionate spread of children of all abilities and no level of ability is substantially over or under represented. The children who apply take a test and are placed into ability bands. The oversubscription criteria are then applied to each band. The school must admit up to its standard number. If an admissions authority wishes to introduce banding, that will require publication of statutory proposals.

Selection by aptitude for a particular subject, is only permitted where there are pre-existing arrangements or the school is a specialist school or the school has a specialism in a particular subject but not within the specialist programme. In the latter cases the number of children admitted with aptitude cannot exceed ten per cent of the total admissions for that age group. The calculation is prescribed by **The Education (Proportion of Selective Admissions) Regulations 1998 (SI 2229)**. For a working definition of 'aptitude' see CPSA 5.15: ' a pupil with aptitude is one who is identified as being able to benefit from teaching in a specific subject, or who has demonstrated a particular capacity to succeed in that subject'.

2) **Grammar schools where all the children are admitted on ability.**
Grammar schools select on general academic ability. The SSFA allows for the selective arrangements to be ended either by a ballot of parents or by the governing body publishing proposals.

Specialist schools

The specialist schools programme started with technology colleges in 1994, closely followed by language colleges and arts and sports colleges. There are 313 technology colleges, 99 language colleges, 67 sports colleges and 57 arts colleges. The Government plans to have 1,000 specialist schools by September 2005 and 1,500 by 2006.

Any maintained secondary school can apply to be designated as a specialist school in one of the four specialist areas. The permitted subjects are modern foreign languages, fine, performing and media arts, physical education or sport, technology, science and mathematics as laid down in **The Education (Aptitude for Particular Subjects) Regulations 1999 (SI 258)**.

A Government Green Paper proposes to increase the number of specialisms. The new subjects for specialisms are likely to be engineering, science, and business and enterprise. Colleges with these specialisms are likely to open in September 2002. Specialist schools can, but do not have to, select ten per cent of their pupils on aptitude for the specialist subject (see partial selection above). The introduction of ten per cent selection by aptitude does not constitute a prescribed alteration and there is accordingly no need to publish statutory proposals. A school wishing to apply must, among other things, raise private sector sponsorship of currently £50,000, prepare four-year development plans and involve other schools and the community.

Inquiries from parents

Many LEAs delegate admission procedures to headteachers, particularly at primary level. In most schools, the school administrators will be the people who field parental inquiries about admissions. A landmark court case, known as the **Rotherham judgment (1998)**, ruled that LEAs must first meet expressed parental preferences before operating any policy of allocating places. In effect this means that parents explicitly stating a preference must be given priority over parents not stating a preference. It is important therefore that schools, in consultation with their LEA where appropriate, ensure that parents are given a proper opportunity to state a preference. In practice this will mean parents filling in an application form rather than merely leaving it to informal arrangements such as asking the school administrator to 'put the child's name down' for a place. Governors should make sure their school automatically gives inquiring parents the relevant admission information and application form whenever they make inquiries. Irregularities at this stage could lead to successful parental appeals. Ideally, all parents should be handed the admission authority's published information about the admission procedures, including information about their right of appeal. Some parents, particularly those for whom English is a second language, may need help in understanding this information. It is very easy for parents to be discouraged by a casual remark about pressure on places. On the other hand, it would be wrong if parents who had little chance of being admitted were encouraged to believe they might be successful.

Schools must not turn away pupils with special educational needs on the grounds that they feel they cannot meet their needs or that a pupil does not have a Statement or is currently being assessed for one. They must be treated as fairly as other applicants and have exactly the same admissions rights as any others. The admissions process for a pupil with a Statement is different and, before it names a school on a Statement, an LEA must consult with the governing body of the school, or with the LEA if it maintained by another authority. If a school is named on a Statement, it must take the child. Parents of children with Statements who are refused a place at a preferred school appeal to the Special Educational Needs Tribunal, and not through the independent appeal process.

Casual Admissions

Governors should be aware that admissions issues arise not just when children start school or transfer at the normal age for their area. Parents often report encountering difficulties with casual admissions. The careful induction that children starting school at the normal time receive is not always offered the late entrant. These children may face difficulties in making friends when their class mates have already established friendships; they can easily start off on the wrong foot if the school's discipline or teaching style is very different from their previous school's. Governors should try to ensure that children get the same welcome whenever they start at their school and extra support in the first weeks of their transfer.

Admissions outside normal entry points are also usually managed by schools themselves and can be a source of conflict with parents. Governors could confirm the agreed arrangements for non-standard entry admissions for their school. Parents can apply for a transfer to another school at any point, and must not be turned down if there is a vacancy in that year (unless the school is fully selective or there are special arrangements regarding religion, or the child has been excluded from two or more schools). If they are turned down, they must be informed of their right to appeal. Transfers without good reason are generally discouraged because they are so disruptive to a child's education, but they should not be denied.

Increasingly the Government and LEAs are encouraging schools to agree arrangements to ensure that all schools have the same proportion of permanently excluded pupils, or perhaps take an excluded pupil from another school after excluding one from their own. The Government has stated in *Circular 10/99: Social Inclusion: Pupil Support and Circular 11/99: Social Inclusion: the LEA role in Pupil Support; (NAW Circular 3/99: Pupil Support and Social Inclusion)* that it expects the local admission authorities to co-ordinate rapid reintegration of excluded pupils and governors may want to initiate debate in the admission forum regarding a co-ordinated strategy between schools. Schools and LEAs should agree local admission arrangements which involve all schools admitting a more even share of children with challenging behaviour, including excluded children, urges the Code.

Parents of excluded pupils often report difficulty in finding a school that will accept them. Concerns about possible bad behaviour are not normally grounds for refusing admission. However certain schools, which already have a high concentration of disruptive pupils and are trying to improve their standards from a low base may refuse to admit a child where to do so would prejudice the provision of efficient education *(see below)*. Although pupils permanently excluded from two or more schools - where at least one of the two exclusions took effect on or after September 1, 1997 - do lose the automatic right described above to a place in a school which has a vacancy, this does not preclude an admission authority from admitting them. Governors may wish to ensure that their school develops policies which allow them to treat each case on its merits.

Parental preference

The law gives all parents a right to state a preference for any school of their choosing. Generally, LEAs and governing bodies have a duty to comply with this preference if there is a place in the school. For admissions outside the normal year of entry, parental preference must still be complied with. Admission authorities should normally use the same number as operated when that year group was at the year of entry to judge whether admission of a child would "prejudice the efficient education or efficient use of resources". If accommodation and/or resources have increased, then the number used could be higher.

When parents can be refused:
Ss86 and 87 of the **SSFA** set out the circumstances when a parent can be refused, these are:

- if compliance with the preference would 'prejudice the provision of efficient education or the efficient use of resources' (the argument that is used when a school is full).

- under **S1** of the **SSFA**, LEAs and governing bodies must ensure that infant class sizes comply with a limit of 30 pupils set by the Secretary of State and may therefore refuse a child a place on the basis that 'prejudice' would arise because the limit on class size would be exceeded.

- the 'prejudice' argument may also be used to deny a place to a child with challenging behaviour applying outside the normal year of entry.

This is only likely to be appropriate, says the Code, where schools have a particularly high concentration of pupils with behaviour difficulties and are trying to improve their standards from a low base (schools under special measures, or which have come out of them within the previous two years, or have been identified by Ofsted or the LEA as having serious weaknesses). Unless the pupil is covered by S87 (see below), parents may appeal against such a decision.

- if compliance with the preference would be incompatible with any special arrangements agreed between the governors and the LEA to preserve the character of the school (usually religious character).

- if the arrangements for admission are based wholly on selection by reference to high ability or aptitude and compliance with the preference would be incompatible with selection under the arrangements.

- where the Secretary of State has approved co-ordinated admission arrangements between two or more schools.

- where a pupil has been permanently excluded from two or more schools (see above) the admission authority does not have to comply with that preference, even if the school has vacancies. The parent has no right of appeal (S87). This provision lasts for two years after the second or latest exclusion but does not apply to exclusions which were overturned or took place before the child was of compulsory school age. Where the admission authority is the LEA and decides to admit the pupil, the governing body may appeal against the admission.

Primary admissions

Generally parents can apply to as many primary schools as they wish. The new duty on LEAs to provide nursery places means many children will start school at age four but a child need not start school until the term following his or her fifth birthday. Many parents are concerned that four is too young for formal schooling but feel they must take up an early infant place for fear the child will lose their place. Where a school admits below compulsory school age and a parent requests that entry is deferred until the child is of school age this may be agreed *provided this is stated in the school's admissions procedure and the child takes up the place within the same academic year.*

In its drive for improved standards, the Government has pledged to reduce class sizes for five, six and seven-year-olds to 30 or below by September 2001 at the latest and is providing funding for extra teachers and classrooms. LEAs have drawn up plans showing how smaller classes are to be provided in their area and should have taken into account parents' wishes for good and popular schools near to home when planning expansion. There will be exceptions to the limit but if a child is refused a place on class size prejudice, it will be very hard for parents to win an appeal for an infant class in future (see below).

Exceptions to the 30 limit are circumstances which "would be prejudicial to [a child's] interests" and examples given in the Code include casual admissions - where a child moves into an area and there is no other school within reasonable distance of his or her home, or where a child moving into the area receives a Statement of special educational needs naming a school which already has reached the class size limit. Another exception is if an error or unreasonable decision by the admission authority prevented the child being given a place. Where an exception is made based on these examples, the class may only be above 30 for the remainder of that school year.

Children with special educational needs, normally based in a unit or special school but attending some mainstream classes, will be excepted if their attendance brings a class above 30.

Secondary admissions

At secondary level there may be some movement towards co-ordination of admission arrangements so parents have only one 'first choice'. However parents can in some areas apply separately to each foundation school or voluntary aided school as a 'first choice'. Where parents make more than one choice, each is valid and there is a right of appeal with each application which is unsuccessful. In some areas this had lead to confusion and difficulties for parents and schools - some parents qualifying for several 'first choices', others having only one. This may be an issue that the governors would wish to raise at the new local admissions forums.

Appeals

Parents who fail to get a place in their preferred school must be told in writing the reason and their right to appeal. LEAs and governing bodies may operate an informal appeal stage in an attempt to resolve the matter, but this does not remove the parent's right to appeal to an appeal committee established by the LEA for all community and controlled schools and the governing body for all others.

Under the Act (**S.94** and **Sched.24 SSFA**) appeal panels are more independent than before and consist of no more than five members. They are established by the admission authority, but do not include governors from the school or members of the LEA. For voluntary aided schools, there is no longer someone from the LEA's list.

The appeal committee will take into account parental preference, arrangements for admission to the school, and prejudice in the provision of efficient education and use of resources. For fully selective schools it must take into account the selection criteria for the school and for each voluntary aided or foundation school, the need to preserve the particular religious or denominational character of the school. Where a secondary, middle or junior age child has been refused a place on the basis that the school was full, the committee will balance the reasons for the parent wanting the school against the prejudice to efficient education that would occur if the pupil was to be admitted. Many parents are not aware that this is the remit of the committee. Governors at primary schools could check that this is explained to parents when their children are approaching secondary transfer or request that the LEA clarifies this in their literature.

Appeal panels hearing appeals for infant places where the class size limit applies can only allow an appeal if they are satisfied that the decision to refuse the child was not one which a reasonable admission authority would make or that the child would have been offered a place if the published admission arrangements had been properly implemented. (**Sched.24** (12) **SSFA,** *SAACP 4.54, Annex B.12-17* and *pars 4.53 - 4.55 NAW COP:School Admission Appeals*) Appeal panels will decide what is reasonable by considering circumstances such as the school's admission policy and the internal organisation of the school - but not the individual circumstances of a child. This means appeals for infant places could centre on whether an infant school normally groups its children strictly by age, or whether it ever vertically groups, and could therefore accommodate more children. For further information see DfEE guidance: *Admissions to Infant Classes from September 2000 and September 2001.*

Appeal panels must have regard to the codes of practice on school admissions and the admission appeals.

Decisions on appeals should be made in writing to the parents and the LEA or governors as appropriate. If the appeal was unsuccessful, the letter should give an adequate explanation of why the committee decided that the individual circumstances of the parent's case were considered insufficient to outweigh the arguments of the LEA or the governing body.

Governors will want to know how many parental appeals the school has faced, and how many were successful. Sometimes appeals are successful by default because the admission authority has failed to act reasonably or legally in carrying out its statutory duties. An example would be if a parent could show that an applicant with less claim on a place than their child was successful when their child wasn't. More and more parents are prepared to challenge their appeals through complaints to the Local Government Ombudsman or the Secretary of State and even through the courts. It is clearly in the interests of admission authorities and governing bodies to do all they can to avoid this happening.

Although the Secretary of State has no locus in relation to the procedures or decisions of appeal committees, parents can complain to the Secretary of State or (in Wales) the National Assembly under **Ss 496** or **497 EA96** if they feel the LEA or governors have acted unreasonably or illegally in constituting the appeal panel, or in presenting their case to it, as well as with regard to their admissions arrangements generally. The Local Government Ombudsman investigates alleged cases of maladministration (**www.open.gov.uk/lgo/**).

Waiting lists

There is often confusion about the status of waiting lists. Schools are not obliged to have one. Governors should ensure that where a waiting list does operate, an explanation of how applicants are ranked is included in the prospectus, and that arrangements are "clear, fair and objective" as set down in the Code. In addition, governors might consider it helpful for the school to provide information about the geographical areas that children have been drawn from over the last two or three years, to give parents some idea of their chances. If admissions over recent years have been limited to a very close geographical area, then it is reasonable to warn parents that there is pressure on places and admission may be difficult. At the same time, all parents have the right to apply. Governors need to strike a balance between providing helpful information without appearing to turn people away.

When places become vacant before any admission appeals are heard, admission authorities should first fill these vacancies from any waiting list.

Withdrawing offer of a place

Places once offered may only be lawfully withdrawn where:
- the place was secured on the basis of fraudulent or intentionally misleading information from a parent which effectively denied a place to a child with a stronger claim

or
- where a parent has not responded to the offer within a reasonable time.

Once a child is attending a school it would not generally be lawful for an admission authority to withdraw a place, except in cases of fraud, and then the length of time the child had been at the school would be taken into account.

Where a placed is withdrawn, the application must then be considered afresh and a right of appeal offered if a place is refused.

Further information

Code of Practice School Admissions, 1999, DfEE, Publications Centre, PO Box 5050, Sudbury, Suffolk CO10 6ZQ (0845 602 2260) free.

Code of Practice School Admissions Appeals, 1999, DfEE, Publications Centre (address above) free

School Admissions – Welsh Office Code of Practice, 1999, David Weale, National Assembly Education Dept, Fourth Floor, Cathays Park, Cardiff CF1 3NQ, (029 20826064) free.

School Admission Appeals NAW Code of Practice, 1999, National Assembly (address above) free.

The Communicating School, 1999, ACE, 1C Aberdeen Studios, 22 Highbury Grove, London N5 2DQ, £8.50.

Appealing for a School, ACE (address above) £2.00.

Pupil Mobility in Schools, Janet M Dobson et al, 2000, Migration Research Unit, UCL, 26 Bedford Way, London WC1H 0AP, £3.

Governors and Spending

Governors have major responsibilities for effective management and spending of school budgets. They are accountable to the LEA which distributes the funding, and to parents and the community for what has been provided. Law and regulations govern the procedure under which these responsibilities are delegated to schools.

As well as explaining the rules for good management, this chapter explains how school budgets are usually spent and where the money comes from. This information will help governors assist schools in using their budget to meet educational targets, and in responding to LEA consultations. There are changes in the pipeline however: a fundamental review of local government finance is underway with a Green Paper 'Modernising Local Government Finance' published by the Department of the Environment, Transport and the Regions (DETR) in late 2000.

The law

Building on Local Management of Schools (LMS) as established by the **Education Reform Act 1988, the School Standards and Framework Act 1998** set out a new Fair Funding framework to "delegate more funds to schools giving them as much power as practicable to make their own decisions about their own affairs", and to "make the allocation of funds as fair, clear and simple as possible" (Framework for the Organisation of Schools, Technical Consultation Paper, DfEE, 1997). The Fair Funding system has been in place since April 1999. **The School Standards and Framework Act 1998 (SSFA)** is less detailed than previous legislation on funding. Requirements are now given in regulations (**Financing of Maintained School (England) Regulations eg SI 2000/478** and **(No.2) SI 2000/1090** and the **Financing of Maintained School Regulations 1999 SI 101** and the **Financing of Maintained Schools (Amendment) (Wales) Regulations 2000 SI 911 (W40)**.

Background to Fair Funding

A key purpose of Local Management of Schools (LMS) when first introduced was to "enhance the quality of education by enabling more informed and effective use to be made of resources". Governors and heads would certainly argue that they are better informed about the needs of their own schools and therefore able to get better value for money, but it is more difficult to show that passing control of budgets to schools has, on its own, enhanced the quality of education. LMS also sought to make the distribution of funds to schools more needs-led, transparent and equitable. LMS was replaced in 1999 with a new system called Fair Funding. The key criteria of Fair Funding listed below show these issues are still very much on the agenda.

Audit Commission figures from 2000 reveal continuing inequalities in funding: the amounts schools receive per pupil vary by up to £1,600 in primaries, and by £1,500 in secondaries. While some variations are to be expected, because of differing local or in-school needs, these large discrepancies are fuelling the pressure for change. One step towards greater equity has been made, however, with the return of grant-maintained schools to the LEA funding mechanism - as foundation or voluntary-aided schools.

The Government says that governors, heads and teachers now feel that responsibility for raising standards rests with them, rather than with the LEA, government or society. As a result there has been a dramatic change over the past ten years with governors managing more of the resources that support their schools. An additional £600m has been delegated to schools with the introduction of Fair Funding and in 2000-01 governors controlled 82% of the total of around £23bn spent on schools in England and Wales. Key questions now are whether the funds are properly managed, can schools and governing bodies also undertake longer-term planning to raise standards, and how much freedom do they have to spend money in the way they think fit? Research by the Audit Commission suggests that most schools have sound day-to-day control of their finances and are good at identifying their priorities for improvement. In some schools, however, a more strategic approach is needed to their management of resources (*Money Matters*, Audit Commission, 2000).

LEAs are also under pressure. After a period of uncertainty their future seems more secure, but they are expected to be more accountable for the share of the budget they retain. There is also a growing debate on whether any further delegation would help to raise standards. The Government has produced league tables for percentages of LEA budgets delegated, with the clear message that maximum delegation is the best. Yet at the same time other league tables put low delegating LEAs at the top of the effectiveness league.

It has long been difficult as a governor to find out how and why the local authority has fixed on its education budget in any one year, so the Government's attempts to clarify the division of responsibilities between LEAs and schools are welcome. Five key areas of responsibility, along with funding needed to support them, are being retained by LEAs. These are:

• strategic management
• access - planning of school places, admissions, transport, etc,
• school improvement (negotiating targets with schools, the LEA's development plan, monitoring and challenging schools and supporting weak ones)
• special educational provision (to include pupils out of school and at pupil referral units as well as those with special educational needs)
• grant-supported expenditure.

Responsibilities and funding for all other school activities are delegated to governors.

Although the SSFA applies to England and Wales, regulations may vary, and are likely to be revised each year. Some differences occur in the categories of funding that English and Welsh LEAs may retain, mainly to do with advisory and inspection services, school meals and strategic management functions. Fair Funding applies to community, voluntary and foundation schools at both primary and secondary levels, but not nurseries.

Seven guiding principles of Fair Funding

• Raising standards in schools

• Self management for all schools

• Clear accountability of both LEA and school

• Transparency of school finances

• Opportunities for schools to take greater responsibility for management decisions if they want this

• Equity between the new categories of community, voluntary and foundations schools

• Value for money for schools and LEAs

The mechanics of funding

LEAs are required to have a scheme, approved by the DfEE, which sets out the financial relationship between the LEA and the schools it maintains (**S47 SSFA** and **Sched.14**). Details, including the rules for delegation and the management of surpluses and deficits, schools' arrangements for banking and borrowing, and what the LEA will do about insurance and legal advice are given in the regulations.

Separate from the scheme, LEAs must also have a formula to divide out delegated funding between schools in line with regulations (made under **S46 SSFA**). LEAs must consult schools on the formula each year and report back on the results of the consultation. Formulae are intended to be "simple, objective, measurable, predictable in effect and clearly expressed" (**Par.10 SI 2000/478,** (England) and **Par.10 SI 911** (Wales)).

LEAs have the right to suspend the delegation of a school's budget where the governing body has not followed requirements, has mismanaged funds (**S51 & Sched.15 SSFA**) or the school is in difficulties following an inspection (**Ss14 – 17 SSFA**). Copies of the LEA's notice of suspension must be sent to the governing body, the head and the Secretary of State, and in some circumstances the school has a right of appeal to the Secretary of State.

Governing bodies are free to spend their delegated budgets as they see fit, subject to the LEA's restrictions under their scheme, and the requirement that the money is used "for any purposes of the school" or other activities set down in regulations (**S50 SSFA**). Other activities may still be controlled by the head and the governing body even if the money has not come out of the school's budget share. For example, any further education provided is not within the purposes of the school, but may be prescribed in regulations. In deciding which responsibilities are delegated to schools and which they retain, the LEA will take account of their own and the Secretary of State's statutory responsibilities.

Fair Funding allows governors and heads to decide which of the services provided by the LEA they want to buy into and which they want to find elsewhere if, for example, the LEA provision has been poor. Existing contracts will normally be allowed to run their course. Care is needed when considering whether to buy into LEA advice on personnel issues. Governors need to remember that they share a joint responsibility with the LEA as employers of staff. If they act on advice from outside sources which conflicts with the LEA's, they may find themselves liable for any legal costs that arise.

Certain activities, including music, and extensions to the curriculum (eg field study work) that are described as 'extra educational experiences', have been identified as being particularly vulnerable if school budgets are under pressure. Regulations allow LEAs to hold back funding for these items so governors will need to check local arrangements.

As well as their delegated budget, schools receive funding for specific government initiatives from a central pot (currently 'the Standards Fund'), distributed through the LEA which usually provides up to 50% match funding. The Standards Fund has grown dramatically over the past few years. As a result of criticism of the bureaucracy generated by having to account for often small sums from different initiatives, the fund has been simplified for 2001 – 2: the requirement for schools to bid has been dropped, and most of the grants are devolved to schools on a formula basis. More of the funds can now be spent as the school chooses as the Government believes schools are best placed to decide their own priorities. LEAs are expected to tell schools before 1 April what their budget allocation will be; the grant has to be spent within the financial year, and schools are required to monitor all projects using Standards Funds, against measurable objectives. For certain grants, up to 20% may be vired into the school improvement category (but not out of it). Governor training is provided with a grant of five per cent of the school improvement fund. Any funds not spent as specified should be returned to the LEA, so governors should make sure they get some training! They should also incorporate the monitoring of Standards Fund grants into their general budget monitoring, and make sure the grants are accounted for separately.

As well as providing for teachers' professional development, the Standards Fund in England covers all kinds of initiatives including support for families through family literacy classes, for social inclusion programmes, support for ethnic minority pupils and travellers (EMTAG), for pupils with special educational needs, school security, enhancing LEA support for music, and support for parent governors elected to LEA committees (up to £1,200 per LEA). The Standards Fund for Wales covers similar activities.

Major projects such as the literacy and numeracy strategies are well defined, as are education action zones and the specialist schools programme. Although the Standards Fund has become fairer by the removal of most of the bidding, the large sums distributed through, for example, the specialist schools programme, are still in conflict with the Government's aim to level the funding playing field. One result of the recent growth in the Standards Fund is the greater control of schools' money it gives to central government.

New statutory instruments on the Standards Fund are published each year with details for the year ahead. (Regulations are now available on the internet and are downloadable: **www.hmso.gov.uk**)

Sources of funding

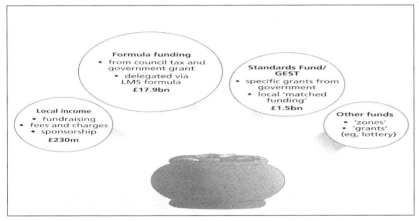

Reproduced with the kind permission of the Audit Commission

LEAs are responsible for most capital funding – money for major building works and developments. Some capital is delegated to schools through a formula *(see below)*, and from time to time the DfEE has delegated extra capital to schools. Capital funding cannot be used for other purposes, but can be added to other money accumulated for capital projects of the school's choosing.

The LEA is required to produce two financial statements, one before the year starts that sets out how their budget will be allocated for the year, and one after the end of the financial year showing actual expenditure. These statements will give details of individual schools' budgets and spending and must be made available to governors who, in turn, are required to make them available for inspection by parents and the public, free of charge (**S52(5) SSFA** and **The Education Budget Statements (England) Regulations 2000 SI576** and **The Education Budget Statement (Wales) Regulations 1999 SI45**).

Consultation

With LEAs given considerable flexibility for their formulae, extensive consultation with schools is very important. Difficulties will arise where too few schools want to buy into a service for it to be financially viable for the LEA to run. This will be more of a problem for LEAs than for schools, as alternative providers will normally be available.

Different types of school

Community, controlled, community special, foundation and voluntary aided schools are all covered by the local distribution formulae, but not nursery schools and pupil referral units (S22 SSFA and Sched.3).

Any new school must be covered by the LEA's scheme from the start, with the date for the delegation of the budget set by the LEA. If this date is after the start date for the school, the Secretary of State has to give approval (S49 SSFA).

Where the money comes from

The bulk of revenue funding for schools comes from taxation at local and national level and most is channelled through local authorities' decision-making processes. Grants for specific items coming directly from central government may also be paid through the local authority. Small but important contributions to school budgets come through the schools' own fundraising efforts from parents, pupils – past and present - local business, sponsorship and lettings of school premises.

The Government decides through the Standard Spending Assessments (SSAs), produced by the Department of the Environment, Transport and the Regions (DETR) and the National Assembly for Wales (NAW), how much money goes to each local authority for a whole series of responsibilities

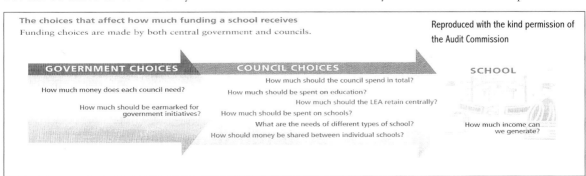

including housing, social services and education. Although SSAs were set up as a mechanism for distributing money to local authorities rather than to define the amount of money to be spent on each service, the education SSA is increasingly being seen as a guideline figure of what LEAs should spend. On top of this, local councils can raise money through their council taxes and then decide how much of their total income to allocate to education. Many education budgets are above the SSA allocation. There have long been complaints that the SSA mechanism is not transparent, or fair to all regions. The current review is looking at these issues, but a national funding formula looks an unlikely outcome.

Having decided how much to spend on education, the LEA puts funding aside for non-school expenditure (under-fives, youth, students and adult education), and for on-going commitments such as capital repayments. The rest is termed the Local Schools Budget (LSB). What this must cover is set out in regulations. This is then divided between LEA responsibilities and the rest which is to be shared out between schools – the Individual Schools Budget (ISB). Government sets targets for the percentage of the budget LEAs should delegate to schools (ie ISB as a percentage of LSB), and the intention is that that this should rise above the 85% target set in 2000. The LEA's formula is then used to divide the ISB into budget shares that are passed on to schools (**S46 SSFA**). LEAs bid for a share of the government-set Standards Fund, and make their own contribution to it before dividing it between schools, mainly through a formula.

New arrangements for school sixth form funding begin in April 2002. Schools will still receive their money through the LEA, but the funds will go to LEAs from the 47 local arms of the Learning and Skills Council (LSC) (or Welsh CETW) set up in April 2001, rather than from central government. LSC will control around £6m per year for funding post-16 education and a range of adult provision.

Consultation started in 2000 on the mechanisms for setting budgets for school sixth forms. Conclusions so far suggest there would be no cuts in the first year, but changes in funding mechanism are likely. Putting school sixth forms on a par with further education colleges, as the new proposals intend would mean schools reporting 'bums on seats' at up to three points in the year, with funding likely to be adjusted downwards if pupils drop out. This is a long game. The funding principles for LSC indicate there will eventually be a national system and formulae for most of the money, but changes will be introduced over a number of years with safety nets along the way. "Money following the learner" will certainly be one of the big changes for schools, as will coherent funding across post 16 provision. The other proposed principles are more familiar – transparency, objectivity, simplicity and flexibility. The key question for schools is how much control they may lose to LSC over the size and range of their sixth form provision.

Deciding the formula

The regulations say what percentage of the school's delegated budget must depend on pupil numbers, and different sums are allowed for children of different ages. Other factors used to calculate the remainder usually relate to the school's circumstances, including special needs, social deprivation, premises, small schools, split sites and possibly allowances for actual salary costs. Funds for school meals must be delegated to secondary schools. Where primaries request delegation for meals the local education authority must also transfer its duties on providing free meals and milk to eligible pupils (**S512A EA96**). In England schools with delegated budgets for providing school meals must see that the compulsory nutritional standards introduced in April 2001, are in place (**The Education (Nutritional Standards for School Lunches) (England) Regulations 2000 (SI 1777)**).

Regulations for England and Wales may differ, for example those published in 2000 give different figures for the minimum percentage of the formula that should depend on pupil numbers: for England 80%, for Wales 75%. The Welsh percentage was reduced in order to give LEAs greater flexibility in dealing with teachers' pay under the performance management arrangements (**Financing of Maintained Schools Regulations**).

Where the money goes

Schools' delegated budgets now cover all their day-to-day running costs, including repairs and maintenance of school buildings, (apart from 'capital works' some management, advisory and legal services). All this is called **revenue funding.** Although schools are responsible for all these functions, they do not have to run all the services

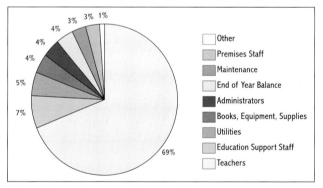

themselves. They can choose to buy back into LEA provision or look elsewhere.

Comparative information on school spending is now more widely available, from the Audit Commission and Ofsted in publications and through web sites.

What this shows is that although governors have responsibility for large sums of money (£2 – £3 million per year for a large secondary school) in the short term there is little room to manoeuvre because so much of the budget goes on fixed costs and staffing. In the longer term, however, the school and the governors can plan for and implement changes in the curriculum and organisation of the school through changes in staffing, as vacancies arise, or if necessary through redundancies.

What is clear is that spending on books and equipment for pupils (capitation funding) is a small but crucial area of the budget. Fundraising that brings in even small amounts can make a significant difference. At the same time, because capitation spending is not committed in advance, it is vulnerable if savings have to be made in school spending.

Whether schools gain financially from increased delegation is a matter of some debate. In the past increased delegation has given schools more cash, but too often this has not matched the extra workload or expenses that went with the delegation. The overall size of the cake to be distributed to schools will continue to be the crucial factor in determining class sizes and the curriculum choices which can be offered.

As governors and teachers take responsibility for new areas of work, for example organising building works, specialist professional help may be needed if contracts are to run smoothly.

Transitional arrangements can be made by LEAs if schools are threatened with large fluctuations in their budgets from year to year.

Strategic Planning

With more than £23bn being spent on school education each year, the strategic nature of governors' financial responsibilities is increasingly emphasised. Schools and governors are now familiar with managing the budget and the annual cycle of setting and monitoring it. A big step forward is now needed for governors to be more comfortable about planning ahead. For many years governors complained that a lack of realistic information hampered the budgeting process – late arrival of LEA figures for example meant schools were unable to set the budget before the financial year began. In this context it has been difficult for governors and schools to plan for more than a year at a time. Now governors are asked to look ahead and plan three year budgets that link with the school's Development Plan. Many governors and senior school staff will quail at producing a future budget when the school faces a huge range of variables – pupil numbers, and changes to the curriculum, government priorities, economic circumstances and political control. New publications from Ofsted/Audit Commission address these issues.

'Best value' is another new concept governors need to understand. Schools are not covered by the legislation on best value that applies to LEAs, but governing bodies are required to consider the four principles of best value when producing their budgets. The principles are:

1. Comparing the school's performance with others
2. Challenging the standards achieved and the nature of the service provided
3. Competing – making sure the school buys effective and efficient services
4. Consulting – with stakeholders on what is provided.

In *Getting the best from your budget* the Audit Commission says most schools are already doing most of these things, so the requirement to report to the LEA each year how they will run a best value budget should not be too onerous.

Managing the budget

1. Defining responsibilities

The law says that school funds remain the property of the LEA until spent, and governors act on the LEA's behalf. The governing body may delegate spending powers to the head, subject to any limits in the LEA's scheme (**S50(6) SSFA**).

Governing bodies need a good structure for managing their financial responsibilities. Most set up a finance committee with membership and clear terms of reference, including delegated powers, approved at a full governors' meeting. Proper minutes must be kept. Non-governors may be co-opted on to this committee but may not vote.

Limits on spending delegated to the head, and the respective responsibilities of governing body and staff should be put in writing. The head is normally responsible for ensuring that LEA and national financial regulations are implemented. A register of pecuniary interests of both governors and staff should be set up and be available for inspection by the school's stakeholders, so all concerned are seen not to benefit personally from decisions that they make.

2. Setting and monitoring the budget

Governing bodies are required to set a balanced budget each year. Key considerations are how to meet targets in the school's Development Plan and getting good value for money. Both issues are monitored during school inspections, which focus particularly on the links between the Development Plan and the budget. In order to meet targets, changes may have to be made in the curriculum or

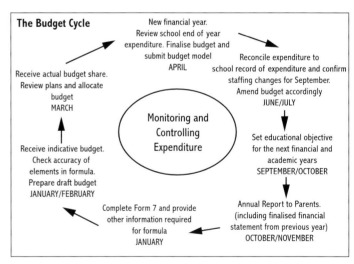

The Budget Cycle

New financial year. Review school end of year expenditure. Finalise budget and submit budget model
APRIL

Reconcile expenditure to school record of expenditure and confirm staffing changes for September. Amend budget accordingly
JUNE/JULY

Receive actual budget share. Review plans and allocate budget
MARCH

Monitoring and Controlling Expenditure

Set educational objective for the next financial and academic years
SEPTEMBER/OCTOBER

Receive indicative budget. Check accuracy of elements in formula. Prepare draft budget
JANUARY/FEBRUARY

Complete Form 7 and provide other information required for formula
JANUARY

Annual Report to Parents. (including finalised financial statement from previous year)
OCTOBER/NOVEMBER

staffing in certain areas. This needs careful planning and may take time to be implemented. Good value for money is not just about getting comparative quotes for decorating or replacing broken glass, but about the educational outcomes of curriculum or organisational changes. This will be easier to demonstrate if the Development Plan includes budget figures and criteria by which success can be measured.

Surpluses may be carried forward to the following year, but schools are encouraged to earmark these for specific activities that fit the Development Plan. In some cases a deficit can be carried forward if the LEA agrees with the governors' plans to make up this shortfall.

If a child is permanently excluded, the law provides for a sum to be deducted from the school's budget, which may be more or less than the sum provided to the pupil's new school (S47(2c) SSFA).

Control

Regular monitoring is needed to see if expenditure and income are in line with spending plans for the year; if not adjustments made need to be made by transferring funds from one area of the budget to another (virement). Governors should expect to see a budget profile which shows the pattern of spending through the year, and a regular cashflow forecast.

Governors may want to check from time to time that financial and management information they receive from the school is relevant, timely, reliable and understandable. They should also ensure that the school has a good accounting system and that written financial procedures are observed; these should include provision for separate accounting of earmarked funding. Other areas of finance that need clear procedures and periodic review include income collection, banking, payroll, petty cash, managing VAT, insurance, records of assets, and protection of computer data – both the back-ups of financial information, and compliance with the **Data Protection Act 1998** for pupil or staff information.

Keeping your balance, published by Ofsted/Audit Commission (2000), has identified 14 key areas to which schools should have regard, so as to manage their budgets effectively. Schools of different sizes are expected to interpret these to suit their own requirements. As well as written materials from Ofsted/the Audit Commission, self evaluation tools are available on the internet. Latest recommendations cover governance, financial planning, budget monitoring, purchasing, internal controls, assets and security.

With growing funds under their control, schools must expect outside scrutiny which comes from auditors and Ofsted/Estyn. School accounts are subject to audit by the LEA and may also be inspected by their external auditor. Ofsted/Estyn inspectors are required to report on "whether financial resources made available to the school are managed efficiently" (**School Inspections Act 1996**) and since January 2000 Ofsted/Estyn have reported on best value in schools.

LEAs should explain their auditing arrangements and how they will keep track of funds used to maintain school buildings. These measures will go alongside LEA monitoring of educational performance and progress towards targets. Schools may now pay for their own external audits if they wish. Any voluntary funds received are also the governors' responsibility (apart from those provided by the PTA), and must be audited by an independent auditor with a report sent to the LEA.

Individual governors in many schools have been very helpful to heads in helping to produce and monitor the budget; their experience of financial management outside school has been highly valued by headteachers. This kind of assistance is being frowned on by the Government in its consultations in early 2001 on reducing the burden on governors.

But small schools in particular have relied on voluntary support because they have felt inadequately funded to pay for professional help.

Withdrawal of delegation

If a governing body is seen to mismanage the delegated budget or fail to comply with delegation requirements, the LEA can suspend delegation. Unless circumstances are extreme, the LEA is required to give one month's notice of a suspension, to explain its reasons and tell the governors they have a right to appeal against the decision. Governors may also make representations when the suspension is reviewed by the LEA before the start of the next financial year and, if the suspension is to be continued, they can appeal to the Secretary of State. Even if an LEA decides to suspend delegation, it may still allow the governing body to decide how to spend some part of the school's budget (S51 and **Sched.15 SSFA**).

LEAs are also allowed to suspend delegation of the budget if a school is falling down on its educational duty towards pupils. This may be triggered by an Ofsted/Estyn report which shows the school has serious weaknesses or requires special measures (S17 SSFA) (*see* **Governors and Inspection**).

Charging policies

Schools are permitted to make charges for certain activities, but only after a policy for charging and remission has been determined by the governors. The policy should say when any charges may be made and the circumstances when the costs may be remitted. Governors should check on the LEA's charging policy before making their own, as the LEA could take account of any differences in its funding formula.

The **Education Act 1996** specifies which items are chargeable, and which are not. In principle, any activity which takes place during school hours must be free, apart from individual music tuition. Activities that take place partly during the school day must also be free if more than half the time taken on the activity is during school hours. Parents can be asked for voluntary contributions towards activities taking place during school hours, but no child should be excluded if their parents do not pay.

Any activities taking place out of school but which are related to the National Curriculum or the syllabus for a public examination must also be provided free of charge. However, charges can be made for exam fees if the pupil has failed to do the appropriate preparation work as specified by the governors' policy. Charges may also be made for costs of board and lodging on field trips, except in particular cases, such as children from families on income support and other specified benefits, where full remission of charges for board and lodgings must be provided for (*Circular 2/89 Charges for School Activities*).

Special educational needs

Under Fair Funding, LEAs have some flexibility on whether to delegate funds for pupils with Statements of special educational needs (SEN). Where this happens, ACE is concerned that parents may have a hard time establishing that their child is being properly supported, particularly where Statements are written vaguely without specific requirements for provision.

Funding for pupils with lower levels of SEN is included within the schools' budget share and normally delegated to schools. The Government is proposing that LEAs extend this to statemented children although there is unease about the lack of accountability when legal responsibilities and funding are separated. Money delegated for SEN is not earmarked which means that governors can decide to spend the money how they choose. What governors cannot do is abandon their legal responsibilities for these children under the **Education Act 1996**. When they account for their spending decisions, governors should be able to show what funds have been allocated for statemented children and other special needs provision. Parents want to be assured that their children's needs are properly supported and they will expect the governing body to be able to demonstrate that this is happening. Greater clarity over funding will help parents judge when the school's resources are sufficient to provide for their child's needs.

Accountability to parents

Governors have a duty to provide financial information in their annual report for parents. The LEA's statement of the school's budget for the previous year must be published alongside a statement of how money delegated to the school has been spent. The spending of any gifts to the school must also be reported.

Governors would find it difficult to consult with parents on the detailed preparation of the budget each year, but if full consultation on the Development Plan has taken place, this will have given parents an opportunity to comment on the framework which sets out priorities for the school's spending.

Control of school buildings

Governors control the use of school buildings at all times except for some voluntary aided and foundation schools where people such as trustees control the premises in some circumstances (such as on Sundays). For community and controlled (but not foundation) schools, any directions from the LEA on use of the premises must be followed, provided these are reasonable, and the LEA should reimburse the costs as an addition to the school's budget. For voluntary aided schools, if no other premises are available, LEAs can give directions for use up to three days a week without payment if the premises are not in use by the school.

Foundation and voluntary aided schools keep any income from lettings. Governing bodies of community and controlled schools normally keep their lettings income through provisions in the LEA's schemes for delegation (**S48 SSFA**). Different arrangements on income may be set up if buildings are run by an outside contractor as part of a Private Finance Initiative (PFI) deal. Significant profits are possible from lettings, but care must be taken in setting charges to make sure the full costs of running the building are covered. Heat, light, cleaning, wear and tear and staff time should be covered, and insurance either included or guaranteed by the

tenant. Governors are advised to agree a policy on lettings to cover these issues. All schools are required to consider whether premises should be available for use by the community, including for sports, youth, adult classes and voluntary organisations. These lettings can be subsided out of profits from other lettings but not from the school's budget. Governing bodies can run out-of-school educational classes for young people as an extension of schooling, but may not themselves provide childcare. Other agencies are allowed to run childcare facilities on school premises, however. Where school facilities are shared with other organisations, Transfer of Control Agreements (TofCAs) can be made for joint control provided community use of the premises is encouraged. LEA approval is required if the transfer affects school hours.

Candidates at elections have rights to hold public meetings in school premises if not in use at the time. The Returning Officer (who organises the election) may also use school rooms at any time for an election and must pay for the costs involved.

The SEN and Disability Discrimination Bill before Parliament in 2001 will require governors to prepare for making their school accessible to disabled people. Government funding for access is being increased year by year to address this need.

Organisations running activities in schools out of school hours must follow the **Disability Discrimination Act 1995**, which makes it unlawful for them to discriminate against disabled people; the Act also applies to governing bodies letting out facilities for sports or other activities to the public. (*See page 17*)

Capital

LEAs are responsible for the majority of capital spending on school premises, but from 2000 the Government has delegated some capital monies directly to schools. This began with a formula-based allocation, plus the opportunity to bid for 'seed challenge funding' where match funds have to be provided by the school. These matching funds have to be 'new money' and not come from the school's delegated budget. Lettings income can be used, for example, or money from fundraising campaigns.

Capital spending for voluntary aided schools is split between the LEA (eg site) and governing bodies (eg buildings), with 85% grants being available through the LEA for governors' responsibilities. The LEA makes a priority list of spending needed by voluntary aided schools and this is submitted annually to the DfEE, separately from the priority list for other LEA-funded schools.

LEA-maintained community, controlled and foundation schools should not incur any expenditure of a capital nature over a predetermined sum without the written approval of the LEA. This includes any leasing of equipment which gives rise to a capital charge against the LEA. Similarly, voluntary schools should obtain approval from the appropriate body, for example the Diocesan Board.

After years of neglect of school buildings, there is at last more flexibility in the amounts of money available for major improvements. LEAs are now required to produce an Asset Management Plan (AMP) based on a review of the condition, suitability and sufficiency of all their schools. Schools should be involved in this process, and governors need to be sure that they agree with the priorities identified by the LEA, as future capital spending, even from funds delegated directly to the school by the DfEE, has to take account of these priorities. Results of the AMPs are being fed back to the DfEE to give a national picture of the state of school buildings. The DfEE may regret opening this particular can of worms but from schools' point of view the realistic identification of needs could be a useful lever with the Treasury for increased spending.

One purpose of the asset management review is to move decision-making on building priorities from the DfEE down to local level. Whoever takes the decisions, health and safety and prevention of serious deterioration to buildings are likely to continue as key priorities, along with provision of new school places. Government does not provide capital for school building but authorises borrowing by LEAs. The amounts available are restricted by the need to control overall national borrowing.

Another source of funds for capital works is the private sector through the Public Finance Initiative (PFI) and Public/Private Partnership (PPP) schemes. PFI is like a long-term leasing scheme. Private companies are encouraged to put up the capital at the start and receive in return an annual payment for a set number of years. It is intended that the contracts include the costs of design, building, financing and operating the new buildings (DBFO). In contrast PPP schemes are likely to be smaller, covering the design, build and finance elements of the arrangement. The DfEE will give priority to capital bids that include a PFI or PPP element, with possible expenditure set aside for these schemes being about 25% of the total. A range of schemes is being pursued at present from wholescale school building to replacement of boilers, contracts for maintenance and school meals provision. The DfEE has a portfolio of examples which schools can access. While there may be financial benefits to LEAs or Government in the long term, it has yet to be seen if these are felt by individual schools, and governors need to weigh up carefully what a PFI/PPP contract would mean for the day-to-day running of the school.

To raise further capital – inside or outside a PFI scheme, part of a school's grounds may be sold. Playing fields may not be sold, however, without approval from the Secretary of State (*Circular 3/99 The Protection of School Playing Fields*). Proposals to further protect school playing fields are currently being considered.

Fundraising

Research by the Directory of Social Change showed schools may have raised around £230 million to add to their regular budgets in 1998. This substantial figure is not evenly spread and adds to the divide between schools in areas of high deprivation, where fundraising is difficult, and the rest. The majority of schools still say that parents and friends are their main source of extra money, but new sources of funding are beginning to be accessed, particularly

for specific support. These include the New Opportunities Fund, where programmes have included training for teachers on IT, and after-school activities. Schools can apply directly for these funds. A growing number of re-generation funds which direct government and private funds towards needy areas are beginning to reach schools, but schools will need to work with local partners for any bids.

Charitable trusts are not yet a significant source of funds for maintained schools, as many rule out providing funds for activities they see as a government responsibility.

Sponsorship from companies is a growing source of funds for schools, but schools should be aware that this is increasingly seen as a hard-nosed marketing opportunity, with obvious effects on pupils. Guidance on sponsorship is available from the National Consumer Council.

There is no shortcut to successful fundraising, so governors with time to put into it can be a great help to their schools.

Further information

Getting the Best from Your Budget: a guide to the effective management of school resources, revised October 2000, Ofsted/Audit Commission, Ofsted Publications Centre, PO Box 6927, London E3 3NZ (020 7510 0180).

Keeping your Balance: standards for financial management in schools, revised October 2000, Ofsted/Audit Commission (address above).

Money Matters: school funding and resource management, 2000, Audit Commission, from Bookpoint Ltd 39 Milton Park, Abingdon Ox14 4TD (0800 502030) £20.

A Guide for School Governors: developing school buildings, RIBA, 66 Portland Place, London W1N 4AD, £5.

School Fundraising in England, 2000, Nicola Eastman and Anne Mountfield, Directory of Social Change Research, 24 Stephenson Way, London NW1 2DP, £9.95.

Schools Fundraising Guide, 2001, Nicola Eastwood, Anne Mountfield and Louise Walker, Directory of Social Change (address above) £16.95.

Sponsorship in Schools, 1996, National Consumer Council, 20 Grosvenor Gardens, London SW1W ODH, free.

Websites
www.schools.audit-commission.gov.uk
www.ofsted.gov.uk

Governors and the Curriculum

The National Curriculum has transformed the content of the education system since its introduction in the late 1980s when, with few exceptions, all children received the same "broad and balanced" diet of core and foundation subjects. In recent years there have been shifts away from the breadth of the National Curriculum at primary school where literacy and numeracy are now the main focus. At secondary school level changes have been smaller but the Government's Green Paper, Building on Success, (2001) points to further major changes at secondary level with significant expansion of the specialist schools programme; fast and slow-track provision at Key Stage 3 for different groups of pupils; and new, more individualised pathways for pupils beyond 14, offering academic and vocational routes or a combination of the two. At the same time the Government is promising greater freedoms over the curriculum along the lines of those which have operated in education action zones.

School governors need an understanding of the legal entitlement of pupils; the opportunities in their school for developing a specialism, or a more individually-tailored curriculum for certain pupils; and the implications which such initiatives have for admissions, inclusion and school ethos. As well as the subjects which are taught, the curriculum embraces the attitudes and values which a school seeks to foster and which ought to be reflected in the atmosphere and ethos of the school.

Compulsory curriculum

The curriculum for every maintained school* comprises:
- the National Curriculum,
- religious education (except special schools)*(see page 41),*
- sex education (in secondary schools) *(see page 41)* and in special schools, sex education for pupils receiving secondary education.

* schools in education action zones may disapply the National Curriculum.

From September 2000 **School Government Terms of Reference Regulations** (2000) ((**SI 2122**) England and **SI 195** Wales) made under **S38(3) SSFA** have required headteachers to formulate a policy for the secular curriculum of the school for adoption by the governing body, to be known as 'the curriculum policy'. This should be reviewed annually. It is meant to be a broad brush document (about one page of writing) specifying the school's values and aims ie the principles underpinning the curriculum. Governing bodies are no longer required to prepare a curriculum statement. However they must see that information about the curriculum and syllabuses, including National Curriculum Orders and Programmes of Study, are kept in the school and are available for parents to look at (**S408 EA96** and **Education (School Curriculum and Related Information) Regulations 1989 (SI 954)**.

Governors' role

The law requires all governors to ensure that the National Curriculum is properly implemented in their school, and entitles all pupils to a curriculum which is balanced and broadly-based and which:

"promotes the spiritual, moral, cultural, mental and physical development of all pupils at the school and of society; and prepares such pupils for the opportunities, responsibilities and experiences of adult life." (S351 EA96)

Most governing bodies delegate responsibility for the curriculum to a separate committee which in turn will normally delegate the necessary checks implied by the above statement to the school's senior management. The committee should ensure that staff have targets for developing each area of the curriculum and that regular reviews of curriculum policies are carried out. This committee may deal with complaints or appeals from parents relating to the curriculum *(see below)*. It may extend to cover special education, out-of-school and after-school activities and provision for highly able children.

Governors have an important role in ensuring that parents are kept informed of curriculum developments and understand any implications for their child. Information sessions can be a useful way of describing, for example, the school's approach to sex education, literacy teaching or the opportunity to study a different language. Important changes - say to the reading scheme - or decisions - such as the availability of 'options' at 14 - need to be properly explained in advance to parents and, when they are old enough, to pupils.

Governors should have an examinations policy covering information to parents, when pupils will not be entered for exams, and the range of examinations which the school offers. Parents often find out too late that their child has been entered for an inappropriate tier for their ability or that their child has dropped a subject, thereby limiting his or her choice for further study or career. Important decisions such as these should be made with full information and this should be made available to all parents and pupils.

Although governors do not have to be familiar with the curriculum in detail, a broad brush grasp of what schools must provide is vital for making strategic decisions, dealing with complaints and appeals and reviewing policies and practice.

Below we describe the statutory framework for the curriculum from foundation stage to post-16.

The Foundation Stage

From September 2000 a new stage of education for children aged three to the end of the reception year was introduced. The Foundation Stage prepares children for learning in Key Stage 1 and is consistent with the National Curriculum. It does not change the point at which education is compulsory, which is the beginning of the term after a child's fifth birthday.

From September 2000 Early Learning Goals (ELG) replaced the 'desirable outcomes for children's learning'. ELG describe what children should be able to do by the time they turn five, but they are not a curriculum in themselves. They are organised in six areas of learning:
- personal, social and emotional development
- communication, language and literacy
- mathematical development
- knowledge and understanding of the world
- physical development and
- creative development.

One experience may give a child the opportunity to develop a variety of skills across several areas.

One of the principles of the Foundation Stage is that children should feel included, secure and valued. There also needs to be a relationship based on mutual respect between parents and practitioners to promote the child's feeling of confidence and security. A child's ethnic, religious and cultural background and home experiences should be noted so that familiar experiences can be used as a starting point for teaching and learning. The need to identify any special educational needs as soon as possible is stressed. Seeing children as individuals is an important part of the Foundation Stage.

The National Curriculum

The National Curriculum was first introduced in the late eighties and had a major revision in 1995. In September 2000, a new version of the National Curriculum was introduced in England with a similar revised National Curriculum 2000 introduced in Wales covering Key Stages 1-3. The DfEE states that the changes are designed to make teaching requirements clearer and to increase the flexibility available to schools to develop their curriculum in ways which best meet the needs of their pupils and local community.

There are two separate handbooks for primary and secondary teachers as well as 12 subject booklets. Each of these contain teaching requirements for the subject at all relevant key stages, the contribution of the subject to learning across the National Curriculum, and general information about the National Curriculum.

The introduction in the handbooks lists two interdependent aims for the school curriculum expanding on the original statement in the **Education Reform Act 1988** (now S351 EA96):
- to provide opportunities for all pupils to learn and to achieve, and
- to promote pupils' spiritual, moral, social and cultural development and to prepare all pupils for the opportunities, responsibilities and experiences of life.

The introduction also lists the four main purposes of the National Curriculum:
- to establish an entitlement
- to establish standards
- to promote continuity and coherence
- to promote public understanding.

There is also a stronger emphasis on inclusion *(see below)*.

The Components

Embedded in the National Curriculum are six skill areas, which are described as 'key skills' because they help pupils to improve their learning and performance in education, work and life:
- communication
- application of number
- information technology
- working with others
- improving own learning and performance
- problem solving.

Five 'thinking skills', also embedded in the National Curriculum, complement the key skills:
- information processing
- reasoning
- enquiry
- creative thinking
- evaluation skills.

There are also other aspects of the school curriculum which should be promoted: financial capability, enterprise education and education for sustainable development.

The three **core subjects** in the National Curriculum: mathematics, English and science, are given more teaching time than any other subjects. They are compulsory in all maintained schools. In Wales, Welsh is also a core subject in Welsh-speaking schools. There are also eight (nine from 2002) **foundation subjects** - history, geography, design and technology, information and communication technology (ICT), art and design, music, physical education and - for 11 to 16-year-olds - a modern foreign language plus from September 2002, citizenship. In Wales, Welsh is also a foundation subject in non Welsh-speaking schools.

These subjects do not need to be taught separately. For example, primary schools may incorporate a number of subjects into a termly class topic, while in many secondary schools information technology will be taught across the whole curriculum. From September 2000, foundation subjects were again made compulsory for primary schools. During the introduction of the literacy and numeracy strategies, the Government relaxed the requirements on primary schools to teach them. Also from September 2000, the literacy and numeracy strategies were put at the centre of the new English and maths programmes of study and the content of the non-core subjects has been slimmed down to make space for this.

There are four key stages (S355(1)(a)-(d)EA96):

Key Stage 1: children in their infant years

Key Stage 2: junior school years

Key Stage 3: first three years at secondary school and

Key Stage 4: final two years.

Programmes of Study (S353(b)EA96) describe what should be taught for each subject and for each key stage. They break the subject down into smaller areas of learning and provide the basis for planning schemes of work. For example, English is broken down into three areas: reading, writing, and speaking and listening.

Assessment and testing

All children entering maintained primary school are tested within the first seven weeks of primary education (apart from some of those who have already been assessed eg at a previous school). Governing bodies are required to adopt an accredited baseline assessment scheme chosen by the headteacher (S16 EA97). They are based on the Early Learning Goals mentioned above. Baseline assessments are intended to give some value-added measure of primary schools' achievements and help identify learning difficulties earlier. Children who have already been identified as having special educational needs, particularly those who have undergone statutory assessment, need not be assessed (S17 EA97). Parents should be offered an opportunity to discuss the outcomes of the assessment with their child's teacher.

The National Curriculum lays down attainment targets *(see table below)* and level descriptions. Attainment targets set out the knowledge, skills and understanding that pupils of different abilities and maturities are expected to have by the end of each key stage (S353(a)EA96). Levels of attainment are obtained from teacher assessments and end of key stage tests and tasks. Teacher assessment is not subject to external moderating but can provide a more considered judgement of a child's performance than the statutory tests which take place at the end of Key Stages 1 to 3. The tests are marked externally and are intended to provide a snapshot of a pupil's achievement.

Teachers measure the progress of pupils by matching their work against the attainment targets. Across Key Stages 1-3 each target is graded

Foundation stage and National Curriculum structure

Age of child	Stage	Year of Schooling	Target NC Level	Tests
3-4	Foundation			
4-5		Reception		
5-6	KS 1	Year 1	Level 1	
6-7		Year 2	Level 2 (a/b/c)	English, maths
7-8	KS 2	Year 3		
8-9		Year 4	Level 3	
9-10		Year 5		
10-11		Year 6	Level 4	English, maths, science
11-12	KS 3	Year 7		
12-13		Year 8		
13-14		Year 9	Levels 5-6	English, maths; science
14-15	KS 4	Year 10		Some children take GCSEs
15-16		Year 11	Levels 6-7*	Most children take GCSEs or other national qualification
			Level 8*	
			exceptional performance*	

* for comparative purposes; equivalent to:

Grades E-C (Levels 6-7)   Grade B (level 8)   Grades A-A* (exceptional performance)

Changes to post-16 qualifications

Type of Qualification	Description	Grades
New Advanced Subsidiary (AS)	First half of full A level; most subjects will have 3 assessments units; a qualification in its own right; coursework can contribute to result; pupils able to take 4 or 5 AS subjects	A-E
Revised A level	made up of 6 modules normally taken over 2 years, or a set of exams at the end of 2 years; includes (usually 3 of) the AS modules taken in the 1st year; 2nd year called 'A2'; A2 modules not qualifications in their own right; coursework can contribute to result	A-E
Vocational A level	taken in subjects related to world of work eg Health & Social Care, Business, IT, Engineering, Travel and Tourism; replace Advanced General National Vocational Qualifications (GNVQ); can be taken in 12 (double award), 6 and 3 unit awards equivalent to 2 A levels, 1 A level & AS level awards respectively	A-E
Advanced Extension Awards	intended to test able students in greater depth than A levels; available for first examination in summer 2002 in 13 major A level subjects	
New Key Skills Qualification	helps students prepare better for work, even if doing academic subjects; made up of Key Skills units of communication, application of number & information technology; certificate for each Key Skill achieved; assessments based on portfolio of coursework & tests; full Key Skills Qualification covering communication, number application & IT will show level achieved for each Key Skill on certificate.	1-4

into eight different level descriptions plus one for 'exceptional performance'. Each level description describes the types and range of performance that pupils working at that level should characteristically demonstrate. At Key Stage 4 there are no levels because the marking system is the GCSE A* to G scale. However, the table includes the NC level for comparative purposes. Pupils at Key Stage 4 will achieve the full range of grades comparable with levels 6 to 8 and above.

You will see from the table that there are three ways of describing children's age: chronological age, key stage and year group; and one way of charting children's progress: NC level.

Level descriptions are designed to help the teacher judge a pupil's performance at the end of each key stage. The Qualifications and Curriculum Authority (QCA) produces examples of pupils' work at different levels in core subjects to help standardise the assessment process. In the case of physical education, music and art, instead of the level descriptions, there is a statement which sets out what children are expected to be able to do by the end of the appropriate key stage.

There has been an attempt to make the demands of the levels of the National Curriculum broadly consistent across all subjects. Progress from one level to the next will usually take two years. Besides the target levels in the table, pupils will be expected to be working in a range of levels at each key stage: levels 1-3 in Key Stage1 [ages 5-7]; levels 2-5 at Key

Stage 2 [ages 7-11] and levels 3-7 at Key Stage 3 [ages 11-14]. However children's performance varies enormously, and the table can only show the typical National Curriculum levels expected of a particular age group.

At the end of Key Stage 3 very few students will achieve Level 8 or the description of exceptional performance. Indeed in knowledge-based subjects, such as science, it will be impossible to achieve a top grade unless a student has covered material from Key Stage 4.

Results of tests and teacher assessments must be reported to parents and must be published in school prospectuses and annual reports. The QCA has devised optional tests for eight, nine and ten-year-olds which schools can use to check children's progress in addition to the end of key stage tests.

There are plans to introduce new national tests for 14-year-olds and the QCA is developing computer-based problem-solving tests for the more able pupils at 9 and 13.

There are proposals for overhauling the GCSE system by expanding vocational GCSEs. More able pupils will be encouraged to take GCSEs earlier. There will be a move away from the emphasis on academic qualifications. Instead, on offer will be a choice of solely academic/traditional GCSEs, or a mixture of academic and vocational GCSEs, or all vocational GCSEs (with the exception of English, mathematics and science).

Significant changes to post-16 qualifications were

introduced in September 2000 (see table above). Students will have the opportunity to study more subjects in the sixth form, to include vocational or a mix of academic and work-related courses leading to new vocational A levels.

The National Assembly for Wales has accepted the advice of the Qualifications, Curriculum and Assessment Authority for Wales (ACCAC) to implement the revised National Curriculum in Wales for Year 10 from 2001 and Year 11 from 2002 (2000 for Key Stages 1-3). The regulatory authorities in England, Wales and Northern Ireland are seeking to maintain a common GCSE system which nevertheless reflects the distinctive curricular requirements of the three countries.

Gifted and talented pupils

Schools are not legally bound to have a policy for gifted children, but the DfEE recommends that they should have clear guidelines. When a school is inspected Ofsted inspectors must evaluate and report on how well the school meets the needs of all its pupils, including the more able. So it is advisable that governors do develop a policy. The Government is developing a national strategy for the education of gifted and talented children ie the most able ten per cent in national terms. It plans to:
• ensure all national education policies include a focus on their needs
• develop effective ways to identify, educate and support them
• ensure these methods are taken up and used in every school and LEA.

Funding should be available to schools to give the provision for able pupils higher priority through various programmes such as Excellence in Cities (EiC), Standards Fund, New Opportunities Fund.

There will not be a detailed, standard curriculum for these pupils as their needs differ. Schools should develop a target-based teaching and learning programme to match individual pupils' needs, build on their strengths and encourage development in areas in which they may not be so strong. Schools will not be expected to establish a separate stream for more able pupils but separate sets, possibly differentiating the curriculum, will be encouraged in maths, science and modern foreign languages. It should be possible to deliver much of the programme in existing mixed-ability classes.

Governors could consider ways their school might develop out-of-hours learning opportunities building on what is available through local networks involving LEAs, businesses, higher education institutions, libraries, museums etc. The range of opportunities which are already underway in some areas include masterclass programmes and summer schools in a range of subject areas as well as university summer schools in science, arts and humanities and social sciences, and mentoring (drawing on the services of students from similar backgrounds, academics and business people).

Literacy and numeracy

As part of the National Literacy Strategy, governing bodies of all English primary schools designated a literacy governor in 1999. A literacy action plan should have been agreed by governors, parents and the LEA and literacy targets drawn up and agreed with the LEA. The general consensus is that the literacy and numeracy strategies have been successful in terms of raising standards, since their introduction in 1998 and 1999 respectively. The structured literacy hour and numeracy lesson are now embedded in the National Curriculum and the Government's aim is for schools to give a clear priority to teaching literacy and numeracy and to meeting literacy and numeracy targets. That is that in 2002, 80% of 11-year-olds will reach the standard expected in English and 75% in maths (level 4 or above in the Key Stage 2 tests).

Reception teachers, now applying the Foundation Stage (not part of the National Curriculum) may choose to cover the elements of the literacy hour and daily maths lesson across the day rather than in a single unit of time. In order to ensure a smooth transition to the literacy hours and daily maths lesson in Year 1, both should be in place by the end of the reception year.

Flexibility at Key Stage 4

The curriculum offered to 14 to 16-year-olds gives greater flexibility to allow young people to choose their 'options' - the academic and vocational courses they follow in Years 10 and 11.

In addition changes have been made by way of regulations, for some young people in these years to drop up to two of the three National Curriculum subjects: science, design and technology or a modern foreign language for three purposes:
• to undertake a work-related learning programme,
• to allow a pupil making significantly less progress than their peers to consolidate their learning and progress across the curriculum by studying fewer NC subjects or
• to allow a pupil with particular strengths to emphasise a particular curriculum area by exchanging NC subjects for further courses in that curriculum area. (Disapplication of NC under **S363 EA96**.)

Schools will meet the statutory requirement for pupils to study the disapplied/modified subjects if they provide a single science course and short courses in modern foreign language and design and technology. These lead to a specified range of qualifications, not all of which cover the NC programme of study in full. These qualifications are separately specified in the annual DfEE circular listing qualifications approved under **S400 EA96**. There is detailed guidance specifying the criteria that must be met for disapplication to be appropriate.

For all other Key Stage 4 pupils in England, from September 2000, the new curriculum for English and information and communication technology will be statutory requirements. From September 2001, the new curriculum for mathematics (foundation or higher programme of study depending on individual pupils' attainment at KS3), science, design and technology, physical education (although pupils can choose other activities instead of competitive team and individual games), religious education and a modern foreign language will be statutory at Key Stage 4. Most pupils will follow full courses in a modern foreign language and technology and a double science programme of study. History, geography, art and music are not compulsory subjects in Key Stage 4.

In Wales, only maths, English, science, religious education and physical education are compulsory in Key Stage 4. Welsh is also compulsory in Welsh-speaking schools.

Schools may decide whether, and when, to stop teaching a programme of study in any subject to any pupil or class, even if this is before the end of Key Stage 4. Such a decision would be on educational grounds such as a pupil already having completed a course leading to a GCSE, a GCSE (Short Course) or other recognised qualification. The only exception to this is PE which must be taught throughout Key Stage 4.

Governors should be active in encouraging alternative curriculum programmes for those young people at risk of disaffection but should ensure that criteria for selecting pupils is stringent so that those pupils with other needs - for example learning difficulties - are not being directed away from vital special educational provision. They should also establish criteria for reviewing the success of programmes to ensure that worthwhile and appropriate provision is in place. A key finding in research carried out by the National Foundation for Educational Research (NFER) was that effective alternative curriculum programmes at Key Stage 4 can make a vital difference between success and failure and social inclusion or exclusion for pupils involved. The research also found that the programmes could also have positive effects on families, schools, the organisations participating and, as a result, on local communities. It was found that the key factors in effective provision for alternative curriculum programmes were for there to be:

- supportive school and local contexts and sustaining collaborative partnerships;
- sound selection procedures for pupils involved;
- encouragement and acknowledgement of achievement;
- monitoring, review and evaluation of programmes and
- a well managed transition for pupils at the end of the programmes for long-term benefits.

Curriculum developments

Citizenship

The Citizenship Advisory Group set up under Prof. Bernard Crick called for compulsory teaching of citizenship in all schools for all pupils to create "a change in the political culture of this country both nationally and locally". The group's recommendations have been taken up and citizenship will be created as a new National Curriculum subject for all 11-16 year olds (Key Stages 3 and 4) from September 2002. A national non-statutory framework for the teaching of PSHE and citizenship at Key Stages 1 and 2 and for PSHE at Key Stages 3 and 4, designed to be taught alongside the revised NC from September 2000 has also been produced. Together these are supposed to bring greater coherence to the way in which schools help young people develop a full understanding of their roles and responsibilities as citizens in a modern democracy, and equip them to deal with the difficult moral and social questions that arise in their lives and in society. Governors might raise the issue of school democracy as a way of encouraging young people

to put their learning into practice. Are there structures in place in the school for all young people to contribute to policy raised at school council and formal links between the school council and the governing body to enable consultation and policy development?

Information and Communications Technology (ICT)

The September 2000 NC has more ICT in it than the previous National Curriculum and includes links between ICT and other subjects to encourage teachers to use ICT across the curriculum. To enhance pupils' learning experiences, the Government intends to connect all maintained schools to the Internet and the National Grid for Learning (NGfL) by 2002. Over £700m for ICT hardware and software is being provided up to 2002. ICT is viewed as the driving force behind the transformation of the teaching and learning environment that will occur in coming years.

Careers Education

Governing bodies and headteachers in maintained schools must ensure all pupils in Years 9 to 11 receive a programme of careers education (S43 EA97). DfEE Circular 5/98: Careers Education in Schools: Provision for Years 9-11 recommends the provision of subject-based careers education within the existing curriculum, as well as discrete provision within PSHE.

The careers adviser is entitled to be given the name and address of every pupil in the equivalent of Year 9 or above. A parent (or pupil if over 18) can object to this. The adviser is entitled to meet pupils at a reasonable time either individually or in a group on school premises to give careers advice and guidance. A pupil can refuse to be interviewed. DfEE Circular 5/97: Careers Education and Guidance in Schools: Effective Partnerships with Careers Services suggests a partnership agreement between the school and the Careers Service. Careers Service staff who work with young people must meet child protection requirements.

Schools must ensure that guidance material and a wide range of up-to date reference materials relating to careers education and opportunities are available to their pupils. They must seek assistance from outside bodies. Where practicable, schools should provide a careers library.

The Connexions Service

This service began in 16 areas in 2001. It is intended to be an integrated support service for all young people aged 13-19 with personal advisers at its heart, some of whom are based in schools. The service's aim is to raise aspirations and to remove barriers to learning by meeting individual needs. The service will take on the careers information and guidance role detailed above and will offer both a universal advice and guidance service to all pupils and personal support to those in need. It will also be involved in work with truants, and will build on effective pastoral and other support that schools already offer. Headteachers will have day-to-day responsibility for the work of Connexions in their schools within partnership agreements between the school and the service.

Special educational needs

The National Curriculum 2000 has a stronger emphasis on inclusion than earlier versions by replacing and extending the previous statutory statements on access with a new statutory inclusion statement. This sets out three key principles for inclusion, which schools should consider at all levels of curriculum planning:
* setting suitable learning challenges,
* responding to pupils' diverse learning needs,
* overcoming potential barriers to learning and assessment for individuals and groups of pupils.

The inclusion statement includes non-statutory examples of action schools might take to meet pupils' particular needs and requirements eg specific reference is made to curriculum flexibility and making available learning opportunities relevant to individual pupil's attainment to enable them to progress and to achieve positive outcomes.

The National Curriculum is intended to be accessible to children with special educational needs (SEN) although some children may have some modification of the curriculum described in their Statements of SEN. Other children with temporary problems may also have the National Curriculum disapplied although the Government is clear that this should only rarely happen. Headteachers have the power to:
* disapply or modify the application of the National Curriculum for pupils with a Statement of SEN (**S364 EA96**)
* disapply or modify the application of the National Curriculum on a temporary basis for any individual pupil for an initial maximum of six months with two further six month directions possible (**S365 EA96**).

Parents have a right to ask the headteacher to give, vary or revoke a direction; if they disagree with the head's decision they have a statutory right of appeal to the governing body, and may also complain formally if they are dissatisfied with the governing body's decision on appeal *(see below)*.

Circulars 118/2000 (for Key Stages 1 and 2) and *84/2000* (for Key Stages 3 and 4) cover all the requirements for disapplication of the National Curriculum in maintained schools. The latter has useful flow charts to show the steps that need to be taken in deciding on disapplication. The Circulars give examples of the types of pupils for whom, and the circumstances in which, disapplication may be appropriate: for example, a pupil from another country needing time to develop English language skills; a pupil returning after a hospital stay, or after being educated at home, or following an exclusion; a pupil with temporary severe emotional problems eg during a family crisis; a pupil with behavioural difficulties requiring different curriculum provision; or a pupil at the transition between different key stages etc.

Religious education and worship

All schools must provide religious education. The law on religious education and worship can be found in **Ss352(a)** and **Ss375-399** and **Sched.31 EA96** and **Ss 69-71** and **Scheds.19** and **20 SSFA.**

In community, foundation and voluntary controlled schools without a religious character, the syllabus must be in accordance with an agreed syllabus designed by the LEA and a local conference of teachers, local churches and faith groups. All locally agreed syllabuses must reflect the fact that the religious traditions in Great Britain are in the main Christian whilst taking account of the teaching and practices of the other principal religions represented in Great Britain.

In foundation and voluntary controlled schools with a religious character (by order of the Secretary of State), the syllabus must be either an agreed syllabus as above or in accordance with the school's trust deed.

In voluntary aided schools, the syllabus must be in accordance with the school's trust deed.

All pupils who attend a state-funded school (apart from special schools) must take part in a daily act of collective worship. Regulations allow for special schools to provide this where practicable.

In schools without a religious character, the required collective worship must be wholly or mainly of a broadly Christian character although this will not be distinctive of any particular denomination. However, schools have the discretion to arrange such worship as may be appropriate to the family backgrounds, ages and aptitudes of their pupils. Headteachers of community and foundation schools without a religious character may also apply to a Standing Advisory Council on Religious Education (SACRE) to determine that the requirement to provide worship of a broadly Christian character need not apply in relation to the whole school or a particular set of pupils.

Governing bodies of all schools are able to make arrangements for an act of worship to take place off school premises on a special occasion after consultation with the head.

In all schools, parents may request that their child be excused from attendance at religious worship and/or religious education. All schools must agree to this request. In addition, a pupil may be withdrawn from the school at the beginning or end of a school session to receive RE or to attend worship of a kind not provided by the school.

Sex and relationship education

The current law on sex education is contained in **Ss S352(1)(c)&(d)** & **403-405 EA96** as amended by **S148** of the **Learning and Skills Act 2000** and statutory guidance in *Circular 00116/2000: Sex and Relationship Education.*

All maintained schools must have an up-to-date sex education policy which parents have the right to see and to have a copy made available free on request (**S404 EA96** as amended). The statutory guidance says the policy must define sex and relationship education, describe how it is provided, who is responsible for this, how it is monitored and evaluated and include information about parents' right to withdraw their child. The *Sex and Relationship Education guidance* stresses the importance of schools involving parents and carers in both developing and reviewing their policies.

The governing body and headteacher must ensure sex education encourages pupils to have "due regard to moral considerations and the value of family life". The Act requires the guidance to secure that sex education lessons include the nature of marriage and its importance for family life and the bringing up of children. However it also goes on to say that teaching needs to be sensitive so as not to stigmatise children on the basis of their home circumstances. Children must also be protected from teaching and materials which are inappropriate for their age and religious and cultural backgrounds (S403 EA96 as amended).

At primary level children are taught relevant sex and relationship skills and knowledge within the Personal Social and Health Education (PSHE) framework which also includes citizenship and which is not compulsory at this level. National Curriculum science, which at Key Stages 1 and 2 covers human reproduction, is compulsory.

Primary school governing bodies are legally obliged to have a sex education policy even though they are not obliged to offer sex education. The guidance recommends that primary schools should have a sex and relationship education programme tailored to the age and maturity of the children, but it is up to governors to decide whether or not to provide more than that set out in the science orders of the National Curriculum.

Secondary schools are also expected to include sex and relationship education within the non-statutory PSHE framework. Offering a sex education programme is a compulsory requirement on secondary schools as is citizenship. National Curriculum science at Key Stages 3 and 4 cover human fertilisation and reproduction. National Curriculum science is compulsory at Key Stage 3 and for most pupils in Key Stage 4.

Secondary schools are required to provide a programme of sex education which includes education about HIV, AIDS and other sexually transmitted diseases (STIs) (S352(1)(c) EA96). The programme should be offered to all pupils including those over 16. A programme should also be offered to young people being provided with secondary education in special schools (S352(1)(d)).

Education about HIV/AIDS and STIs are the only subjects defined by the law as forming part of sex education. Governors will need to be clear about what parts of the programme should be specifically identified as sex education, how much comes under wider personal, social and health education and how the school will teach the relevant National Curriculum science topics. Secondary school policies should say whether information is given on sources of confidential advice, counselling and treatment on contraception and STIs as well as abortion and sexual orientation. Schools' policies on confidentiality, which should be clear and explicit, could be included in the policy on sex and relationship education. Schools with high rates of teenage pregnancy may

find partnerships with local health professionals under the Healthy Schools Programme a useful way of addressing the problem.

Parents have the right to withdraw their children from all or part of any sex education other than that in the National Curriculum (S405 EA96). Alternative arrangements should be made for children who are withdrawn. The DfEE offers schools standard information for parents who withdraw their children from sex education.

Twice in 1999 the House of Lords rejected the Government's attempts to scrap the ban on local authorities promoting homosexuality; the defeat means that the controversial 'clause 28' - now S2A of the Local Government Act 1986 - remains on the statute book. This ban relates to local authorities, not schools. There has been concern that schools who step back from addressing the issues around sexual orientation fail to address homophobic bullying. *Circular 10/99: Social Inclusion: Pupil Support* points out heads' legal duty to take measures to prevent "all forms of bullying" and the need for staff to be alert to the problem. While the Secretary of State says there should be no direct promotion of sexual orientation, he emphasises in the *Sex and Relationship Education guidance* that "...teachers should be able to deal honestly and sensitively with sexual orientation."

Political issues

Political indoctrination in the teaching of any subject in schools is forbidden. LEAs, headteachers and governors must ensure balanced treatment of political issues (Ss406 & 407 EA96). Pupils under 12 must not take part in partisan political activities while at school, or otherwise where the activity is arranged by a member of staff or anyone acting on behalf of the school or a member of staff. This is not a licence to ignore political issues because the National Curriculum requires pupils to understand different political perspectives.

Complaints

LEAs must, with the approval of the Secretary of State, and after consultation with governing bodies of foundation and VA schools, make arrangements for the consideration of curriculum complaints eg NC, RE, collective worship, external qualifications or syllabuses, provision of information, parents' appeals to governing bodies about a head's disapplication direction, charging for school activities (Sched.409 EA96 as amended by Para.107, Sched.30 SSFA). Complaints are limited to those claiming that the governing body or LEA have exercised their statutory powers unreasonably or have failed to discharge a statutory duty.

DES Circular 1/89 on Complaints and DFE Circular 1/94 on Religious Education and Collective Worship are still in force and advise on establishing local complaints arrangements. They recommend that, ideally, complaints should be informally resolved. Failing this, the stages in the procedure are set out and they recommend that for school-based complaints, governing bodies should be involved at the first formal stage of complaint.

Further information

National Literacy Strategy: the second year, 2000, Ofsted, Publications Centre 07002 637833; (www.ofsted.gov.uk).

The National Numeracy Strategy: the first year, 2000, Ofsted.

The Curriculum Guidance for the Foundation Stage, Qualifications and Curriculum Authority (QCA), 83 Piccadilly, London W1J 8QA (www.qca.org.uk) (www.nc.uk.net).

Governors and Standards

Effective governing bodies are at the heart of the drive to raise standards, responsible for helping determine the direction in which their school should develop and helping to create a climate of continuous improvement. Rising standards in pupils' attainment at all levels of education have been reported since the introduction of the SSFA. There has been particular improvement at primary level, where the greatest gains have generally been made by schools with disadvantaged intakes and where attainment was previously low. However, in his annual report for 1999/2000 the Chief Inspector of Schools, Mike Tomlinson, reports that the gap between high and low performing schools remains too high, particularly in secondary schools. The Government is particularly concerned that pupils in Key Stage 3 lose the momentum of their primary years. A new focus on this group is already underway in many secondary schools.

The law

A major responsibility for promoting high standards of educational achievement is imposed on governing bodies with the **School Standards and Framework Act (S38)** - legislation which, as its name indicates, sought to improve standards in schools.

Governing bodies of all maintained schools are responsible for setting and publishing targets each year for the achievement of pupils at the end of Key Stage 2 and Key Stage 4. The legal basis for this is in **S19** of the **Education Act 1997** and the **Education (School Performance Targets) (England) Regulations 1998 SI 1532.** The Secretary of State regulates the specific targets for any of the National Curriculum key stage assessments or public examinations.

The task for governors and schools

Development planning is a key strategy for school improvement, mostly leading to a two or three year forward plan. Schools produce different plans, but all usually include details of the main goals, actions, resources and responsibilities involved. Many say how success will be measured. Broadly governors should support the headteacher and staff in working through a five stage cycle of school improvement which concentrates on pupil performance:
1. evaluating past results and comparing them with similar schools; 2. identifying strengths and weaknesses; 3. setting fresh targets; 4. planning action including resourcing; 5. making it happen - using monitoring and evaluation to analyse progress towards meeting targets.
Governors must be able to-
- take an objective look at pupils' achievements and pinpoint areas of underachievement.

- account for results by identifying strengths and weaknesses in the quality and effectiveness of any part of the school's work, particularly teaching and learning.
- provide information for the 'school improvement plan' which is the vehicle for raising standards and improving quality.
Governors can use the results of this process to celebrate success!

A school improvement programme should set out the priorities for improvement and address any identified weaknesses in three key areas: 1) pupils' standards of achievement and especially attainment and progress; 2) the quality of teaching; 3) the quality of leadership and management.

How well are we doing?

When setting and evaluating targets governors should look at a wide range of evidence about the school's performance and pupils' achievements. These include National Curriculum tests and secondary examinations, truancy and exclusions statistics and, on the more positive side, pupil involvement in out-of-school activities including sporting success and participation. However Ofsted believes that starting with an analysis of the pupils' achievements provides a focus for the evaluation of teaching and learning (*School Evaluation Matters, 1998*). At school level governors should use their own school's performance against any previously set targets, any previous assessment information on the relevant cohorts, Ofsted/Estyn inspection reports and subsequent action plans.

At national level the publication every autumn of national comparative performance information is intended to help governors set realistic targets by measuring their school's achievement with other similar schools. Ofsted produces a 'Panda', short for Performance and Assessment. The data, which is taken from school inspections, gives schools information that rates their performance against other schools that take children from similar backgrounds. The Pandas grade schools according to the standards achieved by pupils; the quality of education; and a category that includes efficiency and management. In the main, the Panda uses publicly available information to construct an analysis of a school and the extent to which it compares to the national picture.

The autumn package also contains 'benchmark' figures designed to help teachers and governors judge their pupils' performance against other schools with similar intakes. From these, schools are required to draw up targets in the three core subjects: English, mathematics and science. The data enables headteachers and governing bodies to judge the achievements of their school against similar schools nationally. The focus in the data is on attainment at the end of the key stages.

Many LEAs provide detailed information to set a school's achievements in context with other local schools (see **LEA role** *below*).

What should we aim to achieve?

On the basis of the above information governing bodies must set statutory targets for pupils at the end of Key Stages 2 and 4. The targets are set by December 31 for the following school year. So governing bodies set targets in autumn 2000 for pupils' performance in summer 2002. Primary schools need to set statutory targets at Key Stage 2 based on the same measures as the national literacy and numeracy targets for 2002.

DfEE Circular 11/98 Target Setting in Schools and DfEE guidance: *Setting targets for pupil achievement; NAW - Target Setting: Guidance for Headteachers and Governing Bodies* give advice on statutory target-setting for pupil performance in schools. Setting school targets fits into the annual cycle of school review, planning and action.

Governing bodies are required to publish their targets alongside performance information (league tables) in their annual report to parents (*see page 77*). Targets are for pupil performance in National Curriculum assessments and GCSE and equivalent qualifications.

Although the Government's emphasis is on academic targets, they have also asked schools to improve attendance and reduce exclusions; and there is nothing to stop schools setting other targets appropriate to their school such as: greater participation in extra-curricular activities and improved links between school and the community. As well as improvements in test results and teaching quality, improving schools are often providing stronger support for pupils' personal and social development (Chief Inspector's *Annual Report 1999/2000*).

Additional targets may be especially relevant to particular groups of pupils; those who have been a cause of concern over recent years include Key Stage 3 pupils, ethnic minorities, children with special needs or high ability, children in the care system and boys (*see **Targeting groups of pupils** below*).

School staff, pupils and parents should all make a contribution to setting targets which need to be SMART: Specific, Measurable, Achievable, Realistic, and Time-related.

National Assembly for Wales (NAW) advice

points out that target setting is especially successful when it is carefully planned and precise, and broken down to the level where individual teachers can take responsibility for setting and achieving the targets.

Action and review

Once the governing body has agreed targets it should consider the strategies needed to achieve them and this will tie into the school's Development Plan which should identify the school's priorities and resources to meet those priorities. School improvement strategies will link into most aspects of the school's work from its ethos, school policies, resourcing, curriculum, and staff training and development.

The governing body's strategies should be translated into action points by the head and senior management; at least one target linked to the achievement of school targets for pupils and performance must be adopted by the headteacher and staff as part of the appraisal process. New arrangements for teacher appraisal (to come on stream later in Wales) enable teachers to play a key role in raising the standards of pupil performance. Continuing professional development and training for school staff is seen as key to raising standards and the governing body should ensure that the Development Plan identifies the needs and resources for staff training. (*see **Governors and Staffing**).

Monitoring of the action and its outcomes will be an integral part of line management of staff and who does what should be clearly defined in the Development Plan. A timetable of reporting back to the governing body on progress will be included. Governing bodies will need to see whether action matches outcomes and make judgements about whether money has been well spent. Governors and staff need a good working relationship so that governors can ask challenging questions about progress without being regarded as confrontational. However, while some specific targets can be measured and quantified, others may require more qualitative judgements to be made.

The LEA role
· · · · · · · · · · · · ·

Over recent years LEAs have taken a more backseat role in relation to schools. However in relation to its standards agenda, the Government has given the LEA a key role, at least where schools are struggling to meet targets. Where schools are successfully managing their own improvement, the Government intends that they be allowed to proceed with the minimum of intervention. According to the Chief Inspector of Schools (annual report 1999/2000) governors often seem to have "an unrealistic and unhealthy view of what the modern LEA could offer, and a correspondingly reduced notion of their own role". If the governing body appears to be failing to promote high standards, the LEA may use its powers to intervene as set out in the *Code of Practice on LEA- School Relations* (England 2001; Wales 1999).

Education development plans (EDP)

The EDP are a key mechanism for local education authorities to meet their statutory duty to promote high standards in schools. From April 1999 LEAs have been required to set out their expectations with respect to the national targets and sometimes set additional targets reflecting local priorities and aspirations. These targets may be for broader areas of pupil achievement. The Secretary of State must give approval for a plan which covers a period of three years and is subject to annual review. A new statutory code of practice sets out the principles of an effective relationship between LEAs and schools and the appropriate use of intervention powers. The code regards LEAs as "the main means through which external support and intervention can be applied in a way which is sensitive to each school's performance and circumstance." (*Code of Practice on LEA-School Relations.*)

For all schools, the LEA has an important role in helping schools to set realistic and challenging targets and in agreeing targets with schools to include in the authority's education development plan (EDP). The governing body must provide information which the LEA requests. This will usually include statutory targets set for pupils as well as pupil turnover and data about pupils with special educational needs. Schools may need to set targets which are above expected projections otherwise standards overall will not rise. The provision to secure those targets may need to be improved or changed particularly in areas where the governing body has identified weaknesses. A change in curriculum organisation, training for staff or extra support for particular pupils are typical examples of the way higher targets can be met. Where schools understand this, LEAs are less likely to need to intervene to set more challenging targets. Where the governing body and LEA disagree over targets, there may need to be negotiation and ultimately the involvement of the DfEE.

Governors who are struggling with the analytical and management skills required for school improvement will have to evaluate whether their LEA can sufficiently support them. The Audit Commission/Ofsted has pointed out the inconsistency both across and within LEAs in this respect. Nor do governing bodies escape their criticism; some are described as having an "anxious dependency" on their LEA. Schools that feel they need more than the diagnosis and recommendations which inspection produces may have to pay for help in acquiring the appropriate skills.

Targeting groups of pupils

Pupils with special educational needs

Governing bodies may wish to use target setting as an opportunity to focus on raising standards among children with SEN. School improvement targets eg for literacy, numeracy, and in test and examination results should be closely related to the SEN policy. Guidance to assist schools in doing this has been recently updated (*Supporting the target setting process (DfEE, March 2001 ref: 0065/2001)*).

In some special schools and mainstream schools with large numbers of pupils with significant SEN, targets will be at levels on the P scales, described by

the guidance. From 2001 schools which set zero rated targets will be required to set measurable performance targets for 2003 at the relevant key stages using the P scales or other performance criteria where appropriate. They will be required to publish their targets alongside performance outcomes in the annual report to parents. P scales provide descriptions of attainment below level 1 and within levels 1 and 2, for English and mathematics. A scale for personal and social development is also included and governing bodies may consider additional targets addressing such areas as behaviour.

The targets on these scales will be set as part of the process of school self review and may be based on needs, for example, if a group of pupils need to make greater progress in communication skills. However, target setting for groups of children should not be confused with individually targeted support set out in a pupil's Statement or individual education plan.

Governors could recognise the achievement of SEN pupils by introducing Progress Files (currently being piloted). They are the planned successor to National Records of Achievement and aim to record achievements, help pupils plan their learning and career development and recognise the knowledge, understanding and skills they are acquiring.

Key Stage 3 pupils

While the proportion of 11-year-olds reaching level 4 and above in English has risen from 57% in 1996 to 75% in 2000 and that in maths from 54% to 72% too many children fail to thrive educationally in their first years of secondary school. For some this can be the root of more serious problems which lead to them being left behind or losing motivation; others may mark time in the first few years and fail to build on the success of their primary years.

In a sense the success of children in Key Stage 3 is the responsibility of both primary and secondary schools. The Government believes that joint training for primary and secondary teachers, better advice and support for parents and improved collaboration between primary and secondary schools could smooth the transition for 11-year-olds.

It intends expanding its summer school programme so that every secondary school can offer provision to pupils transferring in the following autumn. Curriculum initiatives have already enabled secondary teachers to observe skilled primary teachers teaching literacy and numeracy and there is a proposal to extend teaching frameworks and materials across the primary secondary divide. Information is likely to be better disseminated with a common transfer form so that pupil performance data and other information can be transferred electronically and a new Common Basic Data Set to be introduced by 2002 which will enable schools to track each individual pupil's progress even when they change schools.

In its education Green Paper, *Building on Success*, the Government proposes new demanding targets for end of Key Stage 3 tests with ambitious targets in 2007 in English, mathematics, science and ICT with milestone targets for 2004. Some pupils who are advanced may take Key Stage 3 tests early. In March 2001 the Government announced its early secondary strategy which included the following initiatives:

- New frameworks for English and mathematics which include guidance on the inclusion of gifted and talented pupils, those with special needs and English as an additional language;
- More individual provision which will see better catch-up arrangements for those children who need extra help;
- Schools required to audit their teaching and learning practices in English and mathematics;
- Training programmes for teachers;
- Targets to be set by schools for 14-year-olds in English, mathematics and science by the end of June 2001 for the tests in 2002;
- New progress tests for pupils in Year 7 below expected standard for their age in English and mathematics;
- New optional tests in English and mathematics for Years 7 and 8.

Boys' performance

The poor performance of boys in relation to girls, particularly in reading, is a relatively new phenomenon and one which governing bodies will wish to address in schools where the differences are marked. A new trend has also been identified of a minority of boys being disaffected with school itself. New figures show that 83% of permanent exclusions are of boys and that 7,000 more boys than girls left school at 16 with no qualifications.

The Ofsted report into the second year of the Literacy Strategy found that although there has been an improvement in reading at the end of Key Stage 2, attainment in writing lags behind and that boys do less well than girls in all aspects of English at both key stages.

Ethnic minority pupils

Schools which monitor their pupils' performance by ethnicity will be able to check whether there is a need for a greater focus on these pupils. Nationally pupils of African-Caribbean, Pakistani and Bangladeshi heritage are much less likely to succeed. Ofsted has reported that fewer than a quarter of the 25 LEAs visited had a clear strategy for raising the attainment of Black and minority ethnic groups (*Raising the attainment of minority ethnic pupils – school and LEA responses (1999)*). The Chief Inspector has observed that a longstanding obstacle was the reluctance of schools and LEAs to monitor pupil performance by ethnic group. From 2002 the Government is planning improvements to the way schools undertake ethnic monitoring. Since 1990, schools have been required to seek from parents the ethnic group of each pupil on entry to primary education and again on entry to secondary education. National reporting of this information has only ever been in the form of school totals, allowing for little effective ethnic monitoring. The DfEE is planning to issue fresh guidance to schools on the collection and recording of information on pupil's ethnic group.

Ofsted's report identified successful strategies for tackling under-achievement including: curriculum and teaching strategies; pastoral support including mentoring; links with parents and the wider community; and promoting good race relations.

One of the main obstacles appeared to be teachers' low expectations, a factor which was also present in relation to other groups including gypsy traveller pupils and pupils from poor backgrounds.

Children in the care system

The low achievement of children in the public care system is nothing short of scandalous. Around 75% of care leavers leave education with no qualifications and a disproportionate number are excluded from school. A recent Ofsted report has urged that *Guidance on the Education of Children and Young People in Public Care* (DfEE, 2000) be followed by schools and calls for training of governors and regular monitoring of teaching quality as well as each young person's progress.

The targets for this group are modest: the proportion of young people leaving care at 16 or over with at least 1 GCSE or a GNVQ should be increased to at least 50% by 2001 and to 75% by 2003. However Ofsted reports that target-setting is having a positive effect for many looked after children, as their targets are considered on an individual basis alongside their peer group.

The Department of Health's Quality Protects initiative includes collection of performance indicator data on attendance, National Curriculum test results, GCSE grades and permanent exclusions. Governors should ensure that the achievement of looked after pupils is monitored in their school and that there are high expectations of this small but vulnerable group *(see also page 81)*.

National and local initiatives

Education Action Zones (EAZ)

The first clusters of schools to form education action zones aimed at raising standards in schools began in September 1998. Each EAZ receives up to £1m a year, with about a quarter coming from business and other local partners. Forums, which include one or two Secretary of State appointees and a representative of each school (if they choose), run the zones. A forum may take over the functions and most of the responsibilities of the governing body of a participating school. It employs extra specialist teachers and classroom assistants and the Secretary of State may modify the budgets of participating schools. Schools have the choice about whether to be included in a zone. Legislation is already in place to allow other changes in participating schools, such as altering the length of the school day and disapplication of the National Curriculum. Zones will be able to revise teachers' pay and conditions as the **School Teachers' Pay and Conditions Act 1991** can be disapplied.

Although the likely innovation that zones will inspire, is welcome, there is concern about whether parents will be consulted on such matters as changes to the National Curriculum. The lack of accountability is another anxiety if unelected forums take over governors responsibilities.

A report from Ofsted on six zones showed that they had helped bring about considerable improvements in schools, results, particularly in the primary sector, but that there had been comparatively little radical innovation.

Excellence in Cities (EiC)

Schools in EiC areas have shown faster improvement than schools elsewhere both in terms of those pupils achieving five or more higher grade GCSEs and those getting at least one GCSE. Improvements have been fastest in the most deprived schools. The programme directs extra resources to support extension activities for gifted and talented pupils, provide learning mentors to support pupils experiencing barriers to learning; set up learning support units offering provision for excluded pupils, increase the number of beacon and specialist schools in cities and establish small EAZs to raise performance in small clusters of schools. The programme includes strong involvement of LEAs working in partnership with secondary schools. It was launched in March 1999 and by September 2001 will cover around a third of all secondary age pupils across a thousand schools. The Government has announced its intention to extend the scheme to smaller areas of deprivation outside the big cities through new Excellence Clusters.

Beacon schools

The beacon schools scheme has been specifically designed to help raise standards in schools through the sharing and spreading of good practice. The number of beacon schools are to be expanded – by September 2001 there will be 1000, 250 at secondary level. As part of a new package of measures to target writing within the literacy strategy, the Government is proposing to create a network of 300 beacon schools sharing effective practice in the teaching of writing by January 2001. Schools with a good record of teaching skills relevant to the emerging economy – notably ICT skills – are to be given beacon school status along with schools that demonstrate excellence in working with their community including parents.

Governing bodies interested in developing good practice in a particular area could consider whether a beacon school in the area could offer them a model. The 550 beacon schools currently in operation are employing a wide range of activities to disseminate their good practice, including seminars to teachers from other schools; mentoring; workshadowing; provision of in-service training and consultancy. The DfEE website offers links to beacon schools where schools can identify similar schools to their own or get an idea of the range of activities beacon schools are involved in.

The National Literacy and Numeracy Strategies

The National Literacy Strategy was founded on the conviction that effective teaching of reading and writing by primary teachers is the most important factor in pupils' success. A survey of the impact of the literacy strategy on a representative sample of primary schools in 1999/2000 showed substantial gains in standards. (see **Governors and Curriculum**). It is good practice for the governing body to appoint a literacy governor to takes an interest in the strategic implications for the school of the National Literacy Strategy. Similarly, governors should be aware of key issues relating to the implementation of the National Numeracy Strategy through discussions with the headteacher and co-ordinator, and should participate in analysis of the outcomes of monitoring.

Standards Fund

The 2000/01 Standards Fund (*see also page 28*) is aimed to improve standards attained by pupils through school and education development plans, and through a range of initiatives such as the National Grid for Learning, learning mentors, summer schools, and support for parent governors. (**Education Standards Fund Regulations**)

Standards for governors

It has been pointed out that governors are the only group in the education system that do not have formal performance targets, but it must be remembered that they are also the only volunteers in the system. An *Index of School Governance* has been developed by Catherine Burt, an independent governor trainer, which offers a systematic framework for governing bodies interested in assessing their own effectiveness. Twenty standards are grouped together under four Ps: Planning, Progress, Partnership and Practice, and governors gather evidence and discuss what they do under each standard. (Details of the Index from cburt@enterprise.net)

Further information

Improving schools and governing bodies, 1999, by Michael Creese and Peter Earley, Routledge.

Monitoring and Evaluation for School Improvement, 2000, by Mazda Jenkin, Jeff Jones and Sue Lord, Heinemann.

Local Education Authority Support for School Improvement, 2001, Audit Commission and Ofsted, Stationery Office.

Adding value to school improvement, 2000, by Simon Bird, The Education Network (020 7554 2810).

School Evaluation Matters, 1998, Ofsted Publications Centre, 07002 637833.

Circular 11/98 Target Setting in Schools, DfEE, publications centre: 0845 6022260.

Supporting the target setting process, 2001, DfEE.

Raising the attainment of minority ethnic pupils – school and LEA responses, 1999, Ofsted.

Raising achievement of children in public care, 2001, Ofsted.

Target Setting: Guidance for Headteachers and Governing Bodies, 2000, National Assembly for Wales, Publications Centre (02920 898688).

Primary and Secondary School Partnership: Improving Learning and Performance, 1999, Estyn (029 2032 5000).

Standards and Quality in Secondary Schools: The Relative Performance of Boys and Girls, 1997, Estyn.

Standards and Quality in Primary Schools: Improving Primary Schools, 1998, Estyn.

Improving Standards and Quality in Secondary Schools, 1998, Estyn.

Standards and Quality in Primary Schools: Setting Targets for Improvement, 1998, Estyn.

Standards and Quality in Primary Schools: School Development Plans, 1998, Estyn.

How well are we doing? A Survey of Self-Evaluation in Secondary Schools 1998/9, 2000, Estyn.

Governors and Inspection

Although governors have no direct responsibilities during inspection, their involvement in the school's leadership and management does come under scrutiny. Inspectors will be looking for evidence that governors understand their role and are fully engaged in strategic planning. There is no quick fix for governors to come out of inspection well but this chapter provides governors with an understanding of the process and knowledge of what to expect.

Who, why and when

The departments

The legislation set up two independent departments, the Office of Her Majesty's Chief Inspector in England (Ofsted) and the Office of Her Majesty's Chief Inspector in Wales (Estyn) - each headed by a Chief Inspector (HMCI). The Chief Inspectors have a duty to report to the relevant Secretary of State on standards, to offer advice (whether or not the Secretary of State has asked for it) and to report to Parliament each year. They are assisted by Her Majesty's Inspectors (HMIs). Ofsted and Estyn train registered teams and lay inspectors and monitor inspections carried out by Registered Inspectors (RIs) and their teams.

The inspection team

Ofsted allocates an inspection to one of its agreed contractors, who nominates a Registered Inspector (RI) to lead the team. In Wales Estyn allocates a contract after scrutinising each tender. All RIs are required to comply with the Framework including the code of conduct; they must be familiar with their statutory duties, and are responsible in law for making sure inspectors in the team are fit, proper, competent and effective in their work.

Each team has to include one 'lay' inspector, and this can include someone who has been a voluntary helper in a school or a governor. Lay inspectors may take part in all aspects of the inspection but may not lead the reporting on any curriculum subject. Names of all team members and their responsibilities during the inspection must be published in the inspection report.

The inspection team can range from two to about 15, depending on the size of the school, and must include sufficient expertise to examine all curriculum and pastoral issues as set out in the Evaluation Schedule of the Framework. The minimum time the inspection team must spend on each specification is specified for different types of inspection. For special schools the inspectors must be competent to inspect provision for the main disability catered for by the school.

Governors can ask for detailed information about each member of the team appointed to inspect their school. In England, schools worried by the lack of appropriate expertise in one area have been able to negotiate with the RI for a change.

Appropriate authority

Each school has an 'appropriate authority' for inspection. For most schools this is the governing body, but for pupil referral units and schools without delegated budgets it is the LEA. For independent schools, city technology colleges (CTCs) and city colleges for technology of the arts (CCTAS), the proprietor takes this role.

The law

School inspections are governed by the **School Inspections Act 1996**. The **School Standards and Framework Act 1998** made minor amendments to the '96 Act. Regulations made under the 1996 Act are updated regularly - at the time of writing the most recent are **the Education (School Inspection) Regulations 1997 (SI1966)** and **the Education (School Inspection) (Amendments) Regulations 1999 (SI2545)** for England and **the Education (School Inspection) (Wales) Regulations 1998 (SI1866)** and the **Education (School Inspection)(Wales) (Amendment) Regulations 1999 (SI1440)** for Wales.

Section 10 of the 1996 Act states that inspections should report on:

"• the quality of the education provided by schools;

• the educational standards achieved in those schools;

• whether the financial resources made available to those schools are managed efficiently; and

• the spiritual, moral, social and cultural development of pupils in those schools."

In addition, under **Section 23** of the **1996 Act,** governors in certain denominational schools have a duty to arrange for inspection of religious education (RE) teaching and collective worship that is outside the Ofsted/Estyn system. These governors can choose their own inspectors, who need not be registered with Ofsted/Estyn, and are required to publish a report on any 'Section 23' inspection with its own action plan.

Why

The process of inspection is now seen to have three main aims:
• to provide an independent view of the school and its progress to help with its development
• to report to the local community, and
• to collect a national picture of school standards.

When

School inspections are now into their second cycle: all maintained schools, and pupil referral units and some independent schools are being inspected at least once during the six year period. City academies also come under the Ofsted regime. Timing of inspections for individualschools within the cycle is decided by Ofsted/Estyn. Each year they ensure the inspection of a balanced sample of schools.

In England there are now two types of inspection:
• Short inspections, often called "light touch inspections" for schools that are doing well
• Full inspections, for all other schools and pupil referral units.

To qualify for a short inspection, schools must have a good track record and be seen to be performing well against national standards and those for similar schools.

Although Welsh schools will continue to have one year's notice of inspection, in England, alongside the introduction of short inspections, there is now a shorter notice period of six to ten weeks.

The framework for inspection

Despite differences in the detail, the same principles for inspection apply to England and Wales. Each has its *Framework for the Inspection of Schools*, the key inspection document, which gives an outline of the process, explains the roles of participants and provides the evaluation schedules that list what the inspectors must consider.

Guidance on how the Frameworks should be applied and how inspections should be conducted in England is available in *Ofsted Handbooks* for primary, secondary or special schools and pupil referral units, and, in Wales, in the *Estyn Handbook for the Inspection of Schools*. These handbooks now contain guidance on self-evaluation, so that schools and governors can make their own judgements about their progress against inspectors' criteria.

Changes in 2001

From April 2001 Ofsted and Estyn have inspected child care arrangements alongside nursery provision. Inspections of sixth forms also came under a new regime at that time: Ofsted and Estyn will continue to inspect school sixth forms under the 1996 Act, but procedures will be harmonised with the inspection of further education and sixth form colleges under Part 3 of the **Learning and Skills Act 2000.** Ofsted will share a common inspection framework with the Adult Learning Inspectorate. As a result sixth forms will be looked at more closely, and the individual learner's achievements and experiences will be central to the inspection.

The inspection process in schools is steadily evolving. With the volume of comparative data growing all the time, schools are better able to compare their own performance with that of others; self evaluation by heads and senior managers is a growing part of the pre-inspection picture that Registered Inspectors put together. As schools understand more about their own performance, there will be less need for in-depth checks from outside inspectors, and in England more short inspections will be made. The high cost of full inspections is another incentive to shorten inspections.

Short inspections in England

In the first year of short inspections, around ten per cent of schools met the criteria for this 'health check', and the number is expected to grow. The difference between short and full inspections will be felt more by staff than by governors – fewer inspectors will be in school, and for a shorter time, so not all teachers will be seen teaching, and there will be less feedback. Leadership and management of the school will still be important in a short inspection, so governors' involvement is unlikely to be reduced. In effect, what a short inspection does is compare the school's view of itself with the inspectors' findings from information sent in advance and their sampling of school activities. If the two match up, and the school is improving, then the school is given a clean bill of health. If not, and the school is seen to have misread the signs of its own performance, this will be a concern to the inspectors and may lead to HMI monitoring or a full re-inspection. In worst cases this could lead to identification of serious weaknesses or even special measures.

How well is the school doing?

Inspectors now have to consider performance management, the principles of best value and social and educational inclusion. As well as working to help schools improve through the inspection process, Ofsted and Estyn are charged with improving the quality of inspections and the standard of reports. The key question for inspectors is "How well is the school doing and why?" The inspection schedule in England (and to a large extent in Wales) has been simplified into ten key questions :
1. What sort of school is it?
2. How high are standards?
3. How well are pupils taught?
4. How good are the curricular opportunities?
5. How well does the school care for its pupils?
6. How well does the school work in partnership with parents?
7. How well is the school led and managed?
8. What should the school do to improve further?
9. Other specified features - from the school information and, in full inspections –
10. The standards and quality of teaching in areas of the curriculum, subjects and courses.

Key stages of inspection

The governing body agrees its involvement and information to be provided.

Governing bodies have formal responsibilities during inspections but the head and management team will do most of the work. Governors will need an early briefing on the inspection process and should discuss with the head who does what. The Framework documents are useful at this point. Many governing bodies appoint a working group to oversee their responsibilities. Early agreement is useful on issues such as how much involvement individual governors will have, what the headteacher puts into the personal statement (England) or self assessment report (Wales) and what factual information is provided, as well as the timetable for the whole process. A discussion with LEA representatives can also be useful for advice on handling the inspection process and feedback, and establishing what support they can provide.

Ofsted/Estyn must consult the governing body over the specification for the inspection.

In practice a form is completed by the head who gives details of the school, its curriculum and any special circumstances that will call for extra inspection time (for example subjects outside the National Curriculum or extra foreign languages). An inspection may be extended to cover areas such as community provision in schools and this could include further education, although the school may be required to pay for this.

Governors' particular concerns about any part of the school's activities covered by the standard specification should be raised with the appointed inspector in preliminary discussions.

The Registered Inspector should then make contact with the appropriate authority (usually through the headteacher) to agree the actual dates for the inspection.

The governing body must then inform the relevant people and arrange a meeting between parents and the RI. This must be well ahead of the inspection so there is time for the team to take account of parents' concerns in planning the inspection. The people to be informed are the parents of all pupils in the school, and either the LEA (for a community school); or the Secretary of State or National Assembly for Wales (for a foundation school); or the group that appoints the foundation governors (for a voluntary school).

Secondary schools must also inform the Learning and Skills Council (LSC) in England and the National Council for Education and Training (CETW) in Wales. In both England and Wales they should invite representatives of the local business community to send comments to the Registered Inspector. This applies particularly to those business which have recently employed former pupils of the school.

Parents' views of the school

The meeting for parents should be at a time that is convenient for as many parents as possible. All parents of pupils in the school should be invited, with at least one week's notice given. The invitation can be combined with notice of the inspection and can be taken home by pupils. It can include the inspector's own explanation of why the meeting has been called. Standard letters are issued by Ofsted and Estyn, with translations into a number of community languages. Governors and members of staff are not entitled to attend this meeting unless they have children at the school.

A friendly atmosphere is important - sometimes the head or chair of governors welcomes the parents before handing over the meeting to the Inspector, who should explain the inspection, and cover the statutory responsibility to seek parents' views on the school. Parents should be encouraged to make their comments in general terms rather than naming any individuals. The inspector is not expected to comment on parents' views but should take account of significant positive views or concerns both during the inspection and when reporting back to the senior management team and the governors.

The Registered Inspector should ask the appropriate authority to distribute a question-naire to parents, giving time for answers to be returned directly to him/her in confidence before the meeting with parents.

Standard questionnaires are available from Ofsted/Estyn, with translations. Schools may choose to edit the letter and questionnaire (but will incur costs for translations, except in Wales where there is no cost for Welsh/English translations). Before the inspection proceeds the inspector should share with the headteacher and governors the consensus of parents' views from both the questionnaire and the meeting. Parents can be encouraged to write letters to supplement their questionnaires. Inspectors are required to see that parents' responses to the questionnaire are confidential and not seen by the school.

Consultation with parents continues to be given great emphasis in the second cycle of inspections. It is recognised as essential that inspectors hear parents' views and their level of satisfaction with the school, and respond to their comments. Questionnaires and the meeting will be supplemented by comments made to inspectors during the inspection by individual parents, including parent governors, parents who work in the school and others in school or at the school gate. Inspectors can also take account of any surveys the school has conducted, and should make themselves available if any groups of parents request a meeting during the inspection.

Governors can expect to be told about parents' positive or negative views and the inspectors' findings that relate to them in the oral feedback on the inspection and in the final inspection report. In Wales, only views confirmed by the inspection are mentioned in report.

Access to the school and preliminary information

The governors, with the staff, have a duty to provide the required documentation and access to the whole school community. Wilful obstruction of any of the inspection team is an offence under the 1996 Act. Inspectors are instructed to ask only for documents listed in the Framework, and cannot expect schools to provide multiple copies. Before the inspection starts, the school is required to provide information, but apart from the headteacher's forms and statement/self assessment report, this should all be the standard school documents and not produced especially for the inspection. For full inspections in England and all inspections in Wales most of the information is taken away in advance, to allow the RI to build a preliminary judgement on the school which can then be tested out during the inspection. Thus alongside statistics on pupils and their performance, the headteacher's evaluation of the school's position and progress is crucial. Other information required before the inspection includes the previous inspection report and action plan that followed and reports on other external monitoring. The school's own documents which will be needed include the prospectus, development plan, policies, staff handbook and schemes of work. In Wales the development plan, schemes of work and timetables are usually required. Full inspections call for the most evidence, including minutes of meetings of the governing body for the preceding 12 months (not in Wales), structure and proceedings of sub-committees, annual reports to parents and targets set by governors with evidence of progress towards them.

Statistics supplied by schools in England are summarised in Ofsted's PICSI (Pre-Inspection Contextual School Indicator) reports for each school. This is produced for the RI just before the inspection and a copy is sent to the headteacher. It supplements the Panda (Performance and Assessment report) sent to each school once a year as a guideline for self-evaluation. These two documents give useful benchmarking data on national and local achievements and are a great help in understanding what is happening in other schools. (These documents are not available in Wales, however.)

Inspectors must examine an adequate cross-section of the work of the pupils, including all age and ability groups.
Assemblies, off-site units and extra-curricular activities will be looked at, and subjects not being taught at the time will be covered by evaluation of previous work. Since September 1997 inspectors in England have been required to give greater attention to the attainment and progress of minority groups and pupils with special educational needs. This has always been the case in Wales. New guidance published by Ofsted explains what inspectors will be looking for. In Wales, inspectors have been trained in social and educational inclusion and there is useful guidance in *NAW Circular 3/99, Pupil Support and Social Inclusion.*

During the inspection – governors' involvement
Governors have no direct responsibilities during the inspection process but are encouraged to be active and supportive with staff and the inspectors. In England they must meet the inspectors before (possibly at a specific meeting) and during the inspection at times arranged in advance. Individual governors with specific responsibilities can expect to have discussions with inspectors.
Governors' effectiveness will be examined particularly when inspectors consider how well the school is led and managed. Requirements are phrased differently in England and Wales, but all inspectors will be looking at the impact of schools' plans

rather than just their intentions, and how good they are at monitoring what is being achieved. Other key questions are how well governors are fulfilling their statutory duties, and what contribution they are making to the leadership and direction of the school. Judgements will also be made on financial management, including making the best strategic use of resources, and decisions on spending being linked to educational priorities. Inspectors are expected to come to a clear view, supported by evidence, of the school's sense of purpose and priorities, its understanding of its strengths and weaknesses and how to tackle them, and its insistence that all pupils do their best and are able to play a full part in school life. What matters is whether the school is effective in its support for good teaching and learning. Leadership and management will be judged as a whole, with the governing body's contribution being considered alongside that of the staff and headteacher. Inspectors may look to governing body papers and discussions with head and governors for evidence that they understand their respective roles and that the governing body's proceedings enable it to fulfil its responsibilities for strategic planning and raising standards. Inspectors should report on how the various roles are interpreted.

There is no quick fix for governors to come well out of this part of the inspection – good practice, good relationships and compliance with statutory requirements cannot be laid on to order in the week before the inspectors arrive.

Oral feedback
In England inspectors are required to provide feedback for individual teachers after, or soon after lessons are inspected, and during the inspection process to heads of department, course co-ordinators and those with pastoral responsibilities. Professional dialogue between inspectors and teachers is now seen as a valuable part of the inspection process and it is important that enough time is allowed for feedback sessions to enable maximum benefit to be gained.

In Wales only, teachers who are graded consistently very good or poor should be informed orally of it. If other teachers request an evaluation of their teaching they should receive that before the end of the inspection. Oral feedback is given to all staff in primary schools and to all members of departments and senior management teams in secondary schools.

After the inspection the RI must offer to discuss the main findings with the head, at least some of the staff, and separately with the appropriate authority who will arrange the meeting and decide who should be invited, including for example a representative of the LEA or other body such as the Diocesan Board. In Wales the RI should provide translation facilities if required.
The inspector should not report anything to the governing body that has not already been made known to the headteacher and nothing that is published in the inspector's report should come as a surprise to the governors. These meeting should be as soon as possible, and before the report is finalised. Oral feedback is confidential and must not be released to the media until after the inspector's final report has been received by the governing

body. Inspectors should provide clear feedback and allow for discussion and clarification, giving a rounded picture of the school that includes progress since the last inspection, and strengths as well as areas for improvement that should be addressed in the action plan. The school may record feedback sessions if the RI agrees. In Wales agreement does not have to be given. A draft report must be shown to the school so that any factual errors can be corrected. (Schools in England have five working days to respond.) Negotiation on the inspector's judgements is not possible!

The Inspector's report

The inspector must produce his/her report and a separate summary within six weeks of the end of the inspection (or seven weeks if translation is required), and send copies to the governing body, the head, Ofsted/Estyn and the local education authority or other appropriate authority. The report will include judgements on the four key areas for inspection. It will list key issues for action.

The governing body is required to circulate summaries of the report, with copies to the parents of every pupil and others. The 1997 Regulations require that the appropriate authority takes reasonable steps to send this out within ten days of the receipt of the inspector's report. The report and summary must be available for inspection by members of the public. No charge may be made for single copies of the summary requested by a member of the public. Copies of both report and summary must be provided on request, but charges (at cost) can be made for multiple copies of the summary and of the report. Governors should consider whether translations of the summary and/or the report would be helpful. In Wales the specification will state whether the report needs to be in English and Welsh. Schools are advised to publicise the report widely, and send copies to local libraries, newspapers and radio stations as well as local LSCs and businesses which made comments to the inspectors. Careful handling of the media is important so attention is given to the school's good points as well as any problems. Many LEAs offer support to schools over liaison with the Press. Inspection reports for English schools are now available on the Ofsted's web site. If the RI is seriously concerned about standards in the school, special procedures come into play under which the school might require 'special measures' or (in England only) be defined as having 'serious weaknesses'. These involve further review with HMIs and possible involvement by the DfEE/NAW (See below).

The action plan

The governing body is responsible for considering the inspection report and producing an action plan to deal with the points raised. This must be done within 40 working days (or 45 where a translation is required) of the delivery of the inspection report, with some allowance made for holidays. Copies of the action plan must be sent within five days of its completion to parents of pupils in the school, all those working at the school, Ofsted/Estyn, the LEA (or other appropriate authority) and, for secondary schools, the local LSC/CETW. As with the inspection summary, the action plan must be made available to the wider public, with consideration again given to translation, and similar charges being allowed. Anyone living within three miles of the school is entitled to a free copy of the action plan.

The action plan needs to address the inspector's key issues, be clear about what action is proposed, what resources are required, who is to be responsible, the timescales for improvement and criteria by which progress is to be judged. The governing body is then required to include a statement of progress on the latest action plan in its annual report to parents each year, giving reference to proposals and targets dates. Where possible the action plan should be linked to or incorporated into the school's Development Plan, as the inspection report can be a valuable addition to the regular review of school progress. The DfEE and Estyn require that there should be clear identification of the parts of the Development Plan that relate to the inspection, along with the deadline dates for each item.

Action plans are best produced as a joint effort between headteacher, staff and governors. Pupils can be also be consulted through school councils or year heads or tutors. Head and staff are likely to draft the plan for discussion and agreement with governors before circulation. If governors feel the targets and timetables need to be sharpened up or want to make more radical proposals, they may wish to take outside advice from LEA advisers or elsewhere. The most difficult situation for governors is where the inspection report highlights weaknesses in the senior management of the school, and in this case the LEA and the chief education officer may need to be consulted.

Quality and complaints

All contractors that bid to inspect schools have to meet Ofsted/Estyn quality standards, and individual members of the team of inspectors must be named on the reports. English schools, unhappy with their inspection, are encouraged to discuss the problem with Ofsted staff in the first instance, but a formal complaints procedure is now in place. In the first instance schools must raise their complaint with their RI and the contractor. If not satisfied they can write to Ofsted's Corporate Services Group within one year of the inspection. Still not satisfied? The end of the line is the Complaints Adjudicator (OCA), an external arbiter independent of Ofsted, who has to be approached within three months of the final response to the complaint, and whose remit is to review the handling of the complaint.

Complaints over inspections in Welsh schools are handled by HMCI. A complaints procedure is in place and all schools are asked to fill in a questionnaire about the inspection that goes to the RI and Estyn.

Follow-up

In Wales Estyn scrutinises and provides a written response on all action plans to the school. Estyn monitors implementation of all action plans but, because of financial restraints, puts most of its efforts into looking at the progress of schools where deficiencies have been identified. In England, unless a school is a cause for concern, the only follow-up under the law is for governors to report back to parents at the annual meeting, giving details on progress with the action plan targets. These reports will be examined by inspectors during later inspections. In either case, governors should set up their own timetable for follow-up procedures by agreeing with the senior management team when reports will be made to governors' meetings on the various targets in the action plan. On-going monitoring and evaluation can be built into the cycle of governors' meetings, so that the indicators used by inspectors and the governors' own priorities can be checked regularly. The Government's increasing emphasis on target-setting and school self-evaluation is covered in the **Governors and Standards** chapter.

Schools causing concern

While schools are responsible for their own improvement, LEAs or other relevant authorities have a responsibility for supporting them and should be monitoring schools between inspections so that any problems are picked up and addressed at an early stage. The LEA should consult with schools on how it will support school improvement, and set this out in its education development plan (EDP)(England), or education strategic plans (ESPs) (Wales) having regard to the *Code of Practice on LEA/School Relations*. If an LEA judges that the school would cause concern under an Ofsted inspection it is required to intervene to prevent failure. If the LEA and the governors cannot agree on a way forward, the LEA can issue a formal warning to the school. If the school again does not respond effectively, the LEA can set in motion various measures that match what it can do when Ofsted declares a school to have serious weaknesses or is failing. Funding is available through the Standards Fund for LEAs to help schools causing concern. *(Circular 6/99: Schools Causing Concern).*

If the RI or HMI finds a school is "failing or likely to fail to give its pupils an acceptable standard of education", 'special measures' are required. Procedures to be followed are set out in law, and in the last resort the school may be closed, possibly to be re-opened again under new management.

Schools in England providing an acceptable standard of education but nevertheless underperforming in one or more particular areas may be told they have serious weaknesses – the verdict on about eight per cent of English schools recently.

Although not identified as having serious weakness, some schools may be judged to be underachieving. Ofsted /Estyn will decide what follow up is needed after the inspection to make sure that suitable action is being taken.

Special measures

An RI's judgement that a school requires special measures relates to one or more of the following areas of its activities:
- the educational standards achieved, including low attainment and progress with associated factors of poor behaviour and attendance, and significant racial tension.
- unsatisfactory teaching and low expectations, failure to cover the National Curriculum and provide for pupils' spiritual, moral, social and cultural development. Poor relationships that put pupils at risk may also be a factor.
- the management and efficiency of the school, shown through poor performance by head, senior management or governors in their dealings with money and people, including staff and parents.

The inspector and the team must consider whether many pupils are not receiving the education to which they are entitled or if pupils are at serious physical or emotional risk. Even if the school's management team is addressing such difficulties, the inspector must still pronounce the school to be failing.

Informing the school
If the inspection team feels a school may be failing, the RI must warn the headteacher before the end of the inspection. If the inspector then decides the school does need special measures, s/he must first inform the Ofsted's School Improvement Team or, in Wales, Her Majesty's Chief Inspector, before the school is told of the judgement.

Ofsted's/Estyn's view
The school may then be visited by an HMI who will verify whether the school requires special measures, and if confirmed by Ofsted/Estyn this will be reported in the RI's report and summary. The Secretary of State/NAW will be sent the report at this stage. If Ofsted/Estyn does not agree that special measures are required, they will discuss other courses of action with the RI. The school may be visited by HMI in England but will always be visited by HMCI in Wales.

Action plan
When special measures are required, the governors must produce their action plan within 40 working days and distribute it to parents and those working in the school within two days (rather than the usual five days). The plan must also go to HMCI and the Secretary of State/NAW. Governors of schools with delegated budgets (ie almost all schools) are expected to liaise with their LEA when preparing their action plan, and voluntary aided schools with their appropriate authority.

The action plan should provide a timetable for getting the school out of special measures as well as addressing the key issues in the inspection report. In England this should be within two years, while in Wales, it is "as soon as possible". A school in special measures will be monitored by HMIs.

The DfEE may intervene in failing schools by appointing additional governors, by creating a Fresh Start School or by closing the school. *(Pars 62 – 69, Circular 6/99, Schools Causing Concern.)* Similar arrangements apply in Wales.

LEA's role
The LEA is required to comment on the school's action plan, taking account of likely success and possible shortcomings, any omissions in the governors' plan, and how long the LEA has been aware of the problems, with action taken to address them.

The LEA should also give an assessment of whether closing a school is an option, and say whether it will use its powers to suspend the delegation of the budget. This commentary must be sent to HMCI and the Secretary of State/NAW as well as those who normally receive school action plans.

Serious weaknesses

Schools in England which inspectors are particularly worried about but are not thought to be failing their pupils can be defined as having serious weaknesses. This will only happen after special measures have been ruled out. The same characteristics will be examined as for special measures, and a significant weakness in one or more area can trigger the procedures.

If the inspectors decide a school has a serious weaknesses, the RI must first inform Ofsted's School Improvement Division and then the governors and school's senior management team at the oral feedback meeting, and the appropriate authority. The governing body is expected to start straight away on its action plan with close involvement of the head and the LEA giving guidance on the action required. The finding of serious weaknesses will be reported in the full inspection report and the summary. Again the action plan must be published within 40 days and sent to Ofsted and it must give a timetable for addressing the cause of serious weakness **within a year.** The LEA must submit its own statement of action alongside the school's plan which addresses similar points to those for failing schools, including whether the school should be closed because there are sufficient places in the area. The governing body should receive a copy. HMI will comment on the action plan, and any resulting revisions will be required from the school within two weeks. The DfEE may be brought in if HMI cannot agree with the school and the LEA what is required.

Schools can expect the LEA to hold a formal discussion on progress at least once a term. If expected progress is not made within six months, the LEA may intervene more strongly, either by appointing new governors, or removing delegation of the budget. Two years after a school is shown to have serious weaknesses HMI will re-inspect.

Procedures in Wales are similar, but less formalised. The term 'serious weakness' may not be used, but HMIs continue to monitor schools where particular issues such as poor exam results are a matter of concern. A small scale inspection may be instigated with the findings sent to the school in an extended letter. The timescales for a school being improved are similar to those set out for England, but may be less strictly applied.

Closing the school

If the school does not improve sufficiently, the Secretary of State may direct that it should be closed (S19 SSFA). LEAs also have powers to close schools, but in either case there are requirements for consultation with interested parties. The Secretary of State has indicated that failing schools will be given about two years to turn themselves round. Powers are available for new schools to be opened so a failing school may be given a 'Fresh Start' through being closed and re-opened on the same site with new management. Some schools may become city academies, like Fresh Start schools these are set up to replace seriously failing schools. They are managed by partnerships involving government, voluntary church and business sponsors.

What governors can do

The number of failing schools is not large - around two per cent of primaries and secondaries, and seven per cent of special schools in England, and even fewer in Wales (less than 0.5% for all schools). The majority have been able to make satisfactory or good progress but 31 in England have been closed. Around ten per cent of schools in England have serious weaknesses.

Increasingly, LEAs are using Ofsted/Estyn criteria to identify difficulties in their own schools before the RIs arrive. If the LEA is doing its job well, governors should know before their inspection if their school is at risk so expensive 'pre-Ofsted/Estyn' inspections by outside consultants should not be necessary.

If the inspectors decide a school has serious weaknesses or is failing, the governors have a vital role. The first reaction may be disbelief or fury but once the accuracy of the inspector's judgements has been verified, governors should act in the best interests of the pupils in their school. Realism is required and time is short. Morale within the school needs to be restored and frank and detailed discussion of the school's problems need to take place with the LEA or other outside advisers.

The most difficult situation to be faced is a failure of senior management, yet this has to be addressed quickly if the school is to be turned around. Some LEAs have managed this situation by arranging a dignified exit for a headteacher or other key staff. In many cases schools have been effectively rescued by an outside person being seconded in as headteacher. Extra resources may be available both in cash and management support.

Governors can help by spending time in school informing themselves of the situation, discussing a range of options with the LEA, being thoroughly involved in the production of a clear action plan with measurable targets, building relationships with parents, supporting the school in curriculum planning, tackling poor behaviour and attendance and in improving financial management. Ofsted suggests that schools in difficulty need:
* accurate performance information
* sound advice from subject and phase specialist LEA staff
* attention to the quality of teaching and the leadership and management of the school
* clear criteria on which to judge the progress.

Also important is good liaison between LEA and governors. Working out the right questions to ask is more important than ever at this point and governors can insist that LEA officers keep them up to date with progress.

Whatever problems inspection identifies, it can be helpful to remember that all schools have good points that can be the starting point for a revival. Governors can work with teachers to build morale and extend good practice.

Governors and SEN

Governors' responsibilities in this area are likely to increase as new disability legislation is introduced and a new revised Code of Practice, which puts a greater emphasis on school support, comes into force in September 2001. Here we describe how governors can support children with special educational needs and meet these new challenges.

What must governors do?

Part 1V of the **Education Act 1996** spells out the responsibilities that all governors have towards any children in their school who have special educational needs (SEN). These apply equally to governors of all maintained schools. Governing bodies have a legal duty to have regard to the Code of Practice on special educational needs (**S313 EA96**). The governing body must:

- do its best to secure that the necessary provision is made for any pupil who has special educational needs;
- secure that, where the headteacher or the appropriate governor (the 'responsible person') has been informed by the Local Education Authority (LEA) that a pupil has special educational needs, those needs are made known to all who are likely to teach him or her;
- secure that teachers in the school are aware of the importance of identifying and providing for pupils with special educational needs;
- consult with the LEA and other bodies over special needs provision where this is desirable;
- ensure that a pupil with special educational needs joins in school activities with pupils who do not have such needs, so far as is reasonably practical and compatible with the pupil receiving the necessary special education, the efficient education of other children in the school and the efficient use of resources;
- report on the implementation and effectiveness of the school's SEN policy in their annual report to parents (**S317 EA96**).

(The 'responsible person' means the headteacher or the appropriate governor, who may be the chair of the governors or any other governor designated by the governing body for that purpose. In a nursery school, the responsible person is the headteacher.)

The special needs policy

The SEN information regulations for England and Wales require all governing bodies to publish their policy on special education and to make it available free to parents and prospective parents.

The policy must describe the procedures the school uses to identify, provide for and monitor provision for children with special needs.

The SEN policy must contain:

1) Basic information about the school's special educational provision:
- the objectives of the policy
- the name of the school's SEN co-ordinator(SENCO) or teacher responsible for the day-to-day operation of the SEN policy
- the arrangements for co-ordinating educational provision for pupils with SEN
- admissions arrangements
- any SEN specialism and any special units
- any building adaptations and special facilities.

2) Information about the school's policies for identification, assessment and provision for all pupils with SEN:
- the allocation of resources to and amongst pupils with SEN
- identification, assessment, monitoring and review procedures
- arrangements for providing access to the curriculum for pupils with SEN
- how children with SEN are integrated into the school as a whole
- criteria for evaluating the success of the SEN policy
- any arrangements for considering parents' complaints about SEN provision within the school.

3) Information about the school's staffing policies and partnership with bodies beyond the school:
- the school's arrangements for SEN in-service training
- use made of teachers and facilities from outside the school including support services
- arrangements for partnership with parents
- links with other mainstream and special schools, including arrangements when pupils change or leave school
- links with health and social services, educational welfare services and any voluntary organisations.

(**The Education (SEN) (Information) (England) Regulations 1999 (SI 2506) and The Education (SEN) (Information) (Wales) Regulations 1999 (SI 1442)**).

Information for parents

The school prospectus must publish a summary of the school's special needs policy as detailed above and this should indicate how the success of the policy is evaluated and how resources are allocated. It should also outline any complaints arrangements for parents. The governors' annual report must include information on the success of the SEN policy and any significant changes to it. In Wales, in addition, the annual report should describe how, since the last annual report, resources have been allocated to and amongst pupils with SEN and any consultation with the LEA or other schools.

In commenting on the success of the policy, reports should demonstrate the effectiveness of the school's system for identification, assessment, provision, monitoring and record-keeping, and the use of outside support services and agencies. Parents often find explanation of how resources have been spent less than transparent. Diagrams showing the proportion of the budget allocated to each stage of special help alongside information about actual sums spent and total resources available could aid understanding.

The **Disability Discrimination Act 1995** requires schools to describe in annual reports any arrangements for the admission of disabled pupils, facilities provided to assist access and steps being taken to prevent them being treated less favourably than other pupils. Governors should ensure that access to the curriculum, a full range of play and social experiences and extra-curricular activities such as school trips are considered as well as access to buildings and facilities. (*See also page 17*)

The Education (School Information) (England) Regulations 1998 (SI 2526 and The Education (School Information) (Wales) Regulations 1999 (SI 1812).

The Education (SEN) (Information) (England) Regulations 1999 (SI 2506) and Sched. 4 of The Education (SEN) (Information) (Wales) Regulations 1999 (SI 1442).

The Education (Governors' Annual Reports) (England) Regulations 1999 (SI 2157); The Education (Governors' Annual Reports) (Wales) Regulations 1999 (SI 1406)

Terminology

The field of special education is riddled with specialist terminology which can encourage the idea that it is somehow separate from everything else that goes on in schools. Governors need to be aware of the key definitions, and avoid allowing their use to set special education outside their whole-school perspective.

Special educational needs (often shortened to SEN) is the term applied to any pupil who has a learning difficulty which calls for special educational provision to be made.

A child is considered to have a learning difficulty if s/he has "significantly greater difficulty in learning" than the majority of children of the same age; or has a disability which either prevents or hinders him or her from "making use of the educational facilities of a kind generally provided in schools within the area of the local authority concerned" for children of his or her age. The Code of Practice on special educational needs points out that emotional and behavioural difficulties are special educational needs. Governors should bear this in mind when devising behaviour policies and at exclusion hearings.

Special educational provision that is made for children of two and over is any educational provision that is "additional to or otherwise different from" the educational provision made generally for children of his or her age in maintained schools in the area (S312 EA96).

A child with complex and/or significant learning difficulties may have a Statement of his or her special educational needs drawn up by the LEA.

How many children?

The number of children who have a learning difficulty will vary considerably from school to school. As a general rule, it is estimated that one in five, or 20 per cent, of all children will have a learning difficulty at some stage of their schooling, although most of these children will not require a Statement. Currently around three per cent of the school population of England and Wales has a Statement with a little over a third of these pupils placed in special schools. Governors' duties extend towards all children with special educational needs. The Code of Practice describes how schools and LEAs should identify and support these children, and strongly emphasises the importance of working with parents and including the views of pupils.

School stages of help

Special educational provision has commonly been provided in five stages, the first three stages funded from the school's budget and decided by the school, possibly with expert advice brought in at stage three. At stage 4, the child undergoes a statutory assessment organised by the LEA, usually leading to a Statement – which is stage 5 (*see below*).

At time of writing a revised Code of Practice - one for each of England and Wales - is in draft form. It moves from three stages of pre-Statement support to two levels, School Action and School Action Plus. The decision about which level is appropriate will be taken on a case-by-case basis.

The following summarises the new school stages described in the draft Code:

School Action - will be action taken by the school alone. Main provision is by class/subject teacher. Pupil has individual or group individual education plan (IEP) with thorough assessment, planning and differentiation.

School Action Plus - action by the school with support from external agencies. At this level pupils will work mainly in small groups or on an individual basis in ordinary classrooms, a resource base and/or through out-of-hours provision. The pupil will have a more specifically-focused IEP with intensive assessment, and planning, access to adult support and targeted tuition.

As well as a new Code, good practice guidance and guidelines describing thresholds of support for different levels of need is expected later in 2001.

What the changes may mean

The draft Code of Practice appears to shift greater responsibility on schools for pupils with SEN leading to a reduction in the number of Statements issued. It also suggests delegating all money, including funding attached to statemented pupils, to schools. The consequence is likely to be increased pressure on teachers, who will bear greater responsibility for organising provision, and on the SEN governor who will have to ensure the school's systems successfully identify and provide for children with SEN and for monitoring the outcome of interventions at all stages of the Code.

What is a Statement?

A Statement of special needs describes the particular learning difficulties a pupil may have, and sets out the provision that must be made to meet those needs. Both the LEA and the child's parents are bound by the special educational provision that is written into the Statement, which is subject to a regular annual review and can be amended. The Statement is drawn up after a child has been identified (by parents, school, health authority or social services) as having special educational needs, after which a detailed multi-professional assessment is undertaken. Parents are involved in this assessment and should be encouraged to make their views known. An overview of the implementation of the Code of Practice by Ofsted pointed to the need for governors and teachers to remind themselves continually of the importance of working closely with parents and of involving the pupils themselves. A Statement may be made before a child starts school or at any stage during his or her schooling. All children educated in special schools should have a Statement.

To be effective, governors must know about the requirements of the Code of Practice, the assessment and statementing process and how the respective roles of the LEA, the school, support services and parents inter-relate. They will also need to ensure that:
• the school has a written policy on its special needs provision
• all staff are aware of the policy and its implications;
• the policy is summarised in the school prospectus and a report on its effectiveness is provided in every annual governors' report to parents;
• parents are kept fully involved and informed;
• children with special needs are enabled to participate as fully as possible in all aspects of school life.
Ofsted's six-yearly inspections will review and report on the effectiveness of each school's special needs provision and since September 1997 inspectors have had to pay greater attention to the attainment and progress of pupils with special educational needs.

Disability legislation

The **Disability Discrimination Act 1995** (*see page 17*) does not cover provision of education but the SEN and Disability Bill completing its passage through Parliament at the time of writing will bring education under disability law. The Bill will introduce new duties on LEAs and schools. For example, there will be:
• a duty on governing bodies to produce an accessibility plan, for improving the physical environment of their school within a prescribed period to improve inclusion;
• a duty on education providers not to treat disabled pupils and students less favourably, without justification, than non-disabled pupils and students;
• a duty on schools to make reasonable adjustments so that disabled pupils are not put at a substantial disadvantage;
• a duty on LEAs to arrange to provide parents of children with special educational needs with advice and information, and a means of resolving disputes with schools and LEAs;
• a duty on schools to tell parents where they are making special educational needs provision for their child, and a right for schools as well as parents to request statutory assessment of a pupil's special educational needs (thus effectively giving parents the right of appeal even when the school makes the request);
• a strengthening of the right of children with special educational needs to be educated in mainstream schools.

A whole school approach

To be really effective, a school's special needs provision should be developed within the context of the school's Development Plan. This can help to ensure a consistent approach to special needs provision in all aspects of the curriculum and organisation of the school. The governing body can support such an approach through its active work in all areas where it has specific responsibility. In revising the special needs policy, governors should work with staff, parents and LEA advisers. The new Code of Practice will continue to place emphasis on inclusion for the majority of children with SEN.

Governors' monitoring role

The governing body can choose to make one of its members responsible for general oversight of special needs in the school, or form a special needs committee comprising governors and staff with a brief to report back regularly at governors' meetings. This second option can encourage the crucial relationship between the SEN governor and the SENCO, a key to the effectiveness of the SEN governor.

An ACE survey of governors found confusion between the role of the 'responsible person' and the named SEN governor. In general, it is clear that the most effective approach is to agree that the headteacher, who has day-to-day management responsibility, is the responsible person, while a governor (who is not a teacher/staff governor) takes responsibility for keeping SEN on the governing body agenda. Governors can ask to have special education as an agenda item at every termly meeting, and a regular item in each head's report to governors.

Governors might wish to discuss and ask for regular reports on a range of issues including:

- how many children are at School Action or School Action Plus
- resource implications;
- differentiation – matching curriculum and teaching to individual needs;
- training for staff in SEN;
- liaison with support services: educational psychologists, education social workers, advisory teachers etc;
- communication with parents;
- links with special/mainstream schools;
- how the success of the school SEN policy is to be evaluated.

Links with parents

Research has indicated that parents only contact the SEN governor when s/he actively publicises his or her availability. Improving the accessibility of the link governor to parents was seen to be an important way of facilitating partnership between parents and schools. Governors can help parents support their children effectively by ensuring their schools invite parents to termly reviews of individual education plans for children with SEN and provide information on the curriculum and on assessment and testing arrangements.

In their annual report to parents, governors can take the opportunity to highlight the achievements of all pupils, rather than simply reporting the crude league tables that legislation requires. There are other ways in which schools must be accountable to parents – through the school prospectus, pupil records and pupil reports. Governors can use this information to promote the whole-school approach of their special needs policy, and actively encourage parents to become more closely involved in their children's education.

Feedback from parents is one way the governing body can monitor the success of its special education policy. Questionnaires, governors' surgeries, information afternoons/evenings, and complaints procedures are among the ways some schools encourage feedback.

School standards

Governing bodies could use target setting as an opportunity to focus on raising standards among children with SEN. School improvement targets eg for literacy, numeracy, and in test and examination results should be closely related to the SEN policy.

In some special schools and mainstream schools with large numbers of pupils with significant SEN, targets will be at levels on the P scales, described in *Supporting the Target Setting Process* (DfEE, 2001). P scales provide descriptions of attainment below level 1 and within levels 1 and 2, for English and mathematics. A scale for personal and social development is also included and governing bodies may consider additional targets addressing such areas as behaviour.

The targets on these scales will be set as part of the process of school self review and may be based on needs, for example, if a group of pupils need to make greater progress in communication skills. From 2001 schools which set zero rated targets will be required to set measurable performance targets for 2003 at the relevant key stages using the P scales or other performance criteria where appropriate. They will be required to publish their targets alongside performance outcomes in the annual report to parents.

Curriculum

Most maintained schools must follow the National Curriculum. Those in education action zones can choose not to follow it and relaxation at Key Stage 4 may enable secondary schools to offer a more appropriate curriculum to some young people. However, in both cases schools should balance the advantages of a freer curriculum with the entitlement to a broad and balanced curriculum available to the majority of pupils. Although success in the workplace could raise the self esteem of low achievers, schools should not see extended work experience programmes as an alternative to making provision to meet young people's needs.

At primary level all children should have access to the National Literacy and Numeracy Strategies alongside the National Curriculum. Differentiation of learning activities may be needed to meet the needs of all children.

The draft Code points out that learning difficulties may not always result from problems within the child – school practices "make a difference – for good or ill". Governing bodies should examine school policies and practices in the light of any patterns which may emerge in the school's identification and recording of children's SEN or parents' expressions of concern.

Curriculum exception and modification

Pupils with Statements of SEN may have exceptions or modifications to the National Curriculum written into their Statements although it is not necessary for Statements to modify National Curriculum provisions to enable a child to study at a lower level than the majority of pupils of his age group. It is particularly important that a broad and balanced curriculum is maintained even where a Statement includes an exception from the National Curriculum.

Headteachers have the power to except individual pupils from all or part of the National Curriculum, including national tests, for a temporary period in cases where they believe the pupil is unable to follow the National Curriculum for a period of up to six months (renewable for a further period of six months). Heads must prepare a plan to show how they propose to return the pupil to the National Curriculum, or else indicate whether the pupil should be the subject of a formal assessment leading to a Statement (Ss364, 365 EA96). Parents, governors and the LEA must be informed of any such decision and the reasons for it. Parents who disagree have the right to appeal to the governing body. Parents themselves can ask to have a child excepted, and can appeal to the governing body against a headteacher's refusal to do so *(see page 41)*.

SEN funding

In the past most funding for pupils with Statements was retained by the LEA, while funding for other pupils with special educational needs was calculated within the LEA formula and devolved to schools. The draft Code of Practice appears to favour delegating all money for SEN pupils, whether or not they are statemented, to schools. This money would not be earmarked which means that governors can decide to spend more or less than the formula calculation for their school on special educational needs. However children with a Statement are legally entitled to the help set out in that Statement and governors cannot ignore their legal responsibilities under the 1996 Act to ensure SEN provision needed by a pupil is made.

When governors account for their spending decisions they should be able to show what funds have been allocated for special needs provision. They have to make a general report on resourcing for special needs in their school prospectus. Parents want to be assured that their children's needs are properly supported and they will expect the governing body to be able to demonstrate that this is happening.

Currently arrangements vary according to the amount LEAs pass on to schools but greater clarity over funding will help parents judge when a school's resources are insufficient to provide for their child's needs at which point they should be advised to write to the LEA to ask for a statutory assessment for their child.

Under the Schools Access Initiative the Government has made £30m available in 2000-2001 for improving access to the buildings, curriculum and the social life of schools for pupils with disabilities. Funding to schools for this purpose is to rise each year reaching £100m in 2003-4. There is also money available from the Standards Fund for projects that promote inclusion of pupils with SEN into mainstream settings - £82m for 2001-2. The funds will be distributed through the LEA so governors should ensure planning is underway in readiness for new requirements on governing bodies to prepare accessibility plans. These will feed into LEA accessibility strategies and enable them to prioritise improvements (**SEN and Disability Bill**).

Staffing

To meet the requirements of the Code of Practice effectively, all schools should have a member of staff identified to act as the Special Educational Needs Co-ordinator (SENCO). Governors need to establish a clear job description for the SENCO, and agree any additional scale points that are to be awarded for this responsibility in line with the *School Teachers' Pay and Conditions Document*. The draft Code recognises the SENCO's key role in the strategic, curriculum and financial development of schools. While the Government believes that decisions about precise time allocations and facilities are matters for schools themselves, they

will encourage schools to consider carefully how best they can support the SENCO. Practice guidance to be published alongside the revised Code will include advice to help SENCOs manage particular aspects of SEN.

When budgets are tight, SEN support teachers, who may have no specific class or curriculum responsibility, are often seen as the most obvious posts to cut. This should not happen if the school has a clear commitment to special education and this is reflected in the school's Development Plan.

Admissions

Responsibility for school admissions rests with the governing bodies of voluntary aided and foundation schools, and with the LEA for community and voluntary controlled schools. Admissions arrangements have to be published and, if schools are oversubscribed, pupils should be admitted according to the published admissions criteria. Governors should be sure that these criteria are clearly stated and strictly adhered to. The SEN policy must describe the admissions criteria. There should be agreement as to what constitutes 'special social or medical circumstances'.

Pupils with special educational needs but no Statement should not be turned away because of their special needs. However school governors should be consulted before a school is named on a pupil's Statement. The Codes of Practice on admissions state that children with SEN but no Statement must be treated on the same basis as other applicants. Admission authorities cannot refuse to admit a pupil because he or she does not have a Statement or is being assessed for one. They cannot refuse to admit a pupil without a Statement on the grounds that the school considers itself unable to meet the child's needs (*DfEE COP School Admissions* and S*chool Admissions Welsh Office COP*). Admission criteria should not disadvantage these pupils and there may be a case for giving them priority of admission. Governors should monitor admission of pupils with SEN to ensure their fair treatment. Screening of pupils for SEN when they enter the school is another positive step which can be introduced as part of the routine induction but children who come into the school at non-standard entry times should also be screened.

The LEA has a qualified duty to educate children with special educational needs in ordinary schools, so long as this is compatible with the child receiving the special educational provision s/he requires; with the provision of "efficient education" for children with whom s/he will be educated, and with the "efficient use of resources" (**S316 EA96**). There are likely to be changes to this when the **SEN and Disability Rights in Education Bill** becomes law. This would strengthen parents' right to a mainstream place for their child so long as it could not be said to adversely affect the "efficient education" of other children at the school.

Where the governing body is the admission authority it will also have to ensure that the arrangements it makes for determining the admission of pupils to the school do not substantially disadvantage disabled people. It is important that governors are aware of this duty to integrate. They have a significant role to play in influencing attitudes and lobbying for appropriate resources for children with special needs in their schools. Special educational provision can be expressed in terms of specialist or additional teaching, non-teaching support, special equipment like computers or visual aids, and speech or other therapies. There may be implications for the school in terms of organisation and management of the timetable and of the school buildings, support and training for staff – both teaching and non-teaching staff – and working with parents and pupils to create a positive ethos for inclusion.

Exclusions from school

Government guidance (*DfEE Circular 10/99: Social Inclusion: Pupil Support; NAW Circular 3/99 Pupil Support and Social Inclusion*) - has set out how schools should support pupils so that there are fewer exclusions. The headteacher must act within any broad statements of policy on behaviour and discipline in the school that the governing body has agreed. Parents of excluded pupils can 'state their case' to a governors' discipline committee, who must decide whether or not to uphold an exclusion. If governors find the exclusion is not in line with the Circular, they should normally reinstate.

There is a case for the SEN governor being a member of the discipline committee hearing any case involving a child with SEN. Recent research into exclusions, which has included callers to ACE's exclusion helpline, confirmed that a high proportion of exclusions involve children with SEN. Many callers give unmet special needs as a reason for the behaviour which caused the exclusion. Emotional and behavioural difficulties figure prominently and many parents report that schools fail to offer help despite the Code of Practice recognising that such problems are learning difficulties. A significant number of children develop behaviour problems because of frustration with learning. Yet another group of children exhibit behaviour problems following traumatic life experiences such as bereavement and divorce. Governors should always monitor the number and reasons for exclusions and question whether better pastoral care or earlier intervention could prevent some of them from arising. Pupils who have emotional or behavioural difficulties should be referred for support long before exclusion becomes the inevitable outcome. When considering an exclusion case, governors should always ask what support has been provided in the past and whether all possible avenues have been exhausted. Governors should normally expect a pupil who is facing permanent exclusion to have in place either a pastoral support programme (PSP) or an individual education plan (IEP) which includes pastoral support. The LEA Behaviour Support Plan should describe help available for staff (such as behaviour management training) and for pupils (such as counselling services, anger management support or part-time places in specialist units).

One difficulty highlighted by Ofsted - *Improving Attendance and Behaviour in Secondary Schools (2001)* - was the way low-attaining pupils often slipped through the SEN net. Of the young people whose disruptive behaviour was observed by inspectors "Most had difficulties with reading and writing... Often, they displayed a 'don't care' bravado in an attempt to mask their learning difficulties. Too often they were entirely preoccupied with their standing within the peer group and, rather than attempt to gain recognition through achievement, chose to seek it by other means."

Governors could consider whether any of the points identified by Ofsted as key features of improving schools could be adopted by their school:

- teachers work through procedures set out in behaviour policies that give first-level responsibility for intervention to subject departments
- tutors have a detailed and up-to-date picture of their pupils' overall progress and act as an effective link with them, making productive use of tutorial time
- thorough screening for special educational needs of any pupil who joins the school after Year 7
- subject teachers given practical support in adapting their teaching to meet special educational needs in mainstream classes.
- in-school centres or learning support units whose well-defined, short-term role understood by pupils and by teachers, with the pupils involved remaining connected with mainstream.

The Circulars (10/99 - England; 3/99 Wales) state that heads should try to avoid excluding a pupil who is in the process of being assessed. They also say out that pupils with a Statement should only be excluded in the most exceptional circumstances. Governors should check that the school has liaised with the LEA to request greater support be added to the Statement or, if necessary, a new school named in the Statement.

The Government aims to reduce exclusions by one third by 2002 and is collecting much fuller data on both permanent and fixed period exclusions. The information should show which pupils are excluded most. Factors such as age, ethnicity and gender of the pupil and whether they have a Statement will be monitored.

Governors should be aware that under **The Human Rights Act 1998** there may be legal challenges in the area of SEN especially where it is combined with exclusion. Such a test case may alter governors' responsibilities in the future.

Further information

ACE Special Education Handbook, 7th ed., 1996 ACE, 1C Aberdeen Studios, 22 Highbury Grove, London N5 2DQ, £9 (including postage).

SEN Support for Governors, 3rd ed.,1998, ACE (address above) £9 (including postage).

Index for Inclusion: developing learning and participation in schools by Tony Booth, Mel Ainscow, Kristine Black-Harkins et al.CSIE, Redland Close, Elm Lane, Redland Bristol BS6 6UE £24,50.

Developments in Additional Resource Allocation to Promote Greater Inclusion ed. Bram Norwich, Nasen, Nasen House, 4/5 `Amber Business Village, Amber Close, Armington Tamworth, Staff. B77 4RP, £6.

What the Disability Discrimination Act 1995 means for Schools and LEAs, DfEE Circular 3/97, DfEE Publications (0845 602 2260) free.

Governors and Discipline

School discipline is an issue which concerns all those involved in schools – pupils, parents, teachers, non-teaching staff, governors and LEAs. With high exclusion rates, including primary children being permanently excluded, governors have a key role to play in promoting positive behaviour in their schools. And the debate should not be restricted to the governing body: legal requirements require them to consult with parents on a statement of general principles on behaviour. In addition to the legal requirements there is also statutory guidance which in law must not be ignored by governors. The DfEE and the National Assembly for Wales have produced similar, but not identical, guidance. An added dimension which governors need to consider is the impact of the Human Rights Act 1998 on school discipline polices and the exclusion process.

Drawing up a behaviour policy

Governing bodies have a duty to ensure their school follows policies to promote good behaviour and discipline among pupils. Governing bodies of all maintained schools must prepare and review a statement of general principles regarding pupil behaviour and discipline (**S61 SSFA**). In addition, governing bodies have a legal duty to have regard to *Annex B of DfEE Circular 10/99 Social Inclusion: Pupil Support* (England); *Annex B National Assembly (NAW) Circular 3/99 Pupil Support and Social Inclusion* (Wales) which give more details about school discipline policies. Areas that some schools may not previously have included in their policies, but should do so now, are those of bullying and racial and sexual harassment. Legally, the policy must include measures for preventing all forms of bullying (**S61(4)(b) SSFA**). The guidance says schools' behaviour policies need to cover racial and sexual harassment and that parents and pupils should know that the school has an equal opportunities policy and is committed to equality (*DfEE Circular 10/99* in Chapters 2 and 4 and Annex B; *NAW Circular 3/99* Chapter 4 and Annex B) It warns that that 'colour-blind' policies can continue inequality. Schools are advised to have in place an anti-bullying policy (including racial bullying) which is, in line with the **Human Rights Act 1998**, designed to prevent inhuman and degrading treatment. The guidance advises that schools should record all racial incidents and that parents and governors should be informed of these incidents and the action taken to deal with them. In addition governors should report annually to the LEA the pattern and frequency of these incidents. The guidance also points out that racial harassment does not only happen in schools with ethnic minority populations.

Consulting on a policy

There are many different ways a policy can be drawn up – by a committee of governors, staff, pupils and parents; by the governors after consultation with the other parties within and outside the school; or by staff and pupils for ratification by the governors. To be sure it receives support from those that are going to live by it, the governing body will want to take advice from, and consult with, all members of the school partnership. Although there is no requirement to consult with pupils, engaging them in shaping the policy must be one of the most effective ways of sharing values and ensuring good behaviour. Schools that encourage respect in pupils for themselves and others, and demonstrate the importance they give to caring for and helping each child in their care, have a good framework on which to build their behaviour policies. The guidance advises reinforcing school behaviour policies by active involvement of pupils in anti-bullying and anti-harassment policies.

Before producing or revising a behaviour statement, the governing body is required to consult with parents and the headteacher (**S61(3) SSFA**). This could be at the annual meeting or at a specially convened meeting or in writing. It is important that consultation with parents and carers is genuine, giving them a real opportunity to contribute to the policy. Annex B of both Circulars says that governing bodies should take account of parents' and the head's views. Governors could consider using questionnaires, inviting parents to discussions and publicising the availability of governors to discuss the issue.

Parents care as much about good discipline as they do about good examination results but in cases where school and home are in conflict, pupils will favour advice from the home. Thus parental support of the school's behaviour policy is crucial. Parents who have had problems with the way the school approaches discipline in the past may raise important issues which the governing body will duck at their peril. For example, should allowances be made for children whose special educational needs affect their behaviour or for children who have suffered bereavement or serious trauma in their lives? These are difficult questions but they need to be considered if a behaviour policy is to work in practice and win support from everyone involved. The Circulars (England and Wales) stress that behaviour policies should take account of the needs of all pupils including those with special educational needs. Although it is possible for a headteacher to list excludable offences, such as zero tolerance for drug dealing, governors should question whether too much prescription will conflict with a need to be able to consider individual circumstances.

On a day-to-day basis, shops and businesses have a very direct involvement with pupils, before and after school and sometimes at lunch times. By involving shop keepers, local businesses, community groups and the police in discussion on the school discipline policy, governors and schools can encourage support for and confidence in what the school is trying to do.

Discussions with other local schools can also be productive, in that a common approach on a wide range of behaviour and discipline issues, from truancy to drug taking will send strong messages to young people.

Some schools have developed initiatives based on peer mediation and mentoring, and many primary and secondary schools work together to promote a successful transition to secondary school (*see* **Key Stage 3, Governors and Standards,** *page 45*).

Other considerations

Before drawing up or revising the policy the governing body is required to have regard for guidance issued by the Secretary of State (**S61(2) SSFA**). This guidance is found in Annex B of both Circulars (England and Wales). Governors are strongly advised to get a copy.

The Circulars outline what the statement should include:

a) the ethos of the school, its values and the boundaries of acceptable behaviour
b) the school's moral code
c) positive and constructive rules of conduct
d) the rewards and punishments to be fairly and consistently applied.

The role of the headteacher

Responsibility for the setting of an acceptable standard of behaviour is shared by the headteacher and the governing body. The Circulars point out that good leadership is key to successfully promoting good behaviour.

The head must "determine measures" (which may include the making of rules and provision for enforcing them) to be taken with a view to –
i) promoting, among pupils, self-discipline and proper regard for authority;
ii) encouraging good behaviour and respect for others on the part of pupils - (the SSFA introduces bullying into legislation for the first time by adding that measures should prevent "all forms of bullying among pupils");
iii) securing that the standard of behaviour of pupils is acceptable; and
iv) otherwise regulating the conduct of pupils.
(**S61(4) SSFA**).

The head must take account of the governors' statement of general principles and any guidance they give (**S61(5) SSFA**) and is responsible for publi-

cising the measures in a written document, and at least once in a school year bringing them to the attention of pupils, parents and everyone employed in the school (**S61(7) SSFA**). If many parents have a language other than English or Welsh as their first language the policy should be available in relevant languages.

Punishments should be in proportion to offences and enable pupils to make reparation where appropriate. The policy should seek the wide agreement on the standards of the school and the methods of achieving them and ensure that these standards are consistently and fairly applied. There should be a hierarchy of sanctions which are applied fairly and consistently and pupils should be rewarded for good behaviour (*Chapter 4 and Annex B of both DfEE Circular 10/99 and NAW 3/99*). Sanctions should take account of all circumstances including a child's age. Punishments that are humiliating or degrading should not be used (*Circular 10/99 Chapter 4*). Governors should be aware that this is in line with the **Human Rights Act** which prohibits inhuman or degrading treatment or punishment.

Specific discipline issues

Having produced a statement of principles for good behaviour, governors should also consider particular issues that can have a significant effect on pupils' behaviour and achievement in school, and may like to include these in the general policy or have separate statements to cover them. The **SSFA** (**S61(2)**) says that the governing body, if they think it is desirable, must advise the headteacher of their views on any specific measures for promoting good behaviour. The guidance highlights bullying, racial and sexual harassment and maintaining regular attendance as examples. The school behaviour policy should make it clear that racial harassment will not be tolerated.

Another area of concern is that of illegal drugs and alcohol abuse. A comprehensive policy which includes education and support and is not merely punitive will be most useful in maintaining discipline and a safe environment. Good practice in other local schools might suggest ways these can issues can be tackled and the DfEE publication *Protecting Young People, 1998*, is useful. (*See page 81*)

School uniform can be a contentious issue and governing bodies should review their policy on this to ensure it complies with anti-discrimination legislation. The Government has obviously had second thoughts about whether breaches of school uniform policy is an appropriate reason to exclude a child (*see below* **Head's responsibilities**) but governors may wish to bear in mind a report from the National Association of Citizens' Advice Bureaux which recommended that before excluding a child for not wearing the correct uniform, sensitive checks are made to ensure that poverty, rather than defiance, is not the real reason for the breach.

Monitoring the policy

Many school behaviour policies were written or revised several years ago. Governors who have produced a behaviour statement for a school cannot sit back and think this area of their responsibilities will look after itself. Regular and frequent monitoring of how the policy is put into practice is also important. The Circulars state that the governing body should ensure the headteacher's sound maintenance of discipline at school is in line with their policies.

Governors' visits to the school provide an opportunity to observe the way pupils move around the school, behave towards each other, and occupy themselves during playtimes. While a certain amount of experience of observation is required before outsiders can understand the dynamics of a school community, a governor may pick up an aspect of behaviour that the school has come to accept or take for granted. Governors who are unhappy will want to report back in a way that is helpful to the school. Clearly this should be approached with discretion and to the appropriate person, bearing in mind that sharp or public criticism of staff may cause problems if disciplinary measures have to be taken later on.

A special report from Ofsted into high excluding schools, *Improving Behaviour and Attendance in Secondary Schools, (2001)* said that few of the schools in their survey analysed their exclusion data. As a result apparent differences in punishment of some minority ethnic groups had not been picked up and investigated.

The same report highlighted the fact that young people with literacy difficulties were slipping through the special needs net and this sometimes resulted in behaviour problems developing.

Governors' meetings on exclusions offer a good opportunity to check on how well the school records incidents and follows its equal opportunities and other policies.

Whole school strategies

The Green Paper, *Excellence for all Children, (1997)*, in chapter 8 on Emotional and Behavioural Difficulties states:

"Schools need to offer a setting where all children are valued and encouraged to behave well, where there are clear guidelines for behaviour, teaching is positive, and where damaged self-esteem can be rebuilt. Many are working towards whole school strategies designed to sustain this approach, encompassing pastoral systems, specific policies to promote the achievement of boys, and explicit agreement about the role of support services. Such approaches need the support of all staff, and a strong lead from school management".

Schools should try to support all children whose behaviour is causing concern. Pastoral programmes in schools that give good support to individual pupils, and allow time for teachers to attend to unhappy or disturbed children are an integral part of a school that is working to provide a supportive atmosphere for all. The emphasis of the Circulars is on an approach to disaffected pupils (or children from groups that are considered to be at risk of disaffection) that aims to improve behaviour and avoid exclusion. In most cases children should not be excluded from school unless a variety of strategies - including those outlined in Chapter 4 of both Circulars - have been tried first. For children who have been excluded permanently

this would normally include a pastoral support programme (not to be confused with a pastoral programme) which is explained in detail in chapter five of the circulars. It is important that the school's behaviour policy reflects this approach.

While considering a behaviour policy, governors may also like to look at related activities in school such as the level of support the school gives to individual teachers on classroom management through in-service training; the lead given by the headteacher and the senior management team in promoting positive attitudes among staff, pupils and parents; and the appropriateness of the curriculum for the individual needs of all the pupils. The guidance mentions successful initiatives designed to address underachievement including the development of a Black perspective in the curriculum.

Governors should also consider the effects of the appearance and condition of school buildings on pupils' behaviour. Governors now have more control of school premises and staffing and should take account of good maintenance, bright classrooms and litter free playgrounds, as well as adequate supervision at playtimes.

Truancy

The Government sees truancy as a major reason for high levels of youth crime and damaged life chances. It aims to reduce truancy by one third by 2002 and all LEAs and schools have been set targets. It believes that governing bodies and heads have a particular role in considering a whole school approach to non-attendance, particularly unauthorised absence. Governors will want to ensure that, within this, the possible hidden causes of non-attendance are explored such as bullying, caring for a family member, stress in the family and unmet special educational needs including mental health problems. This is particularly important in light of the **Criminal Justice and Courts Act 2000** which has increased the maximum punishment for parents who cannot show that they are trying to ensure that that their children attend school regularly to a fine of £2,500 per parent, and/or up to three months imprisonment. Even if parents can show that they are making every effort to make sure that their child attends school they can still be fined up to £1,000.

However, each truant may have a different reason for non-attendance and governors will need to consider a range of options from improved pastoral care to taking advantage of greater flexibility in the National Curriculum to achieve long-term improvements. Zero tolerance and crack-downs on parents may sound appropriate responses but are not likely to make school more attractive to the school phobic child. The Circular identifies prolonged truancy as an indicator of disaffection and recognises the link between learning difficulties and disaffection. *DfEE Circular 10/99 Chapter 4* and *NAW Circular 3/99 Chapter 2* look at strategies to improve attendance and particularly emphasise working with parents and the community. The school should contact parents on any day that a child is absent without explanation.

The *Social Exclusion Report*, published in May 1998, also detailed measures to tackle the problem. Many are now in operation:

- Parenting Orders which may require a parent to attend special parenting classes or to escort a child to school
- extended work experience for disaffected pupils
- pilot schemes placing education welfare officers in schools
- extended powers for the police to enable them to pick up truants.

The report suggested that increased focus on literacy and numeracy and the encouragement of out-of-hours learning and summer schools could reduce the numbers who truant because they find lessons too difficult.

Home school agreements

(*see also* **Governors and Parents**)
The governing bodies of all maintained schools, city technology colleges and the new city academies and city colleges for the technology of the arts are required to have a home-school agreement.

The guidance on home school agreements, *Home-School Agreements: Guidance for Schools (England ref: PPY984) (in Wales, Circular 27/99)* which governing bodies must have regard to, says that the agreement should be an integral part of a whole school approach to partnership with parents. Governing bodies must consult parents before they produce or revise the school's agreement. As well as spelling out the expectations, responsibilities and obligations of the school, parent and pupil they also cover areas other than behaviour, including the ethos of the school, and the school giving information about the curriculum or the school's homework policy.

A child must not be excluded or disciplined because the parent refuses to sign, or to comply with the terms of the agreement. Nor should the agreement be used in the reinstatement of excluded pupils. This does not prevent individual agreements being drawn up after an exclusion. Similarly, the breaking of the agreement is not in itself reason to exclude a child. A child should only be excluded if the offence itself warrants exclusion. (*Paragraphs 36 and 37* (England); *Paragraphs 31 and 32* (Wales)).

Detentions

Schools may lawfully detain pupils after school on disciplinary grounds, without parental consent (**S550B EA96** as amended by **S5 EA97**). The Circulars explain the law and gives extra guidance. The headteacher must make the fact that detention is used as a sanction generally known within the school and take steps to bring it to the attention of parents and pupils, otherwise parents may be able to challenge the lawfulness of detention on the grounds they were unaware of it. A pupil's parent/carer must also be informed and given at least 24 hours' notice in writing of a detention. This allows time for the parents to put their views. Schools do not have an unqualified right to impose a detention. A detention must also be reasonable and proportionate to the offence. Staff should take into account any special circumstances, including a pupil's age, special educational needs or religious requirements and whether the parent can reasonably arrange for their child to get home from school after the detention. If a parent objects to a detention it could be revoked or deferred. If, despite the

parent's objection, the detention goes ahead, the parent may decide to complain to the governing body. Governors should listen to the complaint but have no power to overturn the detention. Governors will need to monitor the use of such detentions and consider the effect on home-school relations. How the measure is communicated to parents and pupils, and transport arrangements, particularly in rural areas, could be important here.

Corporal punishment and force

DfEE and National Assembly guidance on the use of force to control or restrain pupils lists the circumstances when teachers may use reasonable force with pupils and details the type of physical intervention which might be appropriate. Schools should record all incidents in an incident book. Corporal punishment is forbidden by **Ss548 to 550** of the **EA96**. These sections forbid a teacher to use any degree of physical contact which is deliberately intended to punish a pupil, or which is primarily intended to cause pain or injury or humiliation. This would also be contrary to the **Human Rights Act**. The guidance recommends that headteachers should draw up a policy on this issue, taking account of LEA and Government guidance, and setting out guidelines about the use of force. After discussing the policy with staff and the governing body, a statement on the policy should be given to parents with the behaviour statement. (*DfEE Circular 10/98 Section 550A of the Education Act 1996: The use of force to control or restrain pupils* and *NAW Circular 37/98 The use of reasonable force to control or restrain pupil*.)

The role of the LEA

● ●

The duty on LEAs to prepare, publish and review a statement setting out their arrangements for the education of children with behavioural difficulties was introduced by the **Education Act 1997**. How LEAs carry out local consultation, and publication of the plans are prescribed in the **Local Education Authority (Behaviour Support Plans) Regulations 1998 (S1 644)**.

Behaviour Support Plans were produced at the end of 1998 and must include:
- arrangements for provision of advice and resources to schools for promoting good behaviour and discipline, and dealing with pupils with behavioural problems
- provision for pupils educated otherwise than at school
- assisting pupils with behavioural difficulties to find places at suitable schools.

They must also state how the arrangements set out in the plan interact with those made by the authority for pupils with behavioural difficulties who have special educational needs. (*DfEE Circular 1/98 LEA Behaviour Support; NAW Circular 19/98 LEA Behaviour Support Plans.*)

Consulting governing bodies

LEAs are required to consult the governing body of all maintained schools in the authority's area in the course of preparing the plans and when the plans are reviewed. However since the plans were produced there may have been new initiatives, particularly round exclusion. New governors may benefit from contacting the LEA to see if any new projects in their area are relevant to their school.

LEA services

The Behaviour Support Plan should give governors greater awareness of the services available for supporting pupils with behavioural difficulties and those who have special educational needs as well as support given to schools to prevent exclusions and to reintegrate pupils who have been excluded. A Behaviour Support Plan should set out clearly the circumstances in which the LEA will arrange additional education for pupils and the funding arrangements for such services. This may help governors evaluate whether all "alternative strategies" have been tried prior to an exclusion, as they will know which services could have been provided to help prevent the exclusion. (*DfEE Circular 1/98 LEA Behaviour Support* (England); *NAW Circular 19/98 LEA Behaviour Support Plans*.)

Exclusions

The ultimate sanction against a pupil is exclusion from school. For some years there has been concern about the high level of exclusion. The Government aims to cut permanent exclusions by one third by 2002. There were 10,400 permanent exclusions in 1998/9. There are no current figures for the number of fixed period exclusions which will be much higher. The headteacher is the only person with power to exclude, but governors have a significant part to play in the procedures that follow an exclusion. Currently a governing body must establish a discipline committee of three or five governors to consider exclusions. However, governors should check whether proposed changes to the law have been passed. They would enable the whole governing body to consider exclusions which total less than 15 school days in a term. However this provision may be limited to those which are not

---

The law on exclusions

The law on exclusions is contained in the **School Standards and Framework Act 1998 Ss 64 - 68, 87** and **95, Scheds.18 & 25.** Regulations: **Education (School Government)(England) (Amendment) Regulations 2000 SI 1848; Education (School Government)(Wales) Regulations 1999 SI 2242(W2)); Education (Exclusions from School)(Prescribed Periods)SI 1868** amended by **Education (Exclusions from School)(Prescribed Periods)(Amendment)(England) Regulations 2000 SI 294;** in Wales, **Education (Exclusions from School)(Prescribed Periods)(Amendment)(Wales) Regulations 2000 SI 3026(W.194))**

In the SSFA to exclude means: "exclude on disciplinary grounds".

There are two types of exclusion: fixed period and permanent. Lunchtime exclusions are covered by this part of the law. **The Education Act 1993** abolished the 'indefinite' category of exclusion. **The Education Act 1997** set a maximum limit for fixed period exclusions to total not more than 45 school days in one school year.

---

challenged by the parent. All references to the governing body in exclusion legislation, therefore, may currently be construed as references to its discipline committee.

Exclusion guidance

When considering an exclusion, headteachers must have regard to any guidance on discipline and exclusion produced by the Secretary of State. This duty applies also to governors, the LEA and appeal panels (**S68 SSFA**). The current guidance is found within *DfEE Circular 10/99 Chapters 4, 5, 6 and Annex D; NAW Circular 3/99 Chapters 4, 5, 6 and Annex E*. The Circulars were first published in September 1999. Circular 10/99 was amended in January 2000, August 2000 and January 2001 and Circular 3/99 in February 2000.

Head's responsibilities

It is very important that governors are clear about the responsibilities of the headteacher because when they consider a particular exclusion they should determine whether the head has followed guidance. For instance *Circular 10/99* in chapter 6 specifies where exclusion is not appropriate: minor incidents such as not doing homework or not bringing dinner money; poor academic performance; truancy and lateness; pregnancy; punishing pupils for the behaviour of their parents; breaching school uniform policy - including hairstyle or wearing jewellery.

It should be noted that the August 2000 amendment to *Annex D* of *Circular 10/99* advises that appeal panels should not normally reinstate a child whose refusal to wear uniform is "persistent and malicious". In their guidance on the **Human Rights Act**, the DfEE has advised that to exclude a child for not wearing uniform may be considered as unlawful unless he or she has already flouted the policy repeatedly and has been disciplined for doing so. In Wales, *Circular 3/99* advises that exclusion should not be used for uniform breaches unless it is clear that this is an act of defiance and where all other avenues have been exhausted. *Circular 3/99* also includes incidents which took place out of school hours (unless they represent a serious risk to the welfare of those at the school) in the list of offences for which exclusion is not appropriate.

In all cases, the parents must be informed immediately of the reason for the exclusion, its duration, their right to make representations to the governing body (**S65(1)(a, b and c) SSFA**), and "the means by which such representations are made" (**S65(1)(d) SSFA**).

The headteacher must tell the governing body and the local education authority "without delay" of any exclusion that, when added to all other exclusions that term, totals more than five school days in any one term, exclusions that involve a pupil losing an opportunity to take a public exam, exclusions which are permanent, and fixed period exclusions which the headteacher subsequently decides to make permanent. The headteacher must give information on the reason for the exclusion and the period of the exclusion (**S65(3)(4) SSFA**).

In addition the headteacher has considerable responsibilities conferred by the statutory guidance. In particular, before deciding to exclude, the headteacher should consider all relevant facts and firm evidence and allow the pupil to give their version of what happened. If there is doubt that the pupil did what is alleged, the head should not exclude. Governors will want to ensure that the pupil is interviewed in the presence of another adult and that a signed written statement is taken. In some instances it may be good practice for a tape recording to be made. The same applies if statements are to be taken from children as witnesses. It is important that pupils should be allowed to express themselves as they wish, and care should be taken not to put words in to their mouths. The headteacher must be careful to protect him/herself from allegations of intimidation and inappropriate questioning. Action which involves punishments and discipline should be clearly and chronologically recorded so that an independent observer would agree that the outcome was proportionate to the nature of the incident, particularly in light of the **Human Rights Act.**

The decision to exclude should not be taken in the heat of the moment, except where there is a risk to health and safety. A pupil should only be excluded for a serious breach of the school's discipline/behaviour policy and where allowing them to stay would seriously harm the education and welfare of themselves or others in the school. Before exclusion, in most cases, the school should have tried a range of strategies including those in Chapter 4 of the Circulars. Generally a pupil should not be permanently excluded for a one-off or first offence. This may not apply for a serious offence, for example one which involves violence. In Wales the guidance stresses that the decision to permanently exclude should only be in response to a very serious breach of the school's discipline policy and that all other strategies have been proven to have failed. Governors may wish to monitor the use of exclusion where no help was previously given or where a child has special educational needs but has not received extra help for behaviour prior to exclusion.

The letter from the headteacher to the parents should include considerable amount of information to ensure that they understand their rights and why their child was excluded. Details are found in *DfEE Circular 10/99 Annex D* (England); *NAW Circular 3/99 Annex E* (Wales).

The headteacher is entitled to seek advice from others but should not consult governors who may be involved at a future stage.

Governing body responsibilities

For an exclusion which, when added to any previous exclusions that term, totals five school days or less in any term the parent has the right to make written representations. The same applies for lunch time exclusions which should not normally exceed five school days. However, many parents find it much easier to express themselves verbally and it is often much easier to get to the bottom of a problem at a meeting. The governing body may wish to have a policy that parents can also make oral representations at a meeting. The governing body is responsible for considering parents' representations. They cannot overturn these exclusions, but of course can make their views clear if they feel that an exclusion was inappropriate in some way.

For an exclusion which, when added to all other exclusions in that term totals more than five days, a permanent exclusion, or an exclusion which would mean a pupil losing an opportunity to take a public examination, the governing body must allow the parent to attend a meeting of the discipline committee. The parent may make written and oral representations about the exclusion. The LEA may also attend and make oral representations. The governing body must consider the representations and the circumstances in which the pupil was excluded (SSFA S66 (2a)).

Governors will be aware that many parents would not be able to attend meetings held during the day. The Circulars say that the meeting should be at a time and place convenient to all parties. The watchword should be that governors act fairly and are seen to act fairly. Meeting in the headteacher's study will not feel fair to parents. Parents are entitled to bring a friend or representative. The governing body has the power to direct the head to reinstate a pupil, and to decide whether a pupil should be admitted immediately, or be given a date for reinstatement. There are time-limits set by regulation as to when the meeting should take place - if the child may miss a public examination, the committee should try to meet before the exam. If this is not possible, chair's action may be taken to decide whether or not to reinstate the pupil.

LEAs and parents must be informed of the decision made by the governing body to reinstate or not (S66(4 and 6) SSFA) and must be given reasons where the decision is not to reinstate. The governing body may not attach conditions to a reinstatement and cannot convert a permanent exclusion to a fixed period exclusion. Following the discipline committee meeting, for permanent exclusions, where the exclusion has been upheld, the committee must give the parent notice in writing and must include:
"the reason for the decision, his right of appeal, the person to whom he should give any notice of appeal, that any notice of appeal must contain the grounds of the appeal, and the last date on which an appeal may be made." (S66(6b) SSFA.)
Again considerable responsibilities are conferred by the statutory guidance.

The governors should normally satisfy themselves that other ways (for permanent exclusions *all possible* ways) to improve the child's behaviour were tried before resorting to exclusion including those in the Circulars. Amongst other things the Circulars specify for permanent exclusions a pastoral support programme or amending a Statement of special educational needs. In addition, governors should normally overturn the exclusion if it is not in line with the guidance (*DfEE Circular 10/99 Annex D para.12* and *NAW Circular 3/99 Annex E para.22*). For instance the Circular states that a Head should not exclude a child if there is doubt that they did what they were accused of, so this could be a basis for a reinstatement.

The second amendment to *Circular 10/99* (but not so far to *Circular 3/99* in Wales) changed the remit of the appeal panel in ways that has implications for governing bodies.

One of the main changes mean that if there is an alleged victim in an exclusion case – he or she can send a written statement to the appeal panel, or can attend in person or send a representative.

Clearly, the governing body will need to decide if they wish to make this provision at discipline committee meetings. ACE advises caution. Very clear guidelines will need to be established prior to any meeting to ensure that everyone is clear on procedures and the role and rights of each participant. Any exclusion meeting that includes representatives of a school and a parent who believes that their child has been unfairly treated by that school can become highly charged. The addition of a child who considers themselves to be a victim and/or their parent has the potential to get out of hand, leaving all parties distressed and dissatisfied with the process.

The other changes relate to the independent appeal panel. If the panel decides the child did what they are accused of they should then decide if permanent exclusion is reasonable. The changes have limited the ability of an appeal panel to reinstate a child. For example, a panel should not normally reinstate a child whose action was one that the school's discipline policy makes it quite clear will lead to permanent exclusion. An example would be zero tolerance for drug dealing. Also a panel should consider the effect that reinstatement may have on others in the school and should not normally reinstate if the child's actions included the following:

- Serious actual or threatened violence against another pupil or member of staff
- Sexual abuse
- Significantly risking the health and safety of other pupils by selling drugs
- Persistent and malicious disruptive behaviour. This includes open defiance or refusal to follow the school policies on, for example, behaviour or school uniform.

The governing body is not limited in the same way as the appeal panel. If the discipline committee believes that there are mitigating circumstances, including unmet special educational needs, they are able to consider them and if appropriate reinstate the pupil. Sometimes governors feel torn between loyalty to the headteacher and concern that an exclusion may not have been right given the child's situation. To avoid a difficult situation some would, in effect, leave the final decision to the appeal panel. However, this path is no longer open to governors for exclusions that fall into the circumstances given above.

The need for governors to ensure that the school's discipline policy leaves some room for discretion is also highlighted by these changes.

Time limits

For exclusions which mean that the pupil will be excluded for a total of more than five school days, the discipline committee, after receiving notice from the headteacher for exclusions of 15 school days and less, has between the 6th and 50th school day to arrange a meeting.

For exclusions over 15 school days the discipline committee has between the 6th and the 15th school day to arrange a meeting. (**The Education (Exclusion from School) (Prescribed Periods) (Amendment) (England) Regulations 2000 SI 294** and the **Education (Exclusion from School) (Prescribed Periods) (Amendment) (Wales) Regulations 2000 SI W.194**)

LEA role

The LEA has a right to make oral and written representations where it is informed of an exclusion of over five school days by the headteacher under S65(4). The governing body must consider oral representations made by an LEA officer at the meeting (S66). The guidance does not shed much light on the officer's role at the meeting. Some identify where the school has not followed guidance and this role has been backed up by the covering letter from DfEE introducing amendments to the guidance for appeal panels: "Local education authorities have an important role in making sure that the exclusion process operates correctly" (August 4, 2000). Others compare and contrast the use of exclusion in other local schools. Some will give their view on the exclusion. It is open to governors to ask them for guidance in these and other relevant matters. However the LEA officer should not be asked to stay after the meeting to help governors make their decision.

Advice for governors

Circulars 10/99 (England) and *3/99* (Wales) contain a considerable amount of guidance about exclusion and about the steps that a school should take to avoid excluding pupils. This includes preventative action around children who are in groups which are identified as being at risk of disaffection. Governors, who may sit on their school's discipline committee would be well advised to obtain a copy of the relevant circular and familiarise themselves with the chapters on prevention as well as those which detail the exclusion process.

The circular identifies the need to consider the possibility of racism playing a role in exclusion. Governors should check up on the use of punishment against children from minority ethnic backgrounds and be sure that the school's behaviour policy against racial prejudice and harassment is being fully enforced. If African-Caribbean children are punished or excluded more than other children, governors should make sure that the school takes steps to put this right. Obviously governors will make sure they do not stereotype and are alert to cultural differences and take particular care if there is a possibility that an incident was provoked by racial or sexual harassment.

Pupil record

It is for the governing body to decide what details of the exclusion are included in the pupil's school records. The guidance says that the discipline committee can consider whether more information should be added to the pupil's record. A note of the discipline committee's views should normally be placed on the pupil's record with a copy of the headteacher's exclusion letter and any written material provided by parents in the pupil's defence.

New regulations on school records and enactment of the **Data Protection Act 1998** mean that a governing body can no longer amend the pupil's record if a parent requests it and where governors agree they are inaccurate. The responsibility for school records has passed to headteachers, who can agree to amend the school records. However if they do not agree, parents will now have to go to the courts to request an amendment. Parents could first contact the Data Protection Commissioner for their intervention. The guidance states that is not possible to "clear a pupil's name" and that details of an exclusion may not lawfully be deleted from the pupil record if an exclusion is a matter of fact. However it is arguable that guidance is not correct on this point and a legal action may change this.

Fairness

R v Board of Governors of the London Oratory School ex parte Regis (1988) established that the Rules of Natural Justice apply to governing body meetings considering exclusions. So governors who take part in a meeting arranged to discuss an exclusion must follow the Rules of Natural Justice *(see page 18)*

Discipline committees established to hear exclusion cases must be properly constituted: there must be three or five governors. No governor should have a connection with the pupil or the exclusion. Governors should remember they will be attending the meeting as representatives of the full governing body and, with the other governors present, will be taking a decision on the exclusion or reinstatement of a child. The proceedings of a discipline committee are open to judicial review, although this is very rare.

Governors need to think about the venue and timing of the meeting. Parents' confidence that the meeting will be fair and that governors are making decisions independently of the headteacher will be reduced if the head is already in the room with the governors when the parent arrives or stays after the parent leaves and if it is held in the head's room. In **R v Board of Governors of the London Oratory School (1989)** the judge identified the importance of the headteacher and the governors showing that they were independent of one another. A key issue in the case was that the headteacher had left the room with the parent and had not remained with the governors when they were making their decision. The watch-word for governors should be that "justice is done and seen to be done".

Parents have a right to bring someone with them so should be advised that they can bring a friend or representative with them to the meeting. They rarely know what to expect of the meeting and should be sent information about who will be attending and the order of speaking beforehand.

Governors should work hard to show that they are not just accepting the school's version of events, but are wanting to make an independent decision. In an ideal situation, the parent and friend or representative will be made comfortable enough to explain their views and have a useful discussion on their child's future. In some cases, an educational psychologist and an education social worker will be asked to the meeting to report on and for the child.

The headteacher's reasons for the exclusion will be explained, and should be backed up with documentary evidence of any incidents in which the pupil was involved. The clerk should send out the written statements (for example a report from a teacher relating to the incident that led to the exclusion) before the meeting. If written material is brought to the meeting, parents and their representatives must be given time, either beforehand or at the meeting, to read any reports that are presented, before giving their views. However, almost inevitably, parents will feel disadvantaged if this happens and governors may wish to discourage such practice within their school. To obey the Rules of Natural Justice, any evidence brought forward should be available to all those involved (*see also* **R v Governors of Dunraven School, ex parte B 1999**).

Case law has established that governors should be proactive and not just accept the evidence presented. If possible, where the headteacher's case rests largely or solely on physical evidence, they should see any physical evidence that is relevant to the case. They should ask for written statements and any photographs that may have been taken. It may also be necessary to question important witnesses in person, although the governing body has no power to compel witnesses to attend. They should establish relevant facts and matters in dispute. For example, they should not just assume that if they reinstate a pupil who has bullied another child, that the victim will be able to cope. They should establish this through questioning.

The committee should take account of the school's behaviour policy and whether parents have been consulted about the statement of principles and whether or not the headteacher has publicised the policy during the year in line with (**S61 SSFA**). Governors should consider whether additional support is needed to prepare for reintegration; they should be more aware of sources of additional support as a result of the LEA Behaviour Support Plans. (*DfEE Circular 10/99 Annex D and Circular 11/99 Social Inclusion: the LEA role in pupil support*; *NAW Circular 3/99 Annex E*)

The child's view

An excluded pupil should be heard if they want to be; if the governing body refused this would be contrary to the guidance and the **Human Rights Act**. In light of the guidance to appeal panels the governing body will also need to consider whether they allow the victim or a representative of the victim to be heard in person at the hearing. If a victim were allowed to attend, the situation would need to be handled very carefully. The governing body should be sensitive to the needs of children to ensure that the child's view is properly heard. It would be good practice for training to be requested on working with children and appropriate questioning.

Clerk to the discipline committee

A governor or headteacher cannot act as clerk for the discipline committee. The governing body will need to think very carefully about who takes on this role. They should find out if their LEA runs a clerking service. If a member of school administration staff is used this may cause concern. Their close relationship with the headteacher can make it difficult for them to act independently. At a small primary school staff often have children at the school and therefore their child may be known to the excluded pupil. If a member of teaching staff is used, they may have had previous involvement in investigating the alleged incident. If school staff have to be used, the governing body should ask the LEA for training.

The clerk should keep a record of the meeting and the decision. In cases where the clerk fails to attend, a governor can stand in for that occasion only.

Appeal arrangements

If the governors decide against reinstating a pupil and the case goes to appeal, the governing body is allowed to make written representations to the appeal panel, and a nominated governor may make oral representations. The headteacher may also make representations. The LEA may make representations and send a nominated officer. The governing body is allowed to be represented but should consider if legal representation is appropriate if the parent is not legally represented. A parent has a right to be represented or bring a friend (**Para.10 Sched. 18 SSFA**) but in practice many parents are unsupported. The excluded child does not have an independent right to be represented.

The appeal panel is arranged by the LEA for all maintained schools (**S67 SSFA**).

The appeal meeting must be arranged within 15 school days of the parent lodging the appeal.

If the governing body want to raise matters or produce documents not covered by the statement of decision, these should be submitted to the clerk to the appeal panel in good time before the hearing. However the governing body may not introduce new reasons for the exclusion. The parent and the LEA may put forward new information that was previously unavailable. The governing body should be given an opportunity to respond if this happens. The governing body should also think about appropriate witnesses. This may include the alleged victim or any teacher who investigated the incident or interviewed pupils. The governing body should be told in advance by the clerk who is attending the hearing and the order.

The panel should first decide whether the child did what they are accused of. If the panel think not, they should reinstate the child. If the panel decides that the child did do it - they should then decide whether permanent exclusion is reasonable. For this, they should think about: the interests of others in the school as well as the child; the school's discipline policy and, if others were involved, how fair it was to exclude the child.

If they decide that permanent exclusion is not reasonable they should reinstate the child except in the cases mentioned above. If the panel think that the exclusion was not, or may not be, in line with *Circular 10/99* they should reinstate the child (*Circular 10/99 Annex D para.16-18 – of amended guidance*).

Voluntary/informal exclusions

Alongside exclusions, governors should enquire of their school how many pupils leave the school roll without being excluded. Some will leave because families move or the child is unhappy. In some instances, however, schools suggest to parents that the child would do better with a new start elsewhere. While an exclusion on a child's record is never desirable and schools may want to save parents and pupils from that stigma, governors should be wary of this because parents' rights of representation and appeal are immediately forfeited. Governors should be sure than parents are not removing their child from the school under duress.

Monitoring and review

Has the clerk to the discipline committee received training?

✔ Are discipline committee members dealing sensitively with children attending, is training needed to improve questioning techniques?

✔ Are notes being kept of evidence, the decision and interviews with pupils?

✔ Does the discipline committee have a prepared checklist, to make sure they have asked all the appropriate questions?

✔ What arrangements are there to assist parents who may have literacy problems or ESL?

✔ Is there a pattern to the types of exclusion or group of children being excluded?

✔ Is the school reporting all exclusions of one school day or more to the LEA?

✔ If some groups, ethnic or otherwise, are disproportionately represented, is there a particular reason for this?

✔ When was the school's discipline policy last discussed and parents consulted on its contents? The policy should be reviewed to see it is compatible with the Human Rights Act.

✔ Is the dress code clearly understood and known by all pupils?

✔ Despite Government recommendations to the contrary, are children with special needs being excluded because these needs cannot be met?

✔ Should the priorities on support for special needs be reconsidered, and what does this mean for the budget? Is the LEA's funding formula taking sufficient account of special educational needs?

✔ Are pupils being provided with work (should be set and marked) during a fixed period exclusion? Article 2 of the first Protocol of the Human Rights Act is a Right to Education.

✔ Has the school got legal cover regarding possible compensation as a result of the Human Rights Act?

✔ How easy is it for a parent who requests it to get a copy of the child's school records? Do these procedures need to be reviewed?

✔ What has been the impact of the use of longer fixed period exclusions? For what reasons were they used? Did this allow sufficient time for a reintegration package to be put together?

All headteachers of maintained schools are required to notify the LEA of exclusions totalling over five school days. The guidance also encourages schools to report shorter exclusions termly, unless the LEA asks for more frequent reports.

Admissions and exclusions

(*see* **Governors and Admissions**)

To minimise the time that pupils are out of school, governors can encourage their own and other schools to take excluded pupils. Despite school fears over taking excluded children, a new start can often transform a pupil's commitment and school achievement. This was confirmed by research conducted by the University of Portsmouth which followed up callers to ACE exclusion helpline.

Chapter 7 of the Circulars encourages close co-operation between schools: "rapid re-integration is eased by close co-operation between schools over admitting permanently excluded pupils". For example schools can agree to accept one pupil if they exclude one pupil. *The Codes of Practice on School Admissions* (England and Wales) encourage the idea of local discussions and adjustments made to admission arrangements of both over and under- subscribed schools in their areas. Schools and LEAs should agree strategies in order to allow all schools to admit a more even share of pupils excluded from other schools.

An excluded pupil starting at a new school should have a re-integration plan, drawn up by a LEA arranged re-integration panel (in some cases this could be a named officer). The excluding school is responsible for passing on information about the excluded pupil to the panel.

The guidance acknowledges that re-integration is a challenge and requires intensive support from the LEA. The Government has made available Standards Fund – Social Inclusion: Pupil Support grants to provide support to schools teaching pupils with behavioural problems. The grants can be spent on a range of projects, for example training, multi-agency work, improving home-school liaison, mentoring, involving parents, in-school centres and pastoral support. It is at the LEA discretion to "claw back" between £3,000 and £6,000 of this grant from a school per permanently excluded pupil. This is not the same as the arrangements for money to follow pupils who have been permanently excluded.

The LEA initiatives fund can also be used to fund re-integration officers to work with pupils, teachers and parents to ease the process of finding and maintaining alternative placements for excluded pupils. *DfEE Circular 11/99* (chapter 5) says that LEAs may offer funding to schools receiving excluded pupils for spending on extra classroom support or for buying in LEA or other services to help meet the child's needs. This funding is sometimes referred to as "dowries".

Twice excluded pupils

Where a pupil has been permanently excluded twice, an admissions authority is not required to admit a pupil, even where there is a vacancy at the school, or to arrange for the parent to appeal. This provision operates for two years after the last exclusion took effect (S87(2) **SSFA**). If the LEA is the admission authority, the governing body has the right of appeal against the decision of the LEA to admit such a pupil. The governing body is allowed to make written representations and a nominated governor is allowed to make oral representations. The appeal panel must have regard to the reasons put forward by the governing body as to why the child's admission is inappropriate, and the reasons for the LEA's decision that the child in question should be admitted (S95(2) **SSFA**). Appeal arrangements are set out in **Sched.25** of the **SSFA**.

The *Code of Practice on School Admissions* introduces new hurdles for pupils "with challenging behaviour". Schools can refuse to admit a child, unless it is to the normal year of entry, where "to do so would prejudice the provision of efficient education or the efficient use of resources". However the guidance states that this is only likely to be appropriate in circumstances where a school has a:
* particularly high concentration of pupils with challenging behaviour, and
* where it is trying to improve its standards from

a low base as part of its achievement of targets and its development plan,
that is schools that are under special measures or have recently come out of them (within the last two years), or have been identified by Ofsted or the LEA as having serious weaknesses.

Governors of such schools should consider carefully their policy on this issue before labelling a child or rejecting a child who may have suffered temporary problems and who may benefit from a fresh start. A parent would have a right of appeal is this decision was taken.

Ofsted Inspections

Where Ofsted's inspections of LEAs uncover higher than average exclusion rates, Ofsted will expect LEAs to act to reduce these. LEAs could also consider asking Ofsted to investigate a high excluding school if they have concerns, and appeal panels should draw the attention of LEAs to concerns they have about high excluding schools.

An Ofsted report *Improving Attendance and Behaviour in Secondary Schools, 2001,* based on special inspections of schools with disproportionately high levels of exclusion or truancy pointed to lack of consistency both in teaching and disciplinary interventions as a feature of high excluding schools. Certain minority ethnic groups, particularly Black and mixed race pupils, appeared to have been treated more harshly in terms of fixed period exclusions than other pupils committing similar offences.

Further reading

Outside, looking in, 2001 Carol Hayden, Simon Dunne research following up callers on ACE helpline, Children's Society, ACE, 1C Aberdeen Studios, 22 Highbury Grove, London N5 2DQ, £16.95 including postage.

Permanent Exclusion, Fixed Period Exclusion, Tackling Bullying, 2000, advice booklets for parents, ACE, £2, including postage, address above.

Governors' Pocket Guide to Exclusion, 2000, ACE, £3.50 including postage.

The Anti-bullying Handbook, 2000, Keith Sullivan, Oxford University Press, (0195583884) £9.99.

Bullying: A guide to the Law - how to tackle bullying inside and outside school, 2000, Children's Legal Centre (0946109966) £4.95 (£2.50 to children and young people).

Bullying: Don't Suffer in Silence, 2000, DfEE, £9.95 or available to download from: http://www.dfee.gov.uk/bullying/index.shtml

Towards Bully-free Schools, 1998, Derek Glover et al Open University Press (0335199291) £16.99.

Governors and Parents

The relationship between parents and schools is one that is still evolving but governors can in some circumstances act as a bridge between parents and the school or as a catalyst for greater parental involvement. Some European countries, notably Denmark and the Republic of Ireland, offer parents extensive opportunities to be involved in a wide range decision-making affecting their children's education. In this country parental involvement tends to be focused on a small group of parents who become governors or active members of a school's parent teacher association. Many PTAs are limited in the issues which are debated and parental involvement beyond fund-raising discouraged; even so, it may surprise many governors to learn that there is no statutory right to a PTA. Parent power – if it exists – is mainly limited to parents' power as consumers. The fact that admission authorities have to consider parental preference when allocating school places is the most obvious way parents express their consumer choice. Other parents' rights are largely confined to rights to information through governors' annual reports, the school prospectus and pupil reports.

Consulting parents

Parents have a number of opportunities to ask questions about school policies and their child's progress including the governors' annual meeting, pre-inspection meetings with Ofsted, parent teacher appointments to discuss pupil reports and throughout the process of a child receiving special educational help.

In the past governors were required to consult parents only before making a decision about changing the times when school sessions began and ended (**S41 SSFA**). But now they must also consult with parents about home school agreements (**S110(9) SSFA**) and the statement of principles underlying the behaviour and discipline of the school (**S61(3)SSFA**). Consulting with parents is also an important element of the statutory guidance on sex education which schools must 'have regard to' and cannot therefore ignore.

These growing requirements could provide the impetus for schools to involve parents more in their children's education but in ACE's view they also highlight the need for some sort of formal structure with parents' views directed through parents elected on a class by class basis. This is a view that has been taken up by organisations such as the Campaign for State Education (CASE) and the Education Forum. The Government's Healthy Schools initiative (*see page 78*) recommends schools set up parent forums to comply with its 'whole school' approach so this idea may be gaining ground.

From September 1999 local education authorities have included between two and five parent governor on relevant committees. If such parents are to be effective, they too will need regular and meaningful contact with the parent body. The DfEE *Guidance for Parent Governor Representatives* suggests that the Internet could be one way of making contact with the large constituency of parents. Perhaps LEAs could be persuaded to include a link or page on their own website for parent governors which could invite comments and contributions from parents and other governors.

Both at school and LEA level governors wishing to develop a genuine partnership with parents will need to create many opportunities for parents' voices to be heard and valued. Parents can be encouraged to have a real say in policies and major decisions by planning participation over the year, providing enough information for informed discussion and making the decision-making process clear.

There are equal opportunity issues for some groups such as parents who have English as an additional language. DfEE guidance on home school agreements suggests separate meetings for parents with interpreters present. Access to goods and services for parents with disabilities is covered by the **Disability Discrimination Act 1995.** Schools must take reasonable steps to ensure disabled parents can access the building on parents' evening for example and can take a full part in parents' meetings such as the governors' annual meeting. Unlike the duties associated with employment where reasonable adjustments are made once a disabled person is to join the school staff, the duty to make reasonable adjustments to allow access is an anticipatory duty. This means that providers should not wait until a disabled person wants to use a service before considering adjustments but should take positive steps to make their services accessible to disabled people. These duties do not carry obligations to adapt premises immediately but by 2004 service providers will be required to provide reasonable access for those with disabilities. Governing bodies should consider phasing improvements in over time.

All those with parental responsibility are entitled to be consulted about the child's education and must be treated equally, unless there is a court order limiting the exercise of responsibility. It follows that all who have parental responsibility are entitled to vote in elections for parent governors, in ballots concerning the school's status, and to take part in the assessment and statementing process of children with special educational needs. (*Schools, "Parents" and "Parental Responsibility"* DfEE 0092/2000)

Those who act as parents for children in the public care system also need to be involved in developments at school that impact on those children. Parents of children looked after by local authorities often maintain an active interest in their children's education and need to be kept informed. For children in care, having someone to take a consistent interest is vital - whether this is their parent, foster parent or social worker. Guidance on the *Education of Young People in Public Care* (DfEE 1999) suggests "governors should ensure that carers are treated with as much respect as parents".

Home school agreements

Much controversy has surrounded the introduction of home-school agreements (S110 SSFA). Parents' groups have argued that where such documents are one-sided they have no value but the majority view seems to be that they have no significant impact on home school relations either way. A research project for RISE found that parents feel the agreements state the obvious in terms of responsibilities; schools only put down what is required of them while the responsibilities of parents and students were so obvious they shouldn't need to be written down. Governors have a duty to encourage all parents to sign an associated parental declaration but parents are not legally obliged to sign (S110 (3)(4) SSFA). The law also allows for a pupil to sign the parental declaration where the governing body considers that the pupil has a sufficient understanding of the agreement "as it relates to him". The Government has made it clear that signing an agreement cannot be a condition of admission – indeed the law now expressly forbids this (S111(4) SSFA). The law also forbids exclusion from a school or any other penalty being imposed on any person as a result of any failure to sign the parental declaration. Equally, parents will not be able to sue schools which fail to keep to their side of the bargain. Schools' existing legal responsibilities are not extended by the introduction of agreements.

The idea of home-school agreements stems from the 1977 Taylor Committee which sought greater partnership between parents and schools. Mutuality, reciprocity, participation and accountability were the buzz words in those days. In the more hard-nosed 'nineties the contract was seen as a way of controlling parents – or at least reminding them of their responsibilities. The DfEE refers to agreements in the context of parental responsibility, especially in relation to condoned truancy and parent and pupil behaviour, and it is striking that parents' rights to be consulted are limited mainly to the home school agreement and the governors' statement on school discipline.

DfEE guidance says agreements should include the school's aims and values, the school's responsibilities to its pupils, parents' responsibilities whilst their child is at the school, and the school's expectations of its pupils. Specifically, it recommends that agreements should cover:

- the standard of education; this could include pupils' right to a broad and balanced curriculum and how the needs of children of all abilities will be met. It might include school targets for national assessments and external examinations;
- the ethos of the school;
- regular and punctual attendance – the guidance says that "the Secretary of State attaches great importance to home-school agreements as a means of promoting regular attendance";
- discipline and behaviour – "parental influence is critical in shaping pupil attitude and behaviour";
- homework – the guidance says that parents should have a right to be consulted over changes to or developments in the school's homework policy;
- the information schools and parents will give to one another;
- details of the school's complaints procedure, setting out time limits.

Governors would be well advised, before drawing up an agreement, to consider developing it in the context of a home-school policy (*see below*) drawn up after full discussions involving teachers, governors, parents and pupils. Not only would such a process help the school to build on existing good practice but it would help avoid possible confrontation if parents have no part in its 'terms' or look on the agreement as conferring extra legal rights. Only if the agreement is the product of genuine consultation and is seen to be fair and apply to everyone involved is it likely to win support.

An ACE survey in 1999 found that many schools consulted only in the most cursory way but those that involved parents more fully generally started with a meeting and a blank piece of paper; splitting parents into groups to discuss a range of topics ensured that a wide range of views could be written up and incorporated into the final document. Compare this with the standard form of consultation in which parents are sent drafts of a near-finished document and it's clear why some schools get little response from parents who may feel they have no chance of shaping the final document. One school improved its response rates from parents by employing mailmerge software and using it to direct mail all parents; a follow-up letter went to those who failed to respond first time round. These parents could be under no misapprehension that their views didn't count.

Parent governors

Parents have had an increasing role in the management of schools over the past two decades. The SSFA increased the number of parent governors on governing bodies: one more elected in a majority of schools; in addition two or three members of the foundation group in church schools have to be parents. For the first time, parent governors representatives have been introduced to local education committees (S9 SSFA) (*see pages 11 - 12*).

Parents can be encouraged to keep in touch with the work of the governing body or to become governors themselves if information is provided via a governors' notice board, with a short description of each member's role, name and photograph, and minutes and agendas of meetings; regular newsletters or a governors' section in the school newsletter are also good ways of keeping parents informed. How to contact governors - whether by phone, letter or in person at a governor's surgery - should be publicised. Parents of children with special educational needs should be told the name of the SEN governor and how to contact him or her.

Parent governors are ideally placed to provide the link between the governing body and the PTA. Governors can take the initiative on introducing, developing and monitoring policies with a direct bearing on parents: for instance, the homework policy, equal opportunities policy and home-school policy.

Home school associations

A home-school association, parent-teacher association (PTA) or friends of the school can be of great help to the school but they can be counter-productive if they become exclusive; it is essential that all sections of the school community are equally involved. A school association or forum based on class representatives may be more representative than an ordinary PTA and can feed into the democratic process at local and national level.

Social events and more formal links between staff, parents and governors can help to forge relationships and strengthen home-school links. For instance PTA meetings ought to have a regular slot on the agenda for a parent governor to report matters being discussed by the governing body and this governor should take back any matters of interest or concern raised at the PTA or parent forums.

Home school policy

For parents to be real partners in education, they need to have an equal voice in the policy and direction of the school. It is widely recognised that parents are crucial in their children's attitudes towards education. Involving parents in drawing up a home school policy could be one of the most effective ways governors could improve achievement in their schools.

The process of producing a policy is the first step to carrying it out successfully. Because the parent body is constantly changing it will be necessary to review the policy on a regular basis. Parent representatives should be included in any group or subcommittee set up to develop and review a policy but all parents should be asked for their views through meetings, surveys and questionnaires. Particular attention needs to be given to involving parents from minority ethnic groups who can easily feel excluded by language and cultural barriers.

There is no point in the governing body rubber stamping a policy that has been drawn up by a few people without wider ownership.

Parents are already likely to be participating in many ways with the school so governors could start by asking questions about how and when this is taking place. The policy then can be based on good practice already going on in the school.

A policy need not be very long or detailed but it should state its aims: for example, to encourage partnership with parents and thereby improve children's experience in school; and it should give an outline of the kind of action to be taken to make the aims a reality: such as giving every child a home-school diary with space for parents and teachers to make comments.

Governors should ensure that other policies such as the equal opportunities policy or special educational needs policy are taken into account when drawing up a home school policy and that home school agreements and homework policies are drawn up in the same spirit as the home school policy.

Homework policy

Most secondary schools and many primary schools have homework policies. DfEE guidance advises that every school have such a policy, publicly available on request and that parents and teachers should be consulted regularly about them. A summary could be included in the school's prospectus, home-school agreement, and/or 'welcome pack' when pupils start at the school.

A homework policy would probably include:
- the responsibilities of teachers, parents and pupils
- how often homework is set
- how long it should take
- arrangements for marking the homework

(*Homework: Guidelines for Primary and Secondary Schools*, DfEE 1998)

Ofsted recommend that the procedures for monitoring that pupils complete homework and that teachers set and mark work regularly and appropriately should be included in homework policies, particularly in secondary schools. At primary school a clear overview of the curriculum and what will be covered each term can help parents support their children's learning. The homework policy should recognise that not all parents can offer the same support and alternative sources of help such as the school library or homework club should be offered along with ideas on how parents with limited time, resources or knowledge can support their children's learning.

Complaints

While complaints procedures are desirable, they are unlikely to solve many problems that parents face – good home school communication is the best way of preventing problems turning into disputes. However, even in the best regulated schools disagreements arise and a complaints procedure is one way of handling these in a professional manner.

The education service – unlike the majority of public services – has traditionally offered only patchy statutory complaints procedures. Those schools which have voluntarily instituted complaints procedures regard them as offering feedback which helps to improve policies and practice. They can give parents redress and reduce the number of cases where parents turn to the law. Ultimately a complaints procedure should be seen as an important way of listening to parents' views.

The SSFA requires governing bodies to establish procedures for dealing with all complaints not covered by existing legislation and to publicise those procedures (S39 SSFA). However regulations which would have set out broad principles and were to have defined who should hear complaints, different stages of complaint and time limits for each stage have been postponed indefinitely. ACE is aware that many parents' complaints are dealt with poorly. In the worst cases reprisals are taken against their children and resentment is felt by all parties. Legal provision for two specific types of complaints procedures has been in place for some time:

- LEAs, in the case of all maintained schools, are required to investigate complaints about curriculum issues (S409 EA96).
- **The Education (Special Needs) (Information) Regulations 1999 (Sched.2 (8) SI 2506**(England) **SI 1442** (Wales)) indicate that schools would normally have a complaints procedure for special needs matters.

There are also statutory appeals arrangements against decisions on admissions, exclusions and exceptions from the National Curriculum.

Many governing bodies and LEAs will have procedures in place to deal with complaints on any issue. Governors are likely to be involved if the complaint cannot be dealt with by teachers or senior staff. In some areas an independent panel set up by an external body, such as the LEA, will review governors' decisions if the complainant is still dissatisfied with the outcome.

Checklist for setting up a complaints procedure

The issues to be considered when setting up a procedure include:

✔ deciding who the procedure is for: pupils and staff as well as parents?

✔ deciding the procedure eg beginning with the class teacher and progressing through the headteacher/head of year to the governing body and on to an independent panel

✔ deciding who will hear complaints? – how can a governing body ensure independence?

✔ planning publicity – how to make the procedure accessible and widely known.

✔ planning a timetable – how quickly will complaints be heard?

✔ considering forms of redress – what are the remedies the school can make if the complaint against them is upheld?

Home school communications

Legal requirements to provide information for parents mean schools must already have some communications in place, but there is clearly a difference between merely obeying the letter of the law and communicating effectively with parents using a range of techniques from newsletters and annual reports to telephone calls and curriculum evenings. Many of the calls ACE receives on our advice line show the importance of good home school communications in avoiding misunderstandings and in ensuring all the adults in a child's life are working in the same direction. Often when things go wrong, poor communications are at the root of the problem. Personal communication is at least as important as written communication but in secondary schools parents have less regular contact with schools and rely mostly on letters, newsletters and messages written in the home school diary. Ensuring staff have time to phone or meet parents as necessary should be a consideration when governors are planning staffing levels and resources.

Pupil reports

Schools must provide parents with a written report at least once a year and must include brief details for all National Curriculum subjects studied, the number of absences since the last report and how parents can discuss the contents of the report with the school.

Pupils over 18 must be given their reports directly and the headteacher has discretion to send such reports to parents. New regulations on reporting individual pupil's achievements are made regularly and lay down the minimum information which should be included. The information may be spread over several reports in one year, but all parents must receive statutory information on their child's attainments in National Curriculum tests, teachers' assessments and public examinations. The requirements for pupil reports do not apply to school leavers who are given a report in their own right listing their school achievements. Their report must include brief details of subjects and activities studied as part of the school curriculum, other than those taken at examination level. Many schools use the National Record of Achievement for school leavers' reports which must be produced by the end of the summer term.

The Education (Pupil Information) (England) Regulations 2000 (SI 297) and Education (Individual Pupils' Achievements) (Information) (Wales) Regulations 1997 (SI 573) .

Research conducted for the Research and Information on State Education Trust (RISE) found that the frequency of reports is a key issue in parents feeling informed. RISE's national survey found that the majority of schools report to parents more frequently than legally required but there was wide variation. Some parents will receive only five reports during their child's compulsory secondary schooling whereas other parents may receive 24.

Content of reports was seen as important as their frequency by parents who praised reports that offered clear, accurate and honest information about their child's progress and difficulties. Governors could question whether the language of their school's reports is clear – jargon can be a barrier to parents' understanding according to the survey. Producing reports in different languages should also be considered. Parents for whom English was an additional language said they would like to receive reports in their own home language. Only eight per cent of schools in the survey produced reports in languages other than English. The researchers concluded that pupil reports are an important record for pupils and parents; their contents should be comprehensive and meaningful and cover progress, strengths and weaknesses. For pupils with special educational needs the report is particularly important.

Pupil records

Reports will be kept in the school record which goes through school with the pupil. Parents have a right to a copy of their child's school record (S408, S563 EA96). Under the **Data Protection Act 1998** pupils too are entitled to a copy unless it is clear that they do not understand what they are asking for. An educational record comprises a "curricular record" which is a formal record of a pupil's academic achievements, his or her other skills and abilities and progress in school plus any other educational record (including a teacher's record but excluding teacher's notes processed solely for the teacher's own use) which are kept in school.

If the school record is inaccurate, the parent or pupil can write to the head to have the record amended. In the past parents could appeal against a decision not to reveal, copy or amend a record to the governing body. Under the DPA any appeal would be through the courts.

Not to be disclosed

Certain items which may be contained in a pupil's record must not be disclosed to either the parent or the pupil. This includes information provided by a third person, i.e. someone who is not an employee of the LEA. This will include medical reports. Other documents which are not to be disclosed are:

✔ any information which could identify another pupil who may have been involved in an incident

✔ any information which, if disclosed, would in the opinion of the governors cause serious harm to the physical or mental health or the emotional condition of the pupil concerned or of any other person (but see page 68 Dunraven case)

✔ any information relating to actual, alleged or suspected child abuse

✔ any reference on the pupil provided for a potential employer or other educational establishment to which a pupil may be intending to transfer

✔ any ethnic data on the individual pupil

✔ any school reports written for the Youth Court (although magistrates have the discretion to disclose such reports to the parents and pupils concerned)

School prospectus

The governors of all maintained schools are responsible for publishing detailed information about their schools and this is usually produced in the form of distinctive school brochures. Governors of LEA maintained schools may ask the LEA to publish the prospectus and, if they agree, the governing body must provide the information. The prospectus must be available at least six weeks before the closing date for admission applications or for expressing a preference. If some information is not available, it must be produced as a supplement two weeks before that date. Copies should be available at school for reference and for distribution to parents on request, free of charge.

The Government is currently consulting on changing the legal requirements for school prospectuses and governors' annual reports so that schools no longer have to produce both. Instead they will be required to produce a single document known as the governors' report and school prospectus. The amount of information this contains is likely to be reduced.

While schools are already allowed to combine the two documents, so long as the legal requirements are followed, the Government feels there is currently much duplication and proposes leaving out information on the school's ethos and values and information about the professional development undertaken by teachers.

Prospectus checklist

Your school prospectus must include the following information:

✔ The school's name, address and telephone number

✔ The type of school including any affiliations to a particular religion or religious denomination

✔ Name of head and chair of governing body

✔ Description of school's ethos and values

✔ Details of school's admission policy including any arrangements for prospective parents to visit the school

✔ National Curriculum assessment results, and, where applicable, public examination results at school level and comparative information

✔ Religious education provided and parents' right to withdraw their child from religious education and collective worship

✔ Rates of authorised and unauthorised absence

✔ A summary of the school's SEN policy as set out in the SEN Information regulations including how resources are allocated; and a summary of SEN provision including facilities which increase or assist access for pupils with disabilities (**The Education (Special Educational Needs) (Information) (England) Regulations 1999) and the Education (SEN) (Information) (Wales) Regulations 1999**).

In secondary schools

✔ details of the number of school places available in the current school year and the number of applications received or preferences expressed

✔ numbers of pupils studying for and percentage achieving vocational qualifications

✔ destinations of school leavers.

In Wales in addition the following must be included:

✔ A statement on the curriculum and organisation of education and teaching methods at the school

✔ Information on how to make a curriculum complaint

✔ A summary of the content and organisation of any sex education provided

✔ A summary of sporting aims and provision

✔ A summary of the charging and remissions policy of the governing body under **S457 EA96**

✔ Times school sessions begin and end

✔ Dates of school holidays

✔ Use of Welsh language in the school; whether alternative instruction in English is available where a subject is taught in Welsh and the extent to which Welsh is the normal language of communication; details of any exemption from the National Curriculum in Welsh

Education (School Information) (England) Regulations 1998 (SI 2526) and the Education (School Information) (Wales) Regulations 1999 (SI 1812)

Despite the importance of complying with the legal requirements, the school prospectus is more than a list of facts and figures about a school. How you present your information, the language you use and the view you give of life at your school can all contribute to the school's image. Sometimes a prospectus can reveal a lot more about a school than schools sometimes realise which is why the thought that goes into planning a prospectus is so important if you are to give an accurate picture and one which highlights your school's best aspects.

It's probably best if a committee of staff, governors, parents and pupils contribute to the prospectus. As well as listing legal requirements, the committee could begin with some simple market research: looking at how others have tackled the job and trying these out on parents, for example. A key consideration is to remember the audience particularly in relation to the language used. The Consumers' Association survey found much evidence of jargon and legalistic language which might well be out of tune with the way the school normally communicates with parents. Has your school a sizeable minority ethnic intake which speaks English as a second language? Would it be useful to provide copies of the prospectus in different community languages?

Schools on the web

Hundreds of British schools now feature on pages on the World Wide Web and much of the material produced for your prospectus could be adapted to this. Increasingly parents – especially those moving into an area – will turn to the internet to research local schools. You could consider putting your mission statement, pages from your prospectus, governors' annual report and Ofsted inspection summary on the net. Some schools change their content regularly by including their weekly newsletter, children's news and examples of their work and information about coursework deadlines.

Annual report

Governing bodies are required to publish an annual report to parents describing the activities of the governing body over the last year (**S161 EA96; S42 SSFA**). This must be distributed free of charge to all parents of registered pupils. In addition, the report must be freely available at the school for inspection at all reasonable times.

The annual report is an extremely important element of governors' accountability to the communities they serve. The subject matter, openness of the report, and readability will not only properly acquaint parents with the activities of the governors, but also directly affect the number of parents that attend the meeting to discuss the report.

Governors should ensure that their activities are described in everyday language, avoiding educational jargon, and illustrating points with constant reference to aspects of school life that are relevant to parents. Governors will also need to consider the languages in which the report is to be translated. In the case of community or voluntary controlled schools the report must be translated into a language other than English if the LEA require it.

Whilst the report must contain the name and address of the chair of governors, it could also include the contact details for every governor.

Details of finance and examination statistics can be neatly summarised, but left unexplained they can be dry and meaningless. The statistics could be used to explain the school's spending priorities, drawing out the school's strengths and showing what was being done about areas of apparent weakness.

The Education (Governors' Annual Reports) (England) Regulations 1999 (SI 2157) and The Education (Governors' Annual Reports) (Wales) Regulations 1999 (SI 1406).

The National Assembly in Wales is currently consulting on extending requirements so that annual reports include details on action taken to review school policies and on action taken to implement and review specific school strategies. ACE has welcomed this but expressed concern about another proposal to limit distribution of the annual report to those parents who request a copy - a move which we feel would disadvantage some Welsh parents.

Annual meeting

At least two weeks after issuing the annual report, the governors must hold a meeting for parents (S43 SSFA). The purpose of the meeting is to discuss the annual report and how the governors, the headteacher, and the LEA carried out their duties to the school. Attendance is open to all parents of registered pupils, the headteacher, the governors, and anyone invited at the governing body's discretion.

The proceedings of the meeting are under the control of the governing body, and only those with parental responsibility may vote on matters put to the meeting. Where the total number of parents present is at least equal to 20 per cent of the number of pupils registered at the school, resolutions by individual parents may be put to the vote. Resolutions passed must be considered by the governors (headteacher or LEA if appropriate) and a report given back at the next annual meeting. Governors at their discretion may allow a resolution to be taken if enough parents are not present.

When resolutions are passed by the parent body, most governors would agree that they should be dealt with immediately and not left until the following year until a report back is made.

It is clear from legislation and guidance that the purpose of the meeting goes far wider than a straightforward discussion of the contents of the report. There should be plenty of opportunities to discuss the school issues that parents wish to raise.

As noted earlier, the content and presentation of the report can go some way towards attracting parents. Other strategies are to couple the meetings with a social element or event, or an event that directly relates to the children's progress and opportunities. DfEE guidance suggests governing bodies consider how they send out invitations, the hospitality offered and the type of welcome, and seating.

Despite a recommendation from the Commons select committee on education that the annual meeting be abandoned because of low attendances, ministers have urged governors to be imaginative about their meetings and to discuss issues to be addressed in the year to come as well as looking back on the past year. That way parents may feel their views will have some influence on future policy. (**The Education (Annual Parents' Meetings) (England) Regulations 1999 (SI 2104); The Education (Annual Parents' Meetings) (Wales) Regulations 1999 (SI1407)**).

Governors' meeting and papers

Governors must ensure that parents can see, on request, a copy of the Instrument of the governing body (which deal with membership), and copies of the agendas and minutes of the previous meetings (including draft minutes once these have been agreed by the chair of governors, and any papers or reports considered by the governors – excluding those items deemed to be confidential). Attendance at governors' meetings is at the discretion of the governing body. **Education School Government (England) Regulations 1999** and **The Education (School Government) (Wales) Regulations 1999.**

Governors will need to guard against excessive use of their power to exclude items from public scrutiny on the grounds of confidentiality, as this can give rise to suspicion and mistrust. **Terms of Reference Regulations** (England and Wales)(2000) require governing bodies to be open about the decisions they make and the actions they take and in particular be prepared to explain their decisions and actions. However, governors clearly have to be sensitive to the need to protect the privacy of individuals.

It would be a good idea to put the topic of communication with parents on the agenda for the termly meetings. Although all governors have to be concerned about this, parent governors will have special interest in ensuring parents' concerns are raised and properly considered. They will also feel the need to report back to parents on matters of particular interest.

Annual report checklist

The governors' annual report must contain:
✔ the date, time, place and agenda of the annual meeting

✔ a report of any action taken by the governing body on any resolutions passed at the last annual meeting

✔ the name of each governor and type (parent, co-opted, LEA etc) and the date when their term of office ends

✔ the name and address of the chair of governors and the clerk to the governing body

✔ information on arrangements for the next election of parent governors

✔ the number of registered pupils of compulsory school age at the school on a set date

✔ the dates of the beginning and end of each term and of half term holidays for the next year

✔ a full financial statement, including an account of expenses for governors' travel and subsistence

✔ a statement on the progress in implementing the action plan drawn up following an inspection

✔ prescribed information on public examinations including vocational qualifications. For all except very small schools, information on National Curriculum tests and assessments including the numbers reaching the expected level for their age in the school and numbers of those exempted and those who failed to register a level because of absence. Secondary schools must indicate the destinations of school leavers.

✔ targets for pupils' performance for the relevant year, the two previous years and the following year

✔ information about professional development undertaken by teaching staff

✔ information about school security

✔ information on pupils' absences

✔ a report on the implementation and effectiveness of the special needs policy and any amendments to the policy

✔ a description of the admission arrangements for pupils with disabilities as defined by the Disability Discrimination Act 1995. The provisions of the DDA do not apply to special schools.

✔ details of steps taken to prevent pupils with disabilities from being treated less favourably than other pupils

✔ details of facilities provided to assist access to the school by pupils with disabilities

The Education (Governors' Annual Reports) (England) Regulations 1999 (SI 2157).

In Wales
In addition to most of the above, governing bodies must include:
✔ Steps taken by the governing body to develop or strengthen the school's community links

✔ Progress report on sporting aims including any notable sporting achievements of the school's teams during that period

✔ Information about any targets for improving pupils' performance and for reducing unauthorised absences

✔ The dates of the beginning and end of each school term, and of half-term holidays, for the next school year

✔ A summary of any changes to information in the school prospectus since the previous governors' report was prepared

✔ Information since the last governors' report on the success of the school's SEN policies, significant changes in the policy, outcomes of any consultation with LEAs and other governing bodies on co-ordinating SEN provision, and on how resources have been allocated to and amongst pupils with SEN.

The Education (Governors' Annual Reports) (Wales) Regulations 1999 (SI 2157) and The Education (SEN) (Information) (Wales) Regulations 1999 (SI 1406).

Governors and Pupils

In many respects all the chapters of this handbook are about the pupils of the school. As the ultimate 'consumers' of education, the staffing arrangements, curriculum, inspections and so on are there ultimately for their benefit. On some issues, however, the governing body must focus directly on the pupils' welfare and development – and their rights. These issues are covered here in A-Z format.

A new approach

One way governors can ensure their school is a model of good practice on all issues concerning the emotional and physical development of pupils is to encourage their school to sign up for accreditation under the National Healthy School scheme. This initiative - involving both the DfEE and the Department of Health - is aimed at improving the health of schools in its widest sense. The Government hopes that all schools will be working within a nationally accredited local programme, supported by a co-ordinator, by March 2002

Under the scheme, a National Healthy School Standard has been drawn up aimed at assisting schools seeking accreditation for their work. A whole school approach to education and health improvement will be a key element to any local programme. This means that governors will need to ensure that school policies and publications reflect the Standards, for example checking policies are in line with legal requirements and guidance. The governing body could take the lead in establishing such mechanisms as parent forums for involving the whole school community in policy development and implementation. Consulting parents and pupils will be an important way of monitoring the success of the school's healthy school work.

Local programmes may work with schools on local and school priorities, for example reducing the number of teenage smokers. Specific themes described in the guidance include PSHE, citizenship, drug education (including alcohol and tobacco) emotional health and well-being (including bullying) healthy eating, physical activity, safety, and sex and relationships education. Many themes will involve governors taking an active role, for example the guidance recommends that a governor work alongside a named member of staff on drug education.

Bullying

There is now a requirement for schools to draw up behaviour policy which addresses bullying; this needs to be kept under review. One of the most common complaints about schools and bullying is that the policy is not followed so governors should

consider ways they can involve the whole school in the development of the policy and monitoring its effectiveness.

A survey of over 4,000 teenagers reported in 2001 by the charity Young Voice found that more than one child in ten has experienced severe bullying, including physical violence, blackmail and racism. The survey found that bullying caused serious physical and mental problems, including depression, suicidal instincts and drug taking. All too often the impact of bullying is dismissed or underestimated.

The law and guidance on bullying

Governing bodies must produce and review discipline policies in consultation with parents **(S61 SSFA)**. Headteachers have responsibility for day-to-day measures (such as school rules) including those "to prevent all forms of bullying among pupils" **(S61(4b) SSFA)**. DfEE guidance Bullying: Don't Suffer in Silence (2000) gives advice on different approaches schools can take to tackle bullying as well as a range of steps which schools should take to ensure pupils' journey to and from school is safe. The police may use the **Protection from Harassment Act 1997** and other criminal law to charge and prosecute bullies.

DfEE Circular 10/99 Social Inclusion: Pupil Support and NAW Circular 3/99 Pupil Support and Social Inclusion acknowledge that bullying can prejudice achievement, lead to lateness and truancy and, in extreme cases, end in suicide.

Not our school

For a variety of reasons, schools find it difficult to admit that children are bullying and being bullied. "Oh no, it doesn't happen in out school!" is a very common response from staff. This contrasts sharply with what children and parents say about bullying. For children, it is the major fear they have about transferring from primary to secondary school.

Schools in which bullies are allowed to operate become stressful and unwelcoming places, not just for the victims, but for all those who look on and feel threatened and helpless – other children, teachers, class and playground assistants, and parents. In addition bullying has a direct causal link with truancy and academic underachievement. In extreme cases it can lead to pupils taking their own lives.

Government guidance states clearly that schools must act, and importantly be seen to act, firmly against bullying. The DfEE's *Bullying: Don't Suffer in Silence* guidance suggests a range of anti-bullying strategies ranging from circle time and co-operative groups for younger children to mediation, counselling and quality circles for older pupils. Some approaches such as assertiveness training, can be used with all age groups. The no-blame approach is one option recommended in the guidance – although it is now called the Support Group Approach – but the Government also feels that a range of sanctions may also need to be employed where the bullying is persistent and violent. Circulars 10/99 (England) and 3/99 (Wales) say pupils who are racially harassed at school or outside may need support. The guidance suggests pupils can be actively involved in developing anti-bullying policies and older pupils can act as mentors.

What can governors do?

Although responsibility for the day-to-day running of the school rests with the headteacher, governors have a very important role to play in making sure that their schools are welcoming places where children are relaxed and happy enough to take advantage of all the educational opportunities on offer.

The first thing for a concerned governor to do is get the issue put on the agenda for the next governors' meeting. You can do this by asking the headteacher to cover bullying in the next report, or you could ask for a special meeting devoted entirely to bullying. Either way, you need to establish how bullying is being tackled in your school. To have an informed discussion, ask the headteacher to provide information about current policies and strategies and information about bullying incidents over the past year or two. You could ask whether they have anything in common and how they have been resolved.

Anti-bullying policies

Governors must make it clear that they want practical strategies and curriculum plans which can be delivered. It is much better to have a strategy of limited but achievable goals than a nebulous all-embracing policy with no direction.
The DfEE's guidance says policies should include
- a definition of bullying
- aims and objectives
- procedures to follow - who to tell, recording incidents, sanctions
- intervention techniques
They should be reviewed annually.
Governors should therefore make sure that any formulation of discipline and anti-bullying policies are informed by the views of
  - the pupils
  - the parents
  - the teachers
  - the class and playground assistants
  - the dinner helpers
  - the caretakers.
Such policies should make a clear anti-bullying statement which applies to each and every member of the school community. Governors should ensure

their discipline policies spell out what sanctions the school would use against persistent bullies and what steps the school will take to investigate complaints and to protect victims. But a paper policy is no good if no-one knows of its existence and if it isn't implemented anyway. So governors need to make sure that the school handbook contains a clear anti-bullying statement and that the statement is clearly displayed around the school. What is under the microscope here is the whole ethos of the school – the values which shape the way in which it is run and the manner in which pupils and adults work together.

The policy should relate to everybody in the school, adults and students alike. One of the things that pupils have said about bullying is that some adults continually pick on or humiliate particular children. Sometimes they are the very children who are being bullied. If adults bully then they give licence to bullies.

Some groups of children may be more vulnerable than others - those from particular racial groups or children with disabilities, for example. The policy should explicitly refer to racial and sexual harass-

---

A bullying checklist for governors

✔ Does the ethos of the school - its general atmosphere and purpose - encourage or discourage bullying?
✔ Does the school already have whole school policies and strategies which specifically identify and address bullying?
✔ If so, how are they being implemented and are they effective?
✔ How do the pupils know what the school's policy on bullying is?
✔ Does the policy apply to staff and parents?
✔ Are the policies explicit about sanctions?
✔ How do pupils complain about bullying and are complaints dealt with effectively and quickly?
✔ Is there someone that a victim can talk to in confidence and is support provided for victims?
✔ How are pupils encouraged to take responsibility for themselves and others?
✔ How does the school work with bullies?
✔ How does the school involve parents in its anti-bullying work?
✔ Does the school keep a record of bullying incidents to look for common themes and to pinpoint areas in which specific intervention would be useful?
✔ Does the school link with outside agencies such as the police and bus companies to minimise bullying on the way to and from school?
✔ Do staffing policies take into account supervision of areas where pupils are more vulnerable to bullying?
✔ Are training needs including those of playground supervisors kept under scrutiny
✔ When did the school last look at how the playground is being used and whether it is a place which caters for the variety of play needs which pupils have?
✔ Does the school clearly set out its complaints procedure in the school prospectus or annual report? Do governors monitor parents' complaints on bullying? Could the governing body justify the school's responses in court?
✔ Does the school's insurance cover the school for negligence claims by pupils?

ment and bullying of children with SEN. It should link with the school's equal opportunities and behaviour policy on these issues. Under the **Race Relations Amendment Act 2000** governing bodies are required to develop strategies to prevent and address racism in schools.

School rules, so often a catalogue of 'thou-shalt-nots', can miss the chance to describe the kind of behaviour which we would all like to see and give no examples of non-confrontational methods of resolving conflicts. A policy should lay down positive values of how we should relate to each other.

Even though it may mean constantly having to 'reinvent the wheel', whole-school involvement in developing and reviewing an anti-bullying policy could be the catalyst which sparks off real democracy in schools. Rules are usually imposed on pupils rather than developed and evaluated by them. It is important that pupils own and respect the rules by which they are expected to behave.

Is there someone to talk to?

When something is wrong most children will first try to sort it out for themselves. Only later will they complain to the class teacher, and even then often with reluctance. As they get older they are less likely to complain to a teacher, particularly if they are being bullied. Governors should:

1 Try to ensure that children are actively encouraged to talk about bullying, not only in the classroom but also on an individual basis. They need to know that it is OK to speak to someone they can trust. Some schools offer mentoring support from older pupils or a drop-in club where they can talk and feel safe at lunchtimes.

2 Try to ensure that there is a named person in the school whose job it is to listen to victims and/or their parents in confidence. This person should be able to offer a range of solutions to the child and support them in the course they choose to take.

3 Publicise the name of this person in the school handbook, on the school noticeboard, at assemblies and at any appropriate time during class or at parents' meetings.

Bullying complaints

All schools have a duty of care towards their pupils, and breach of that duty of care is grounds for a claim of negligence. A governing body and/or LEA could be regarded as vicariously liable for an employee's negligence if a complaint of bullying was not taken seriously (*see negligence, page 13*). For many years negligence cases involving bullying have either been unsuccessful or have resulted in out-of-court settlements. However, in October 2000 a case taken by a former pupil of a north west grammar school resulted in damages of £1,500 being paid after an 18-month campaign of verbal abuse culminated in a sexual assault during a school trip. The judge found that the teachers could not have foreseen the assault but concluded that the school had fallen down in its procedures and was therefore in breach of its duty of care as far as the verbal abuse was concerned. "A school must take reasonable steps to minimise bullying," he said.

Governors should make sure that a log of all reported bullying is kept and that both bully and victim have follow-up sessions to give them both the opportunity to discuss any progress or deterioration. Schools should record and monitor reported racist incidents and how they are resolved. An incident book should record different types of bullying including racial harassment. Termly reports to the governing body could highlight any pattern which the incident reports throw up. Parents should also be kept informed of action to deal with incidents. (*Annex B Circular 10/99* (England).

Since governing bodies are charged with a responsibility for the discipline and conduct of the school, failure to deal with a proven case of bullying could leave them open to legal action or to censure by the Secretary of State for Education for unreasonable or unlawful behaviour under **Ss 496** and **497** of the **Education Act 1996**. No complaints procedure should cut across, compromise or pre-empt the right of the parent or victim to make a direct complaint to the police. This possibility should be addressed in the complaints procedure.

Children in public care

Most children in public care will be facing separation and loss; many will have experienced numerous and often unplanned moves of home. Sixty-five per cent live in foster placements, and the rest live in residential provision or with their families with social work support.

The term 'looked after' refers to children who are subject to care orders made by a court and those who are accommodated by voluntary arrangement between the local authority and parent/s. If a child is in care, then the local authority has parental responsibility with the parent/s and can exercise parental rights. If a child is accommodated, the Social Services Department does not have parental responsibility but in either case they can act as 'corporate parent'.

The serious underachievement of looked after children is, in many ways, testimony to the value and power of parents but evidence too of the shortcomings of corporate parenting. A range of professionals, individuals and agencies are involved in corporate parenting and this includes governing bodies whose strategic role can be important in ensuring that this small minority of children are not overlooked or stigmatised.

DfEE guidance *Education of Young People in Public Care (2000)* points to the importance of educational planning and support for these young people. At individual level a care plan will set out the child's educational history, the need for continuity and the need to identify and provide for any special educational needs. The statutory part of this guidance also requires that every child and young person has a personal education plan which acts as an achievement record; identifies needs; sets out short-term targets and long term plans. The PEP will be an integral part of the care plan and reflect other plans such as a Statement of SEN, individual education plans and pastoral support programme.

On a strategic level governing bodies are crucial. They should ensure that school policies for instance, anti-bullying strategies, SEN policies and equal opportunities polices promote supportive practice for this group. Admissions and exclusions are other areas which have adversely affected looked after children. Delays and discrimination result in many spending unreasonably long periods out of school because of resistance to their admission. Local authorities are being set a maximum time limit of 20 school days within which they must normally secure a school place for children in public care. Governors should ensure induction of all pupils joining the school outside normal periods is high priority as these young people are recognised as being at risk of disaffection by *Circular 10/99 Social Inclusion: Pupil Support.* The Circular also recognises looked after children as a vulnerable group. Governors should check whether truancy and exclusion affect them disproportionately.

Quality Protects is a major three year programme to overhaul children's services in response to reports on the low quality of services for children with the public care system. One of its key objectives is "To ensure that children looked after gain maximum life chance benefits from educational opportunities, health care and social care." Having a designated teacher who understands care issues is critical to making joint working across social service, health and education boundaries successful. DfEE guidance suggests it would be desirable that the person who fills this role has sufficient authority to influence school policy and practice. It may be that working with a designated governor would be a 'joined-up' way that schools could contribute to improving practice at school level.

The Government has set targets to improve the educational attainment of looked after children *(see page 46)* to bring them closer into line with other local children. There is evidence that raising their profile is beginning to make a difference in some LEA areas and some schools. Ofsted in a recent report *(Raising achievement of children in public care, 2001)* found there was still a significant minority achieving at an unacceptably low level. However, in its examination of the work in 26 local authorities where targets were set to raise achievement of looked after children, many pupils were making good progress. It recommends that training of governors, key teachers, social workers and others could focus on shared knowledge of the requirements of the education and care services.

Child protection

All schools should have a child protection policy setting out their procedures for dealing with allegations of abuse against children or in situations where a child is considered to be at risk from abuse. Advice on drawing up a policy is set out in *DfEE Circular 10/95: Protecting Children from Abuse: the Role of the Education Service.* This says that schools should appoint a senior member of staff as designated teacher for child protection. Their role is to liaise with external agencies such as social services, the Area Child Protection committee and the police.

Police may on occasions disclose information about known sex offenders in the neighbourhood and should discuss with headteachers how to warn parents of the risk.

Clear guidelines for staff will need to cover issues such as confidentiality, parental involvement, staff and governor training, record keeping, monitoring and supporting children on the Child Protection Register and physical contact with pupils. The policy should be reviewed annually with a report to the governing body on its operation.

The Circular recognises that children with special educational needs, especially where these include communication difficulties, are particularly vulnerable to abuse and staff guidelines will need to "maintain a balance between providing support and preventing abuse".

Schools' procedures should also include action to be taken if a member of staff is accused of abuse *(see* **Governors and Staffing***).* The Government is currently proposing that there should be a 'named governor' for liaising with the LEA or Social Services Department where a headteacher is accused of misconduct under child protection procedures.

Governing bodies should consider whether education on personal safety is included in the school's sex education programme. Decisions on how to provide this in a way which is sensitive to the maturity of the children will be a matter of professional judgement. "Teaching children possible ways to prevent or tell about abuse must be done carefully so as not to cause anxiety or upset normal, stable relationships between adults and children," says Government guidance.

Sexual relationships involving pupils and teachers at the same school or college would constitute serious misconduct on the part of the teacher and may lead to dismissal or the teacher being barred from further employment in the education service by the Secretary of State. Sexual relationships involving children under 16 are a criminal offence, and **Chapter 44 (3)** of the **Sexual Offences (Amendment) Act 2000,** creates a new offence to protect those under 18 from abuse of trust in the form of inappropriate sexual relationships. A teacher having a sexual relationship with a full-time pupil in the same school who is under 18 will therefore be committing an offence.

Drugs

Every school is likely to be affected by the impact of drugs in the community although a 1999 survey by the Schools Health Education Unit found that the percentage of young people that have tried an illegal drug may have peaked.

The Government is encouraging schools to approach drugs education through the personal, social and health education (PSHE) curriculum and the Healthy Schools initiative *(see above).* At the same time the White Paper *Tackling Drugs to Build a Better Britain* considers the wider context and sets out a ten year strategy for tackling drug misuse with a reduction in exclusions from schools arising from drug-related incidents as one of the main objectives. *Protecting Young People, 1998,* DfEE guidance which underpins the strategy, says that governors have a central role to play in determining the approach to discipline and general ethos of a school and their training needs should not be neglected.

The need for a policy

With the pressures placed on young people to use drugs, it is essential that schools have a policy in place to ensure that children and young people have access to drug education and are fairly dealt with if they become intoxicated or bring substances on to school premises.

An over-reaction by school managers may mean pupils worried about drugs will be less likely to seek help. It may also perversely glamorise the use of drugs amongst pupils. Exclusion leaves the young person bewildered and parents distraught and worried about future schooling. Other parents who have a sneaking suspicion that their young-sters may be involved will be reluctant to turn to the school for fear of landing their child in a similar situation.

It is possible, however, to develop a measured and sophisticated approach towards drugs, with strategies which include appropriate disciplinary action, pastoral responses and realistic education, and balance as much as possible the needs of the institution, parents, young people and staff.

Working with other agencies

Governing bodies may decide to appoint a lead governor to work with the school drug co-ordina-tor and external agencies on developing the school's policies and practice on this issue.

The DfEE recommends that schools work with 'other services concerned with young people to offer appropriate advice and support'. Locally appropriate support may come from the youth service, the community drugs and alcohol service and the local youth offending team. *DfEE Circular 10/99: Social Inclusion: Pupil Support* encourages schools to contact their local drug action team for advice on handling incidents, on criminal offences committed within the school and on helping to support pupils involved in drug-related incidents.

A number of LEAs have provided guidance to help schools construct a policy. If an agreed local framework can be used as the basis of individual school policies, the general disciplinary approach for all young people in one area will be consistent. This will strengthen acceptance of the schools' policies, and minimise difficulties over exclusions.

A policy working party could include a member of senior management, the PSE co-ordinator, head of science, local youth worker, governor and parent representatives, students, police school liaison officer, worker from a local community drugs team, and the LEA drug or health education co-ordinator. It is particularly advantageous to have representation from external agencies as they can contribute to drug education and support if incidents occur. It is vital that young people are included; their experience and concerns will help the adults focus on the issues affecting them.

What the policy should cover

An audit of existing drugs education and practice is a good starting point with school policies, publi-cations, schemes of work and exclusion records as evidence of existing practice.

There are two key elements that need to be covered: 1) provision for drug education and 2) responses for dealing with drug related incidents

Drug education

Drugs education should take place across the age range and is especially crucial within Years 7 and 8. Young people making the transition from primary to secondary schools expand their contacts overnight to include pupils who will have access to street drugs. They need to be informed about the outcomes of taking a variety of drugs. Primary schools too need to address the issue. A Schools Health Education Unit survey found that about 20 per cent of nine to 11-year-olds were fairly sure that they knew someone using drugs for non-medicinal purposes; more than two-thirds wanted their parents to talk to them about drugs and a third would have liked their teachers to do so.

The Ofsted report, *Drug Education in Schools* (1997), found that while many schools had access to a wide range of drug education materials, insuf-ficient attention was given to selecting those materials. Guidance on this subject, *The Right Choice (1998)*, has since been published by the Standing Conference on Drug Abuse (SCODA).

Statutory requirements for drugs education under the National Curriculum are included within the science orders at all key stages while the adoption of drug education within a framework of personal, social and health education should ensure that young people see the connection with other life skills and health issues. SCODA's good practice guide *Quality Standards in Drug Education (1999)* helps schools put their drug education in the context of the Healthy Schools Standards *(see page 78)*.

Managing drug related incidents

There is much conflicting advice on this subject and governing bodies need to be well-informed on drug issues before they decide their stance. A zero-tolerance policy may seem attractive but can be a blunt instrument where the overlap between pupils selling or sharing their drugs among their peers makes it difficult to distinguish between 'dealer' and 'pupils with drug misuse problems'. Policies which treat the child who may have been pressured into trying cannabis with the same severity as a pupil dealing hard drugs are unlikely to win the respect of pupils. Research shows that many teenagers have experimented with alcohol and cigarettes – governors will need to decide its disci-plinary approach where drug abuse is of legal, but arguably equally harmful, substances.

The main Government guidance on managing drug-related incidents is found in Circulars 4/95 and 10/99 (England) 3/99 (Wales).

Circular 10/99, Social Inclusion: Pupil Support (amended in August 2000) says that permanent exclusion is a last resort, a final sanction when all other reasonable steps have been taken. "Reasonable steps" could include a pastoral support programme or other strategy. (A list of strategies employed by schools is described in the SCODA publication *Managing and making policy for drug-related incidents in schools*.) Although the Circular accepts that permanent exclusion may make a young person more vulnerable to exposure to drugs, an amendment to the guidance to appeal panels makes it clear that they should not normally reinstate where a pupil presents a significant risk to the health and safety of other pupils by selling illegal drugs.

Circular 4/95 Drug Prevention in Schools points out that just because certain behaviour could constitute a violation of the criminal law it should not, in itself, be taken as automatically leading to the exclusion of a pupil. It goes further by arguing that schools should develop a "repertoire of responses", and that permanent exclusions should be seen "as a final sanction when all other reasonable steps have been taken". Fixed term exclusions provide an opportunity for a pastoral response to be arranged through an external agency. Those schools which have already involved local agencies in the process of developing a policy can benefit from those relationships if and when the policy needs to be applied.

A referral system for young people worried about drugs should be in place. The ethos of the school should be one where students feel able to talk in confidence to a member of staff about a drug related problem without fear of reprimand. It is important however that they are aware of the limits of confidentiality, and appreciate the difference between voluntarily confiding a concern and being discovered with drugs while at school. Staff with a counselling role should be left to judge at what point parents should be informed and this should be made clear to the young person.

The Drugs Policy should include

- an explanation of the justification of the drugs policy with reference to current trends and the potential risks to children and young people. Reference to national and local policies and guidance. Links with other policies developed in the school, especially the school's behaviour policy.

- a brief description of the drugs and other substances to be included in the policy, including their characteristics and legal status. Policies should ideally cover all types of drugs.

- the organisation of drug education at all key stages, how it is delivered and who is involved, including the role of visitors.

- procedures for dealing with the following situations:

    when suspicion is aroused or rumour encountered

    incidents out of school but perhaps on the way to and/or from school

    the discovery of a substance

    when a disclosure is made (a statement on confidentiality will be needed here)

    in an emergency such as illness or intoxication the arrangements for counselling and support for a child or young person in trouble with drugs.

- the sanctions that would be applied in a given situation. NB Staff should be aware of the disciplinary action that would be taken if they contravene the code of conduct concerning drugs.

- plans for in-service training of staff and governors.

- plans for occasional but regular parents' evenings, perhaps to coincide with the drug education work with pupils.

- an appendix could include teaching and information resources together with a list of local and national agencies which can help.

Once the policy has been prepared it may well be useful to prepare versions for pupils in their induction packs, provide a summary for parents, and plan a launch. The policy working party could continue meeting on a termly basis to monitor and review the policy, evaluate new resources and plan particular projects.

Similarly governors need to be clear about their role; it would be inappropriate for a governor taking part in a case conference to decide what action to take against a pupil involved in, for example, a drugs incident to then sit on the discipline committee which hears a parent's representations.

Health and safety

Serious incidents at school and on school journeys over recent years have resulted in new legislation and guidance covering outdoor education, school transport and school security. Governors need an understanding of both to inform policies which will help make their schools as healthy, safe and secure as possible.

Under the **Health and Safety at Work Act 1974 (HSWA)** employers are responsible for the health and safety of their employees and anyone else on the premises – such as pupils and visitors. The Act places duties on the employer which is the LEA, except in voluntary aided and foundation schools, city technology colleges and independent schools where the employer is the governing body. Governors of voluntary aided schools may seek help from the diocesan authority.

The Management of Health and Safety at Work Regulations 1999 (SI 3242) made under the 1974 Act require employers to assess the risks to which their employees and others – such as pupils – might be exposed, and introduce measures to control those risks, including preventive and protective measures. These include evaluating risks which cannot be avoided and adapting the work to the individual, especially as regards the design of workplaces, the choice of work equipment and the choice of working methods.

Employers' duties

The main actions employers must take under the above law are to:
- provide safe and healthy working conditions for employees and others
- provide information and training about health and safety
- draw up a health and safety management policy, which describes who does what and details the monitoring expected of them
- assess the risks to health and safety to which employees and others are exposed
- make sure that appropriate safety measures are in place eg sufficient first aid kits
- ensure that staff are aware of the safety policy, and any responsibilities which stem from it
- make sure that staff are properly trained to meet their responsibilities
- ensure that employees are informed of risks, safety measures and procedures
- monitor and review safety measures.

Health and Safety Management Policy

This should:
- name the key person responsible for the policy, its implementation and development
- explain who is responsible for the different aspects of health and safety identified in the policy

- describe when training will be provided
- describe any procedures to be followed
- give details of standards to be met
- describe reporting arrangements and record keeping
- describe any monitoring arrangements in place
- explain how pupils, parents, staff and visitors will be alerted to health and safety issues and kept informed.

Delegating responsibility

Delegation of responsibilities does not remove the legal duty of governing bodies and LEAs which should monitor carefully decisions taken on their behalf. Governing bodies often delegate health and safety matters to individual safety representatives and committees which take responsibility for:

- keeping up-to-date on health and safety requirements,
- checking that legislation is complied with eg that cleaning materials are stored safely
- responding to day-to-day problems which may arise
- liaising with outside bodies eg fire officers
- monitoring accidents, procedures and practice
- anticipating health and safety issues
- suggesting improvements which can be made.

Governors must ensure their school follows the guidance laid down by the LEA, where applicable, in its health and safety policy. This will include duties which are delegated to the governors. The main health and safety functions falling to the governing bodies of county and controlled schools are likely to be:

- purchase and maintenance of equipment (including firefighting equipment).
- non-structural repairs (eg to doors and windows)
- cleaning
- first aid (covering numbers of trained first aiders and appointed persons, those responsible for taking charge when someone is injured or becomes ill, ensuring that help is called when appropriate and looking after first-aid equipment).
- Ensuring risk assessments for school outings and trips are carried out and that public service vehicles are carrying first aid equipment.

(**The Education (School Premises) Regulations 1999 (SI 1999/2)**;*Circular 2/94 Local Management of Schools; and Guidance on First Aid for Schools, DfEE 1998*).

Health and Safety Executive inspectors have the power to prosecute organisations or individuals who break health and safety law and the courts could hold to account either the LEA or the governing body, or both, for a breach of the health and safety legislation (*see* **negligence** *page 13*)

Other relevant legislation includes the **Occupiers' Liability Acts 1957** and **1984**, **Environmental Protection Act 1990, Food Safety Act 1990; Health and Safety (First-Aid) Regulations 1981; Health and Safety (Workplace) Regulations 1992, Control of Substances Hazardous to Health Regulations 1988**;[2] **Reporting of Injuries, Diseases and Dangerous Occurrences Regulations 1995.** Summary guidance on workplace regulations is available from the Health and Safety Commission; DfEE *Safety in Science Education (1996)* gives useful information on safe practice in the science laboratory.

Medical issues

Increased inclusion of children with special needs – some with medical conditions requiring regular monitoring or care – has meant schools are beginning to develop policies for dealing with children requiring medicines and health care, whether regularly or in an emergency. In law schools owe a duty of care to their pupils and have a professional duty to safeguard their health and safety. Yet teachers cannot be required to administer medicines and some are naturally cautious about taking on the responsibility. It is helpful, therefore, if schools, in conjunction with LEAs, adopt a school policy discussed with staff and parents, and this is recommended by Government guidance – *Circular 14/96: Supporting Pupils with Medical Needs in Schools.* Schools should have a clear policy with formal systems and procedures, drawn up in partnership with parents and staff, and drawing on advice from the School Health Service, says the Circular.

Policies and procedures should take into account

- **The Medicines Act 1968** which places restrictions on dealings with medicinal products, including their administration
- storage, handling and disposal of medicines
- staff training
- emergency medication and emergency action
- special medical needs of pupils
- medical problems arising during off site activities
- co-ordinating and disseminating information
- confidentiality

In some cases the Circular suggests schools draw up an individual health care plan for a pupil with special medical need to identify the level of support that is needed at school. Some, but not all, of these children will have a Statement of special educational needs (*see* **Governors and SEN**, *page 56*).

Play safety

Play safety is best achieved by providing good-quality and stimulating play opportunities. And the challenge for schools is to make the playground a resource which promotes healthy child development but does not expose children to unnecessary hazards.

Governors will often see playtime in the context of complaints about bullying and accidents – but before the governing body acts to restrict lunch and playtimes, they should consider the importance of play in a normal healthy childhood. Play or break-time has an important social value, because it provides time for children to interact, to express themselves through games and to learn social skills.

Installing play equipment is often a favourite fundraising objective for PTAs which recognise that play equipment can offer children physical and intellectual challenges. In meeting these challenges, children will take risks and therefore risk injury. Risk taking is essential for children – it is how they learn to make sound judgements concerning their own safety. But this is not the same as exposing children to hazards – if not properly chosen, installed and maintained, equipment can introduce hazards. Schools should have in place systems involving keeping records of inspection, maintenance and supervision as well as keeping accident and equipment log books.

It's worth bearing in mind that the Health and Safety Executive has identified the main causes of playground accidents as (in order of frequency):

- poor design and layout of equipment
- the lack of impact absorbing surfaces
- poor maintenance
- poor installation.

Besides the obvious consideration of safety of playground equipment and surfaces, governing bodies should consider whether lunchtime supervisors have training needs and if they and pupils are fully involved in decisions made about playtimes. A lot of bullying takes place in the playground yet very often the adults nearest the scene, the playground assistants, are the least supported workers in the school. They are excluded from staff-room discussions, often have no training and are badly paid. Because of this, they may not feel responsible for the children's behaviour. But the support and experience of playground supervisors is essential if bullying is to be tackled.

The quality of the school environment is also important. Governors need to improve play opportunities and limit the opportunities for bullying in the playground by:

- exploring what changes can be made to improve the playground environment
- increasing the play opportunities for all children – both those who want to rush around and those who want to sit and talk
- opening up hidden corners where bullies can operate unseen
- making sure that the playground assistants deal with bullying in a consistent manner
- involving non-teaching staff in staff discussions about bullying.

Playgrounds characterised by aggressive, rough games have been dramatically improved by changes to their design; by empowering playground supervisors to promote greater play opportunities; and by the development of whole school play policies.

School outings

Headteachers have a legal responsibility to ensure that there is a safe and reliable system of supervision of pupils in all authorised school activities, both on school premises in school hours and on school trips. Governors also share this legal responsibility as part of their overall responsibility for the conduct of the school. They should ensure that a risk assessment takes place before any school trip and that preventive and protective measures are considered. This might mean increasing supervision for a particular group or changing the nature or type of activities undertaken to ensure no pupils are excluded because of disability or cost for example. It's important that health and safety policies distinguish between risk which is dangerous and avoidable and risk which is anticipated and built into a well-planned, challenging activity.

The duty to act as any reasonably prudent parent and duties under the **Management of Health and Safety at Work Regulations 1999 (SI 3242)** in making sure that children are healthy and safe extends to teachers leading activities taking place off the school site, such as educational visits, school outings or field trips. Some of the recent tragedies involving school parties have involved teachers taking on an unfamiliar role of long-distance driver (*see* **Transport** *below*) or outdoor guide. Governing bodies should consider whether training would be advisable before extending teachers' roles or whether using a licensed activity centre with trained personnel would reduce unnecessary risk.

The Lyme Bay canoe tragedy exposed the difficulty of schools and governing bodies fulfilling their duty of care when choosing activity centres. That responsibility is less difficult now the **Activity Centres (Young Persons' Safety) Act 1995** and the accompanying **Adventure Activities Licensing Regulations 1996 (SI 1772)** are in place. Twenty-six activities including caving, climbing, trekking and watersports are regulated through the licensing scheme, which is enforced by inspection. The scheme covers the operators of centres run mainly by commercial organisations and local authorities. Voluntary bodies and schools providing for their own members and pupils are exempt as are operators whose activities fall outside the scope of the regulations.

Security

A number of violent incidents in schools – most notably the tragic massacre at Dunblane Primary School - made security a major issue in the mid-nineties.

Although such serious incidents are rare all schools now must consider their security arrangements and governing bodies are required to describe in their annual report to parents any steps taken to improve security.

For community and controlled schools, the LEA will have an overall policy for security, but governing bodies will need a more detailed school policy based on their school circumstances; this may be part of the school's wider strategy for health and safety and management of school premises.

For voluntary aided and foundation schools the governing body as employer has responsibility under health and safety legislation to ensure schools are safe and secure; management responsi-

---

Checklist of issues for school security review

✔ Access including signposting and reception arrangements, out-of-hours access, rights of way: procedures as well as security equipment.

✔ Premises issues including design of buildings, secure doors and windows, fire detection systems, fencing, CCTV, car parking, lighting, alarms and patrols

✔ Personal safety including after-hours activities, trespassers and intruders, community involvement

✔ Property including security marking, secure storage, vehicle security

✔ Dealing with incidents and emergencies including when to contact the police, media interest

✔ Links with other school polices eg discipline policy, anti-bullying strategies

✔ Reporting and recording incidents, including keeping parents informed, liaising with police

✔ Insurance.

bility for security will be shared between the governing body and the head.

A sub-committee of governors or an individual governor might take on the role of ensuring security is kept under review. Over a number of years the Standards Fund has supported security measures based on LEA security strategies and priorities identified by schools through risk assessments.

DfEE guidance *Improving Security in Schools (1996)* advises that everyone in the school should be involved in maintaining security and that regular open reviews will help keep everyone aware of current risks. The guidance covers risk management, security measures and includes a useful checklist for a security survey and risk assessment. It also covers access control and the visitor reception procedures which can deter unwanted visitors and help direct those who are welcome.

Most schools aim to strike a balance between security and creating a welcoming environment and wider strategies can play as important a part as narrow physical improvements to security. Opening schools to community use both in and out of school hours can improve better security by the presence of more adults on the premises. Home-school policies which ensure parents know the mechanics of approaching a school about their concerns and feel they will be listened to can prevent disagreements turning into disturbances on school premises when parents become angry and frustrated.

A head has the power to decide who may have access to school premises and on rare occasions may ban parents. However parents should be given written warning and the opportunity to put their case before such a draconian action is taken. The Court of Appeal (in the case **Wandsworth v A, December 1999**) pointed out that a parent's legitimate interest in being informed about the work of the school, generally made them a more significant figure in the public activities of the school than a 'mere visiting tradesman'. The parent therefore should have the right to a hearing – however informal – before a decision to ban them is taken.

The DfEE's *Dealing with Troublemakers (1997)* gives detailed advice on trespass including school's use of **Section 547** (**EA96**) which means trespassers creating a nuisance or disturbance on school premises can be removed and/or prosecuted.

The Offensive Weapons Act 1996 extended the law on weapons to schools. Where it is suspected that someone is carrying a weapon, generally the police should be contacted. According to the guidance, teachers have authority to search a pupil but if the pupil declines to co-operate a search should always be undertaken by the police. Random searches would contravene the right to privacy under the **Human Rights Act 1998**.

While schools may represent oases of safety in some difficult areas, the murder of 10-year-old Damilola Taylor on a Peckham housing estate showed that schools cannot ignore the risks which their neighbourhoods present. Governors will need to consider to what extent the school takes responsibility for pupils travelling to and from school in relation to the school's policies on behaviour and security. In some circumstances bad behaviour by a pupil may reflect badly on the school and heads may feel justified in taking disciplinary action. However this concern for out-of-school behaviour of pupils is discretionary; a school's duty of care

was said not to extend outside school in the case of a school girl who had been bullied on the journey between school and home (**Leah Bradford Smart v West Sussex CC, 2000**). Even so, the DfEE encourages schools to try prevent such bullying (*Bullying: Don't Suffer in Silence, 2000*) and personal safety of both pupils and staff must be considered when after-school activities are planned or pupils kept late in detention. Transport difficulties may make lunchtime clubs and detentions a better option in some areas. Parents should always have 24 hours notice if their child is to be kept late.

Record keeping of incidents, however minor, is a crucial element of security management. Analyses of the incidents may reveal a trend or pattern which requires a particular response; sometimes a number of small incidents may provide early-warning of a greater risk and aid the police in cases involving vandalism, theft, assaults or other criminal matters. Good liaison with the police will provide a useful guide to how the school should respond to different types of incident and appropriate security measures for a particular school.

Supervision

The organisation of a safe system of supervision is primarily the duty of the headteacher.

LEAs or schools should have rules about the ratio of teachers to pupils when supervising activities off-site. The DfEE recommends that the level of supervision required for school journeys should be considered as part of the risk assessment for the journey. Under normal circumstances it suggests that at least two teachers should accompany parties of primary pupils visiting local swimming pools; at least one teacher for every 15 secondary-aged pupils, and for every six pupils under the age of eight on local visits to museums, historical sites etc; for overnight visits and trips abroad the general guidance is 1:10 secondary-aged pupils and 1:5 pupils under the age of 10.

Playground supervisors will mostly cover the lunchtime period in school but children must also be supervised before and after school as they gather to enter or leave school. While most schools believe it is reasonable for teachers to supervise children arriving at school up to ten minutes before the session begins, the general rule is that there can be no responsibility for the supervision of pupils before this. Schools no longer have a legal duty to publish times of morning and afternoon sessions in the school prospectus although it is in their interests to make sure the times are well known to pupils and parents. Governing bodies of community and voluntary controlled schools are required to consult parents about any changes (**S148 (f) EA96**; regulations under **S41 SSFA**). Any changes should be well-publicised so parents can make new arrangements for the delivery and collection of their children to and from school.

Legal cases involving accidents on school premises outside of normal school hours usually hinge on whether supervision would have prevented an accident or whether it would have happened anyway. Liability could arise under the duty of care owed to pupils as 'visitors' under the **Occupiers' Liability Act 1957** *(see page 15)*.

The issue of when a school /LEA may be held

liable in negligence for supervision of pupils will depend on the facts of the case. There are two contrasting cases where the issue of what was reasonable to expect was discussed.

In the case of **Barnes (infant) v Hampshire CC [1969]** pupils were let out of school earlier than the scheduled 3.30pm. A five-year-old girl wandered into the street before her mother arrived and was injured in the road at 3.29pm. Parents had not been informed of this in advance and the LEA were held liable.

However in the case of **Nwabudike v Southwark LBC [1997]** it was held that provided the school had taken all "reasonable and proper steps" to ensure that its children were safe, there would be no liability. In this case a six-year-old boy had run out of the school gates during the lunch hour after having been disciplined for poor behaviour. He was run down by a car but the claim was dismissed. The standard of care expected is high but a balance has to be struck between security and turning a school into a fortress. Whatever precautions are taken there is always a risk that accidents could happen, particularly if a child is determined to act in a way which avoids any safeguards in place.

Generally schools have no responsibility for children arriving at school before the usual time for the beginning of the school day. Where pupils are allowed into the grounds from a certain time there may be responsibility and liability. Prudent schools should ensure that school gates are not opened unless or until a member of staff is present in the playground to supervise activities. Pupils should not be let out into the playground at lunch break until there is adult supervision in place. Schools do not have to provide adult supervision at the end of the school day.

Transport

Specialist training should be provided for any teachers volunteering to drive children on school outings and the whole journey should be planned to ensure that teacher drivers do not face unrealistic demands. Schools drawing up their own guidelines should consider the following safety points:

✔ setting out a staff pupil ratio for outings and ensuring someone other than the driver is responsible for children during the journey
✔ determining who ensures passengers are wearing seat belts
✔ ensuring teacher drivers are trained (ROSPA provides minibus training)
✔ limiting the hours teachers should be allowed to drive in a day when they are also working
✔ensuring the school uses safe coach operators. All coaches and minibuses transporting children must have seat belts fitted under Department of Transport safety regulations. Minibuses and certain public service vehicles must have first-aid kits.

School guidelines should also include common sense provisions such as checking the oil, water and tyre pressures; checking traffic conditions and weather before setting out; and ensuring the teacher in charge is clear about who to contact and what to do in an emergency.

Work experience

Risk assessment involving a health and safety check of a workplace prior to placement is the key to good planning for work placements for secondary school pupils **Health and Safety at Work Regulations 1999 (SI 3242)**. For most pupils a placement will involve two-weeks with a local business or service and issues such as safety training, protective clothing and safety equipment should be arranged before placement. Special arrangements may be needed for pupils with medical conditions or special educational needs but the relative inexperience and possible immaturity of all young people in the workplace must be taken into account.

From September 1998 certain young people in years 10 and 11 have been able to undertake an extended work-related learning programme. Long-term placements may involve wider exposure to risk and schools should ensure there is adequate supervision with regular debriefings covering health and safety issues.

Further information

Bullying

Bullying: Don't Suffer in Silence, 2000, DfEE, DfEE Publications, PO Box 5050, Sudbury, Suffolk CO10 6ZQ (0845 602 2260).

Tackling Bullying, 2000, advice booklet for parents, ACE, £1.50 + 50p p&p.

Child Protection

Developing your Child Protection Policy, 1998, CEDC, £5.95.

DfEE Circular 10/95 Protecting children from abuse: the role of the education service, free.

Children in Public Care

DfEE guidance **Education of Young People in Public Care**, 2000, DfEE, free, (address above).

The Education of Children who are Looked After by Local Authorities: a guide for governors, 1996, Who Cares? Trust, Kemp House,152-160 City Road, London EC1V 2NP, £5.

Raising Achievement of Children in Public Care 2001, Ofsted (07002 637833).

Drugs

White Paper, **Tackling Drugs to Build a Better Britain**, 1998, Stationery Office, £7.50.

The Right Response: Managing and Making Policy for Drug-related Incidents in Schools, 1999, SCODA, 32 – 26 Loman Street, London SE1 0EE, £12.

The Right Choice: guidance on selecting drug education materials for schools, 1998, SCODA (address above), £12.

The Right Approach: Quality standards in drug education, 1999, SCODA, (address above) £12.

Health and safety

Circular 22/94 Safety in Outdoor Activity Centres, DfEE, free (address above).

Circular 14/96: Supporting Pupils with Medical Needs in Schools, DfEE, free (address above).

Guidance on First Aid for Schools, 1998, DfEE, free (address above).

Health and Safety of Pupils on Educational Visits,1998, DfEE, free (address above)

Managing Health and Safety in Schools, HSE Books, £5.95.

Security

Improving Security in Schools, (1996) DfEE Guide 4 in **Managing school facilities series** (address above).

Dealing with Troublemakers, (1997) DfEE (address above).

Governors and Staffing

Effective management of staffing issues is one of the most important and most responsible jobs that a governing body carries. A key objective for governors is raising standards and this can best be achieved through strong and effective leadership from the head and senior management and professional good practice from the teaching staff.

It is important for governors to understand the context in which they operate in relation to personnel issues. Many schools find it difficult to recruit and retain staff. The teacher unions blame teacher shortages on stress, workload and poor pay. The Government has responded with above-inflation pay rises but has also sought to introduce an element of performance related pay. Governors can be caught between the drive to raise standards in schools, tensions about performance related pay and the need to be able recruit and retain teachers.

As part of the drive to make schools take responsibility for their own improvement, governing bodies are being made responsible for some aspects of performance management once undertaken by the LEA. However, the role of the governing body in relation to staffing matters is currently under review. A proposal that governors should lose responsibility for the selection and discipline of staff below deputy heads has been criticised by teacher unions and governor organisations and looks unlikely to be taken up. A major criticism is that governors would still be liable to defend actions in court or at tribunal even if they had not taken the decision themselves.

Staffing committee

As with other functions of the governing body, certain decisions such as staffing can be delegated to a committee. The appointment of a head or deputy cannot be delegated but **Scheds.16 and 17** permit committees or the headteacher to make decisions about staff appointments. (**Para.17 Sched.16**)

Ideally, all governing body committees should be agreed at the first full governors' meeting of each academic year, together with details of each committee's terms of reference. These should be in line with the **Education (School**

Law and Guidance

The law relating to the employment of teachers is contained in general employment law such as **Employment Relations Act 1999, The Disability Discrimination Act 1995** and legislation specific to education and regulations. These include the **School Standards and Framework Act 1998 (Scheds. 16 and 17)**, the **School Teachers' Pay and Conditions Act 1991, The School Teachers' Pay** and **Condition Document 2000** and its annual successors and **The Education (School Teacher Appraisal) Regulations 2000**. Circulars issued by the DfEE, for example, Performance Management in Schools(0051/2000) supplement the law. The National Assembly for Wales is currently consulting across various areas including induction of new teachers, appraisal and performance management. Changes broadly in line with those in England are expected later in 2001. The DfEE is responsible for teachers' pay and conditions in both England and Wales.

Government)(England)Regulations 1999 SI.1999/2163 and the Education (School Government)(England) (Amendment) Regulations 2000 (SI 2163), or the Education (School Government) (Wales) Regulations 1999 (SI 2242).

Many governing bodies prefer committees to be made up of at least one parent, one teacher, one LEA member and one co-opted member, to reflect the make-up of the governing body as a whole.

Details of the function and proceedings of the committee must be agreed, and meetings must be formally minuted. These measures will help to avoid complaints or grievances about the conduct of the committee.

The staffing committee should
- agree which powers it will delegate to the head-teacher alone;
- appoint separate committees to hear any appeals concerning individual staff grievances or discipline.

Staffing committees are required to report back on their activities and the decisions to the next meeting of their governing bodies. Governors also need to consider how information can be relayed between committees to ensure they are working to common purposes. Once a committee structure and membership have been agreed, the personnel committee should elect a chair and then timetable a series of meetings over the academic year. Governors need to arrange meetings at times which tie in with key calendar dates in the school year such as pay review, with other committee dates and governing body meetings.

Governors will find they can discharge their personnel duties most effectively if the following are in place:

- School Development Plan and supporting budget
- Equal opportunities policy
- Pay and appointments policy
- Grievance and discipline policy
- Comprehensive insurance cover
- Planned programme of staff training and support
- Planned programme of governor training and support
- Performance management policy for teacher appraisal.

Dismissal committees

Decisions relating to staff dismissal and appeals must be delegated to staff dismissal and dismissal appeal committees. The staff dismissal committee and the dismissal appeal committee must contain three or more governors but, exceptionally, the quorum can be two. The appeal committee must have no fewer members of the governing body than the dismissal committee. A separate committee with different members must consider appeals against decisions made by the dismissal committee. The headteacher cannot be a member of either committee (**The Education (School Government) Regulations 1999 and reg7 Amendment Regulations**). These committees must be clerked (reg 51). Draft amendment regulations have been published in Wales and will make similar changes when introduced.

Equal opportunities policy

Governors with responsibility for decisions about all personnel issues, including appointments, appraisal and pay, clearly need to demonstrate a commitment to equal opportunities. The schools performance management policy offers a useful opportunity to promote equal opportunities, and to encourage all teachers to develop their professional skills, their careers and to share good practice across the school. Schools are bound by the **Sex Discrimination Act 1975**, the **Race Relations Act 1976**, and the **Disability Discrimination Act 1995**, (*see* School Government page 15) but issues of social class and age should also be considered. The school's equal opportunities policy provides an opportunity for addressing discrimination in all its forms, and for confirming that both staff and pupil needs are taken into account. The policy should describe specific action, and how it is to be implemented and monitored.

In Wales a duty to promote equal opportunities and good relations emphasises the governing body and headteacher's need to eliminate unlawful discrimination (**The School Government (Terms of Reference) (Wales) Regulations 2000 (SI 195)**).

Appointments

The normal procedures for the appointment of all teachers are laid down in **Sched.16** of the **SSFA** for community and voluntary controlled schools and **Sched.17** for foundation and voluntary aided schools.

Appointments policy

The governors' appointments policy should describe the process of identifying vacant posts, advertising – both internal and external posts – shortlisting, and interview. It should address:
- the need for job descriptions for all staff
- who is to be involved at each stage (headteacher or headteacher and governors' committee);
- any procedures for de-briefing unsuccessful candidates

Governors' role

Governing bodies of voluntary aided and foundation schools must ensure each member of staff has a contract of employment. Although the LEA (in community and controlled schools) is responsible for issuing teachers' contracts, the school may send a letter to successful candidates confirming their appointment, salary, and starting date. The governing body fulfils most of the roles of the employer even in community and controlled schools.

Governors of schools with delegated budgets (the majority of schools) decide on the number of staff and have responsibility for all appointments; in the case of community and controlled schools the LEA must accept these appointments provided the staff concerned satisfy the requirements of appropriate qualifications, health and physical capacity or fitness on educational grounds (**Para.15 Sched.16 SSFA**). Teaching vacancies (other than those for a head or deputy) for a period of not more than four months are exempt from these requirements. The governing body draws up a job specification with the headteacher and sends that to the LEA. Other vacancies must be advertised unless the governing body decides to appoint a person nominated by the LEA or decides to recommend an internal candidate.

A vacancy for a headteacher, deputy head or any teacher post which has not been filled using the normal appointment procedures can be filled by the governing body employing someone from an agency. In this case the contract of employment is between the agency and the individual teacher rather than the LEA (**Par 16**).

LEA role

In the case of appointments of all teachers in community schools, the LEA's Chief Education Officer (CEO) is entitled to attend all proceedings (including interviews) of the governing body and the selection panel (in the case of head or deputy) in an advisory capacity. In the case of appointments and engagements of headteachers, deputy headteachers and acting heads or acting deputies, the CEO offers whatever advice s/he thinks appropriate. In the case of other categories of teachers s/he gives advice if the governing body requests it. Whether or not such a request is made, the governing body must consider it (**Para.18(4) Sched.16 SSFA**). Headteachers have similar rights to give advice and have that advice considered, unless the appointment is for a headteacher (**Para.19**).

The governing bodies of foundation and voluntary aided schools can make an agreement with the LEA giving the CEO the same rights as in community schools (**Para.2 Sched.17**). If the school is a voluntary aided school with a religious character, the governing body must give the appropriate diocesan officer the same advisory rights as the CEO. If the school is a foundation or voluntary controlled school with a religious character, it is at the governing body's discretion. *(COP on LEA School Relations (One for each of England and Wales))*

The governing body of any school where the LEA is the employer is required to consult the CEO before selecting any non-teaching staff to enable the authority to ensure that comparable staff are employed on comparable terms. (**Para.20(3) Sched.16** and *COP on LEA School Relations.*

The appointment of a headteacher or a deputy headteacher

"The importance of high-quality leadership cannot be overestimated," says Mike Tomlinson HM Chief Inspector of Schools in Ofsted's 1999/2000 annual report. This comment draws on the experience of many inspections of individual schools and underlines the importance of the governing body's responsibility for appointment of an effective headteacher. The law, also, reflects the seriousness of the decision by setting out the procedures which schools must follow, including LEA involvement in all types of maintained school.

In the case of the appointment of a headteacher or a deputy, the governing body of all schools must notify the LEA of the vacancy in writing. The governing body must appoint a selection panel of at least three of its members; the appointment of a headteacher or deputy may not be delegated to a committee. The full governing body must endorse the decision of the selection panel. Whatever the category of school the panel must notify the LEA of applicants selected for interview (**Para.6(2)Sched.16** and **Para.7(2) Sched.17**) Where the LEA objects about the suitability of any of the shortlisted applicants, the selection panel may only recommend that applicant to the governing body for appointment after it has considered those representations, notified the LEA in writing of their response and made a copy of both the representations and their response available to the governing body . The LEA in determining whether a person is suitable for appointment as a headteacher shall have regard to any guidance given by the Secretary of State. This guidance is contained in **Annex 3** of *The Code of Practice on LEA- School Relations* which lists examples of the types of concerns that may or may not trigger the making of representations by the LEA.

The Government will require in due course that all new heads have a National Professional Qualification for Headship. Regulations are allowed for under **S18 Teaching and Higher Education Act 1998**. As part of the induction of new headteachers, all heads appointed to their first post are entitled to The Leadership and Management Programme for new headteachers (HEADLAMP). This programme entitles heads to an additional budget of up to £2,500 for two years. There is also a professional development programme for existing heads - the Leadership Programme for Serving Headteachers. The

increased support for headteachers goes hand in hand with the increased expectations of their role in raising pupil achievement and scrutiny of that role through performance review *(see below)*.

The procedures for the appointment of a deputy head are the same but the LEA has no right to make representations about candidates' suitability.

Background checks

All offers of employment are subject to satisfactory completion of background checks and this should be clearly stated to candidates. The procedures apply to all teachers, ancillary staff and volunteers who have contact with children. The DfEE hold a list of people (List 99) who are medically unfit, barred on grounds of misconduct or 'on educational grounds'. Volunteers who spend substantial unsupervised time with pupils are included to ensure they are not using their volunteer status as a way of avoiding background checks.

The LEA or employer must arrange for the following background checks to be made:

- Check against List 99. The list is made available on a confidential basis to LEAs and other bodies, or via the DfEE.

- Qualified Teacher Status or equivalent (a legal requirement for heads and deputies) **The Education (Teachers' Qualifications and Health Standards) (England) Regulations 1999 (SI 2166); The Education (Teachers' Qualifications and Health Standards) (Wales) Regulations 1999 (SI W18).**

- Health and Fitness and Mental Capacity to Teach. **Reg 6.** This can be carried out for teachers on their first appointment by asking the medical adviser to the training provider; for teachers changing schools, the previous employer should be approached with the candidate's permission. *(See Circular 4/99, Physical and Mental Fitness to Teach of Teachers and of Entrants to Initial Teaching Training.)*

- Registration with the General Teaching Council. **The General Teaching Council for England (Registration of Teachers) Regulations 2000 (SI 2176; Teachers (Compulsory Registration) (Wales) Regulations 2000 (SI W200).**

In addition the following checks should be made:

- Academic qualifications (where appropriate)
- Previous employment history
- Professional and character references
- Criminal background in posts that involve substantial unsupervised access to children (Written permission should be sought.)
- Identity

Under the **Education (Restriction of Employment) Regulations 2000 (England SI 2419; Wales SI W186),** the Secretary of State has the power to bar people from relevant employment on the following grounds:

- medical
- misconduct
- that the person is not a fit and proper person to be employed as a teacher or worker with children under the age of 19
- that the persons concerned is included in a list kept by the Secretary of State under the **Protection of Children Act 1999.**

Relevant employment means employment by local authorities, schools and further education institutions as teachers, including agency or supply teachers or workers with children and young people under the age of 19.

The Criminal Records Bureau will help schools make safer appointments by providing a one-stop shop for criminal background and List 99. For more information about this recently set up agency, see **www.crb.gov.uk/index.htm**

Pay

Pay policy

Governors should have a clear pay policy which is discussed with staff at the school. The policy must be informed by the **School Teachers' Pay and Conditions Act 1991**, and any local agreement entered into by the LEA. Each year the DfEE issues a new *School Teachers' Pay and Conditions Document (STPCD)* accompanied by a related circular after the Pay Review Body has made its recommendations, and the governors' pay policy will be based upon the current document. The document applies to all teachers (in England and Wales) unless the school has an exemption eg some schools in education action zones.

The policy could be drawn up using the following headings:
- Aims of policy
- Statement of general principles: including reference to equal opportunities, School Development Plan, school budget cycle and salaries review cycle, consultation, teacher appraisal and staff support, staff access to records and training and continuing professional development.
- Support staff: refer to any national or locally agreed structures that have been negotiated with unions and professional associations that governors will adhere to. (It would be sufficient to refer to such agreements, rather than spell them out in detail.)
- Teaching staff: refer to *School Teachers' Pay and Conditions Document*; describe those discretionary pay flexibilities that the governing body expects to be using; list criteria for awarding increments or extra allowances, and process of informing staff of pay point.
- Heads and deputies: criteria for awarding annual increments (not automatic for heads and deputies) including performance reviews and the required annual pay review.

Once the committee has drawn up its draft pay policy it should circulate it for consultation among staff and the governing body. A copy should also go the LEA for comment. Once consultation is complete, the committee should consider any responses and then draw up a final policy for ratification by the full governing body. Pay levels and the policy should be reviewed once a year and a timetable planned for this, keeping in mind the time of year the annual STPCD is issued, the academic year and the need for consultation.

Conditions of service

Conditions of employment for all teachers are laid down in the annual *School Teachers' Pay and Conditions* document. They include pay, professional duties and working time arrangements.

Governors should also have access to the Burgundy Book, (*Conditions of Service for School Teachers in England and Wales*) which sets out other aspects of conditions of service for teaching staff such as sick pay, maternity leave entitlement and periods of notice. Others may be covered by 'collective local agreements' on such matters as time off for public or trade union duties.

Governors have considerable discretion on the actual conditions under which staff work, and will need to take care to be seen to treat these issues with sensitivity. The pay policy should include a commitment to consult with staff over any plans for significant changes.

Pay structure

The structure of the teaching profession has changed and there are now different categories of teachers. Previously there were heads and deputies who were paid according to a different pay structure or spine than classroom teachers. Now there are classroom teachers who may or may not have passed the performance threshold, advanced skills teachers and the leadership group.

The Leadership Group The leadership group is a designated group of senior teachers who have substantial strategic responsibilities for school leadership. Within this group there is a new category of teacher called an assistant headteacher. Heads, deputies and assistant heads have separate pay ranges drawn from the leadership group pay spine. The head's individual school range is related to the size of the school. Members of the leadership group are not covered by classroom teachers' working time provisions. Guidance of how the leadership group operates is contained in *Leadership Guidance for Schools*, DfEE 0127/2000. Important detail is also contained in *School Teachers' Pay and Conditions of Employment* – DfEE guidance note 0105/2000. Governors and the headteacher will play a key role in identifying which posts in the senior management team should be paid on the leadership group's pay and conditions, appointing to the leadership group and calculating individual salaries. The salary costs for all members of the leadership group will be met from the school's budget but there is additional funding available for the initial years through the Teachers' Pay Reforms Grant.

Advanced skills teachers (AST) The grade of advanced skills teacher has been established to provide a career path for teachers who wish to remain in the classroom rather than become heads or deputies. In addition to classroom duties ASTs are required to train, mentor and assist other teachers. They are paid on a separate pay scale out of the school's budget and the working time provisions are not applicable to them. It is open to the governors to create one or more AST posts but teachers must have passed a national assessment procedure.

Classroom teachers are paid on either the main pay scale or the upper pay scale if they have passed the threshold assessment with additional allowances in some cases.

Fast track teachers are those who have passed a national selection procedure. For newly qualified teachers on fast track, there is a higher starting salary and accelerated progression up the pay scale if performance merits it. These teachers are expected to perform at a level that will merit annual double jumps up the scale. This scheme is under consideration in Wales but not yet introduced.

The School Achievement Awards Scheme

This government scheme funds bonuses for staff at successful schools in England and the awards will be made annually. If the school is in receipt of an award the Government will supply guidance on how it should be distributed. For more details of how the scheme operates see: DfEE 159/2000, *The School Achievement Awards Scheme*.

Salary reviews

The governing body must undertake an annual salary review for every teacher in service as at September 1 each year. The teacher must be given a clear written statement of how their salary was calculated. The salary is determined by the teacher's position on the main or upper pay scale and any additional allowances. The teacher's point on the pay scale is determined by points for qualifications, experience, any additional points for a fast track teacher and finally any additional points for performance. Additional allowances are awarded for management, teaching children with special educational needs, recruitment and attendance and, if relevant, London allowances.

Unless the previous year's service has been unsatisfactory, a teacher will automatically proceed up the main classroom teachers' scale by being awarded one experience point. They can only move through the upper scale if their performance merits it. A decision not to award a point for experience would normally only be appropriate if competency procedures had been put in place.

From September 2001 it will be possible for a teacher to make a double jump up the pay scale to reward excellent performance. The decision to award such a point should be informed by the result of the teacher's appraisal.

Threshold assessments

Classroom teachers in England and Wales are able to apply for a performance threshold assessment which gives access to an upper pay scale. Teachers who are eligible to apply have nine years teaching experience, or a good honours degree with seven years' experience. The applicant will have to demonstrate qualities in the following: knowledge of teaching of their subject; effective planning, classroom and teaching management strategies; clear and well grounded expectations of pupils; pupils achieving well; professional development, active part in school life and professional characteristics that challenge and support all pupils. Once a teacher is on the upper pay scale, progression up that scale is not automatic. The threshold assessment is carried out by the headteacher and verified by an external assessor. The contents of threshold applications are confidential and governors will not have access to them. (**Education (School Teachers' Pay and Conditions)(no4) Order 2000 (SI.3106)**; *School Teachers Pay and Conditions of Employment June 2000 0105/2000* as amended by DfEE guidance dated 22 November 2000: Restart of Threshold.)

The professional duties of headteachers include reporting back to the chair of governors annually on the professional development of all teachers at the school and the procedures for dealing with incompetent teachers.

Performance management

Performance management is seen by the Government as an additional route to school improvement and an important way of promoting high standards. Governing bodies have two statutory duties under the new arrangements (currently operating in England only).

- To establish a performance management policy and monitor its effectiveness
- To review the performance of the headteacher with the help of a DfEE accredited external adviser.

The governing body's performance management policy should set out how teacher appraisal at the school shall be implemented having first consulted with the teachers at the school. The policy must be reviewed every year. (*See* **The Education (School Government) (Terms of Reference) (England) Regulations 2000 SI 2122**) The policy can be developed by the headteacher after consultation with the teaching staff and presented to the governors for consideration and agreement. It is the duty of the governing body to secure that appraisal takes place and to determine the exact timing of the review cycle. The length of the cycle is one year. (**Regs.4 and 8, The Education (School Teacher Appraisal) (England) Regulations 2000 (SI 1620)**). Governors need to make sure that sufficient resources including staff and senior management time is available for the implementation of the policy. Standards Fund grants are available.

In Wales the LEA is currently the appraising body in all but former grant-maintained schools and must secure appraisal of teachers' performance (**Reg.8 The Education (School Teacher Appraisal) (Wales) Regulations 1999 (SIW25)**). These regulations are to be replaced in December 2001 when governing bodies take over responsibility.

The DfEE has produced guidance and a model policy. It is called *Performance Management in Schools 0051/2000*. *Performance Management: Guidance for Governors (Guidance 59/2000)* details governors' responsibilities.

Appraisal of headteacher

It is the duty of the governing body to appoint two or three governors to be appraiser for the headteacher. These cannot include a teacher governor and in the case of voluntary aided school or a school with a religious character, one or more must be a foundation governor. If there are three appraisers, two shall be foundation governors. In addition, the governing body must appoint an accredited external adviser. An adviser is provided to the school free of charge for eight hours a year. This covers 'core' advice on setting objectives and assessing the head's performance and the adviser's presence at the review meeting. Governing bodies must involve the adviser in the performance review and provide him or her with the headteacher's objectives and other relevant information. It is up to them how they might further involve the adviser. The DfEE guidance suggests the adviser could help prepare for the review, conduct the review and draft the review statement. However decisions are a matter for the governing body, and cannot be delegated to the adviser.

Governors appointed to carry out the head's performance review should:
- Recognise the head's achievements
- Review, discuss and confirm the head's essential tasks, standards and objectives and determine whether they have been met
- Confirm action and any changes agreed
- Identify areas for training and personal development
- Agree new objectives which should include at least one objective relating to school leadership and management and one to pupil progress.

In Wales, under current regulations, the LEA is involved in deciding who appraises heads in all but former grant-maintained schools (**Reg.8 The Education (School Teacher Appraisal) (Wales) Regulations 1999 (SIW25)**; to be replaced with similar regulations to those in England in December 2001).

The cycle of appraisal starts with the setting of objectives relating to school leadership and management and pupil progress. The appraisers, the external adviser and the head meet to plan and prepare for the appraisal and agree a written statement of objectives. The cycle is completed by a review meeting and the setting of new objectives. The governors write a review statement and give a copy to the headteacher within ten days of the review meeting. The head can make written comments. The headteacher can complain about the conduct of the performance review to the chair of governors or a review officer if the chair was involved in the performance review.

Appraisal of other school teachers

The appraiser for other school teachers is appointed by the headteacher and can be another teacher or the headteacher. The appraisal cycle starts with a meeting of the teacher and appraiser to set annual objectives, including objectives relating to pupil progress and ways of developing and improving teachers professional practice. Progress towards achieving those objectives is monitored throughout the year and includes classroom observation. At the end of the year a review meeting is set up and new objectives are set. A teacher can also make a complaint about the review to the headteacher or if the headteacher was the appraiser to the chair of governors.

Appraisal procedures are not to be part of any disciplinary or dismissal procedures.

They are not to be used for teachers in their induction year where the LEA is responsible for deciding whether the teacher has met the required standard on the basis of the recommendation of the headteacher. NB induction is not currently required in Wales.

The arrangements do not apply to teachers employed for under a year.

Appraisal statements

Appraisal statements are confidential documents held by the headteacher with a copy for the employee. The appraisal statement of a headteacher is given to the chair of the governors. Regulations set out who may receive a copy and this will include those governors who make decisions about pay.

Staff development and training

Continuing professional development and training for headteachers and teachers is at the heart of new initiatives to raise standards and the governing body should ensure that the Development Plan identifies the needs and resources for staff training.

The action plans drawn up after appraisal can help identify the training requirements of individual teachers. The part of the appraisal statement dealing with training and development needs can be passed to those responsible in the school for planning training. At least once during each school year the headteacher must report to the governing body about the operation of the appraisal and report back on the training and developmental needs of the teachers (**Education (School Teacher Appraisal) (England) Regulations 2000**).

Discipline and grievance

The policy should state that accepted discipline and grievance procedures will be used where appropriate. These may be described in the staff handbook or other school documentation. Governors should confirm that such procedures do indeed exist in the form of written guidance and should be clear about the governing body's role. With teacher appraisal now in place, this is a sensitive area and governors must clearly define the relationship between appraisal, pay and discipline.

The procedure should give guidelines as to what constitutes misconduct and gross misconduct, and describe the stages to be gone through should a disciplinary case arise. This would usually begin with informal counselling by the headteacher or line manager to agree measures to secure improvement (including supervision and an agreed period of review), followed by a formal oral warning, a formal written warning, and then a final written warning. At each stage, the nature of the offence and the reason for the disciplinary action should be stated, together with the improvements needed, how they might be achieved, and the appeal arrangements. The governing body should make a clear distinction between capability and misconduct. The capability procedures stress the need to identify performance problems early on, to support and set targets for struggling teachers, and to start formal action if these fail to produce improvement after a specified period. After formal procedures have been begun the normal period for improvement will be two terms and in extreme cases, four weeks.

The written policy should describe the personnel who would be involved at each stage (senior management, headteacher or governing body), procedures for appeals and staff grievance and the policy for recording information on staff files.

In cases of gross misconduct, immediate suspension (usually with full pay) should follow, with a hearing within 20 days. Only the governing body or its committee can terminate a contract. In community and controlled schools, the LEA must be consulted in advance and must issue a notice on behalf of that school within 14 days (**Para.25 Sched.16**).

The General Teaching Council (one for each of England and Wales) established by the **Teaching and Higher Education Act 1998** has the power to investigate the wrong doing of individual teachers and to deregister a teacher.

Dismissal, suspension, retirement and redundancy

Governors are also responsible for dismissal, suspension, retirement and redundancy of staff. The governing body determines whether any payment should be made by the LEA and the amount to be paid in respect of a dismissal of any member of staff. These costs will be met by the LEA unless it has good reason to deduct them or part of them from the school's budget share (**S57(5) SSFA**). However, the costs incurred by the LEA in respect of any premature retirement are now met from the school's budget share for one or more financial years unless the authority agrees to meet the costs in writing (**S57(4) SSFA**).

The governing body has control of the regulation of conduct and discipline in relation to staff in the school and for the procedures for giving staff the opportunity to redress grievances in relation to their employment. The governing body must also establish disciplinary rules and procedures which include disciplinary measures to be taken with regard to the lack of capability of the member of staff (**Scheds.16** and **17 SSFA**). To determine whether a member of staff is not capable of doing his job the governing body must consult and follow guidance issued by the Secretary of State. The guidance consists of a model procedure and is contained in *Capability Procedures for Teachers, DfEE125/2000*. The governing body must inform the LEA immediately when imposing or ending a suspension and must notify the LEA and give reasons in writing if they determine that a member of staff employed by the LEA should be dismissed. The member of staff must be given an opportunity to make oral or written representations and to appeal prior to the governing body notifying the LEA of their decision. These rights are not available to a person on a fixed term contract where the reason for the ending of his or her employment is the expiry of the term of the contract, unless s/he has been working continuously at the school for over one year (**Para.27 Sched. 16** as amended by **S40 Employment Relations Act 1999**). Before making a decision to dismiss, the governing body must consider the advice of the CEO or other person who is entitled to attend the proceedings. Where the LEA has serious concerns about the performance of the headteacher of the school it makes a written report to the chair of the governing body and sends a copy to the headteacher. The chair must notify the authority in writing of the action s/he intends to take. The statutory guidance for LEAs is contained in Annex 3 of the Code of Practice (*as above*). The CEO is entitled to attend and give advice at dismissal proceedings at a voluntary aided or foundation school (**Para.25 Sched.17**).

The appointment, discipline, suspension and dismissal of school meals staff are subject to regulations (**Para.30Sched.16 SSFA; the Education (School Meals Staff) (England) Regulations 1999 (SI 2258); the Education (School Meals Staff) (Wales) Regulations 1999 (SI 2802)**).

Natural Justice

During all the governing body's proceedings, the Rules of Natural Justice apply:

* Consultation should be open and genuine, allowing a reasonable time to respond; in any discipline or grievance hearings the case should be clearly stated and the evidence produced but confidentiality should be respected;
* a right of reply and time to prepare;
* the right to be represented or accompanied;
* both sides should be able to ask questions and call witnesses;
* a right of appeal to a committee of governors which has not been part of the original decision.

Failure to follow these basic 'rules' can, in itself, be grounds for a challenge.

Some governing bodies may have members with experience of personnel issues, but it is likely that most governors will be tackling these important issues for the first time. Careful planning is essential. Governors should take advantage of any LEA guidance where applicable. Governors of voluntary aided schools may, in addition, seek help from diocesan authorities on a range of staffing issues. Governors not taking LEA guidance must be prepared to conduct their own negotiations with the unions and may find themselves liable for any legal costs that arise.

Further information

The Best for Teaching and Learning in Wales, 1999, Green Paper NAW Publications Centre (02920 898688).

Circular 4/99, Physical and Mental Fitness to Teach of Teachers, DfEE (0845 602 2260).

DfEE 159/2000, The School Achievement Awards Scheme

Proposals for Appraisal Regulations for Performance Review, 1999, NAW Consultation, NAW Publications Centre.

Performance Management in Schools (0051/2000) DfEE

Performance Management : Guidance for Governors (59/2000), DfEE (phone number above), free.

Governors working together

The responsibilities of governing bodies can only be effectively exercised if governors work together as a team and in harmony with the head and staff of the school. When a governing body gets into the news on account of some major dispute, muddle or mismanagement, it is either because individuals or small groups of governors have tried to act alone, or because the governors and heads are in conflict over territory. This chapter suggests how governors themselves can work better as a team. It also offers some guidance on how they can keep hold of their responsibilities while understanding, negotiating and managing the boundaries between their work and that of the professionals within the school.

Nowhere in education law will you find any reference to the powers or duties of a school governor. A school governor as an individual has no power at all: the wide and weighty responsibilities of governors belong to the governing body corporately. They exercise these responsibilities by means of decisions taken, by majority vote if necessary, at properly convened and conducted meetings. Even the chairperson has no power to act except in a dire emergency or when specifically asked to do so by the governing body. All this may seem elementary, and yet whenever governors get themselves into trouble the most likely reason is that they have forgotten it.

Governors represent different interest groups – the LEA, the founding body in voluntary schools, the parents, the teachers, the wider community. They bring different viewpoints to the work of the governing body, and they have an obligation to listen to the group they represent, carry their concerns to the governing body (but not necessarily vote as advised) and report back. Governors' decisions are influenced by these different viewpoints. It will not always be the decision which an individual governor – or that governor's interest group – would have wanted, but it is the corporate decision and all must be loyal to it however hard that may sometimes be.

Negotiating the boundaries

Even when a governing body has fully accepted the corporate nature of its responsibility it may still find it hard to establish a proper sharing relationship with the professional staff of the school. But a governing body which is well-organised within itself, and strong in the loyalty and unity of its members, can much more easily tackle these difficult territorial issues. Later we look at a rough and ready demarcation of responsibility between governors and headteacher. Here it is only necessary to remind governors (a) that they cannot expect to get it right straight away; (b) that there are grey areas where boundaries have to be negotiated; (c) that patience and understanding are needed for that negotiation; (d) that every governing body has to start from where it is. The important thing is to make progress.

What makes a good team?

A good team has a common purpose. To achieve that purpose it accepts certain discipline and observes certain rules. Every member is concerned to perform well on a personal basis, but not at the expense of others. All must feel that their contribution is equally valued and the skills of members will complement each other. This may mean that individuals hold back sometimes. Members will respect and protect each other. They will all accept responsibility for their own learning, and will share the work.

A common purpose

Few people would accept the responsibilities and frustrations of being a governor without a deep commitment to education and to the well-being of their own school. All members should start from this assumption about each other, and it is very important that heads also accept it. Too many heads are suspicious about 'where governors are coming from' and talk of private agendas is common. Some governors may have private agendas and governing bodies must work to avoid this. But the only healthy starting point for relationships is to assume that people become governors because they care about the school: high expectations bring good outcomes, and vice versa. Every governing body is under such pressure that time is rarely found to share the feelings which have brought its members together. To do so is not a sentimental orgy, but a framework for decisions. Without a shared understanding of the special things about that school and its priorities, the governors will lurch through the long agendas and make some bad decisions. Sharing of goals and values should also include the staff from time to time: it demystifies governors and makes teachers feel good about what they are doing.

Equality of all members

There must be no A and B teams and no private agendas. This is easy to say but most governing bodies suffer to some degree from inequalities and mixed motives, which can easily lead to a power drift away from the governing body as a whole into the hands of individuals or small groups – a destructive and dangerous process. A governing body which values its unity will be watchful all the time for evidence of such tendencies, will search for the causes and try to deal with them. In general the keys to success are:

- regular sharing of aims (discussed above);
- good and rapid induction of new members;
- delegation of work on a basis which spreads the interest groups and strengths over the whole committee structure;
- work-sharing of all kinds; equal or equivalent involvement in the school's daily work;
- good working practices and rule-keeping;
- care for groups or individuals who for any reason are prevented from making a full contribution;
- willingness of all to learn;
- a commitment to open and democratic working.

These issues are examined in more detail below.

Effective induction

In general – and not only in the work of governing bodies – the induction of new colleagues into any club or voluntary activity is poor. At worst they are left to pick up the names, the roles, the in-language and in-jokes as they go along. No effort is made to find out what they think and what they can do, and they could end their period of service without ever having contributed and with colleagues having little knowledge of their attitudes or skills. This process needs planning, since it is a serious matter for a group with important responsibilities and a limited period of involvement if everybody doesn't get on board at once. As soon as a new governor is appointed or elected the chair should make contact, say something about the main current issues before governors, and find out a little about the new colleague. The head should invite new governors into school before the first meeting, make them welcome, give them a list of staff with responsibilities, a plan of the building, and a few basic papers eg the prospectus, the last annual report to parents, a calendar of school activities, evening meetings, big events, sporting fixtures etc. as appropriate. S/he should then suggest a further visit with a clear focus later on. The governor whom the new recruit is succeeding should donate a well-weeded file and any good advice, and one serving governor should be delegated to make contact, invite the new governor(s) for tea or coffee, offer to go to the first meeting with them and perhaps go through the agenda, lend them any material or books s/he has found helpful, and perhaps arrange to accompany them to a training session.

The meeting at which one or more new governors are present should start early with some refreshments and a chance to meet informally. The chair should ensure that new and old colleagues introduce themselves clearly and fully. In finding out what skills the new governor has, colleagues must be careful not to intimidate them by implying that they only mean word-processing or accounts, but that organising, listening, peacemaking, contacts, access to any kind of facilities, knowledge of the neighbourhood or involvement in any other community activity, are all valuable assets. Acronyms should always be explained and the background to difficult issues sketched. Early involvement in a committee, with assurance that they can just watch for a bit, is essential.

Making sure every governor contributes

It isn't only new and old who constitute A and B teams. There are many reasons why some governors never fully emerge, and colleagues must be ever-watchful for this and the reasons. Shyness and a feeling of not being well enough informed are the simplest. Every governor should try to make each under-contributing colleague feel both at ease and important. Never assume agreement just because someone is silent. If the issue is important, go round the table to make sure no-one is holding back. Language problems – including problems of understanding – should be sensitively treated, and jargon banned. A word is necessary here about parent and teacher governors who often have particular difficulties arising from their representative role. There may be someone who does not even accept that they have a representative role – the head, the chair, the LEA – and this must be dealt with. These governors are not delegates – who would have to vote on instructions – but being elected makes them representatives, with a duty to listen to and convey the concerns of their group to the governing body. They must also ensure that their constituents are well-informed on all activities of the governors apart from confidential items. Establishing this role may need the help and support of colleagues.

Teacher governors have additional problems in that they often feel inhibited from speaking freely and confidently for fear of upsetting the head, being unwittingly disloyal, or rocking the boat. After all they work there – don't forget that. But it is still important that they are able to make an independent contribution, far more important in the long run even to the head than any occasional embarrassment it may cause. Governors need the professional expertise confidently represented. All governors can help to protect and promote the contribution of colleagues.

One source of inequality is raising issues for the first time at meetings, either by tabling papers or by wrongly using 'Any Other Business'. Remember that every time an issue is sprung on people at short notice, it increases any natural inequalities, disadvantaging even more those who are new, those whose first language is not English, those who don't read so fast, and those who are unfamiliar with the jargon or the background so need more time to understand an issue.

Sharing the work

A sure sign of an A and B team is one all-powerful committee with a preponderance of dark suits making decisions on finance. Every governor manages money in private life. Those who might describe themselves as 'only a mum' have managed quite a lot of money. If these people are excluded (or exclude themselves) from strategic decisions, money will take on a life of its own in the school and become the master not the servant of children's learning. The role of experts is not to make a mystery of money but to make it easier for other to make decisions about it. All interest groups should be equally spread over all activities in delegating functions. Remember that individuals can only be excluded if they or their close relatives stand to gain personally from the outcome: teachers and to a lesser extent parents are often excluded quite unnecessarily from sensitive activities.

Every governing body should try to develop a 'culture' in which each member is expected to pull his or her weight. Firm expectations by the group are the best way to squeeze out passengers.

Learning and developing

A good team is concerned about the development of each member and the growth in the skill and knowledge accessible to the group. This should be part of the culture too. Information and sources of information should be shared, not kept as a source of private power. The group should expect each member to undertake training and it should be on the agenda.

No amount of learning and training, however, is a substitute for familiarity with the school at work. Without this governors cannot make wise decisions or be good ambassadors. Every governing body, as part of its expectation of members, should introduce and monitor a system for every governor to commit some regular time to visiting with a purpose. It could be a duty governor of the month who takes on any tasks or events for that month and also plans a visit to look at something specific (grand tours are a poor use of time). It could be an attachment to a subject or activity or, in a primary school, a class.

Effective meetings and rule-keeping

An effective meeting is one in which time is used well, with less important items kept within bounds to allow time for major ones. It is one which leads to clear decisions, leaving no doubt what action is to be taken, by whom, by when, and in consultation with whom. It should be clear how governors will be informed that their decision has been implemented. At an effective meeting there will have been restraint on rambling or irrelevant contributions, without hurting anyone. This is not easy. But it is important that nobody should leave the meeting feeling aggrieved at not having been given a chance to speak, and indeed that everyone should have contributed. Combining this with efficient despatch of business requires good chairing, bearing in mind that on a governing body a chair is a team leader and not a chief executive. A good chair will have a rough plan for a meeting so as to get through the really vital items, but will

negotiate this with colleagues before beginning, making sure that nobody's agreement is taken for granted. The rules by which governors work together are crucial. Details of the legal requirements applying to governors' business are given in the chapter on School Government. Please do not see these as dry bureaucracy. If you study them carefully you will see that they are designed to ensure (a) that the governing body holds on to its corporate responsibility, that delegation of power is limited to certain subjects and is undertaken consciously, thoughtfully and precisely; (b) that conversely power is not allowed to drift to individuals or small groups, and that vital decisions are made by a stated minimum proportion of members; (c) that in general all governors have an equal right to participate; (d) that in general governors' business is democratically and openly conducted, with confidentiality kept to a minimum and decided only by the governing body itself; and (e) that where any decision might lead to an appeal to governors at a later stage, involvement in the initial decision is restricted so as to leave enough governors 'uncontaminated' by knowledge or involvement in that decision to hear an appeal.

It is important firstly that all governors are familiar with these rules, since unequal knowledge leads to more serious inequalities. It allows individuals or groups to take advantage of the innocence of others. How often a governor will say 'I don't think that was the right way to proceed, but I don't know where it says.' Every governor should know 'where it says', and it is a good idea if governors can evolve some system of reminding themselves, while they are all together, of what the rules are.

Outside the governing body two rules of self-discipline are paramount. Firstly if something has been classified as confidential it will be because it affects the private life of an individual, and honouring this is vital. Neither should governors report even a non confidential decision in an unprofessional way: it is enough to say what was decided and what the main arguments were.

Relations with the head and staff

All the staff of a school must understand that the governors' role is here to stay, supported by all political parties and deeply rooted in history. They must understand too that it is legitimate that a service which is publicly financed and whose quality affects everybody should be subject to public oversight. Without this understanding relationships with governors are bound to be wary and suspicious, if not exactly hostile. More positively, it is important for staff, including the head, to realise that governors can make school decisions more robust and be powerful ambassadors for its policies and methods in the community. Even more important, governors at school, community or national level can be a powerful protection for those public service values which professionals hold dear and find it hard to promote on their own. As far as heads are concerned, it would transform relationships if they could see the effective development of a governing body as a professional challenge worthy of the most outstanding talent. Their professional pride would then be engaged, and that is a strong motivator.

No opportunity should be lost of 'demystifying' governors for the staff. Teachers and support staff should be regular visitors in turn to governors' meetings, getting to know governors and saying something about their work. Opportunities for social contact and for discussing school issues less formally than a meeting allows should be created. Teachers should be co-opted as appropriate onto committees and working parties. Governors should always take an interest in teachers' working conditions and welfare, and remember to praise any special initiatives or efforts in the curriculum, in school activities or in obtaining additional qualifications.

Territorial limits

Governors will be familiar from this handbook with their legal responsibilities. The degree to which they are accepted in their role will vary from school to school, and there is no doubt that in some schools heads have been slow to accept that role and it is quite difficult in these circumstances for governors to fulfil it. Patience and tact will be needed, but there must be progress. One of the most helpful ways of making progress is to plan the work and to look forward. Otherwise issues are often brought to governors either to approve retrospectively or when they are too far advanced to change. The way round this is to structure meetings to face the future, always asking the head in his/her report to sketch the issues coming up for consideration and the deadlines to meet. The agenda should always have space for a looking-forward item of some kind. Governors should avoid ever by-passing the head or springing things on him or her at a meeting. They must remember always to say the positive things and pass on the positive comments.

Governors and heads often say that they would welcome more specific advice about their respective roles. Often the law gives governing bodies a choice as to whether to carry out their functions themselves or delegate them. **The Education (School Government) (Terms of Reference) (Regulations) 2000** and the DfEE guidance, *Roles of Governing Bodies and Headteachers*, help clarify who does what and suggests that governing bodies should delegate as many functions as possible but should take into account factors such as the experience and wishes of the head; how much support is available to the head; the availability of good management information to enable the governing body to monitor effectively and any special skills or experience which members of the governing body can offer. The Regulations give the governing body power to give the head reasonable directions in relation to any function they delegate, and oblige the head to provide sufficient information for governors to feel confident that responsibilities taken on by the head have been properly carried out.

The Government has attempted to encapsulate the desirable relationship between governors and heads – going so far as to include the colloquial term "critical friend" in the regulations

The guidance speaks of governing bodies and headteachers working in partnership to develop key policies with heads as "lead professional"

responsible for implementing policies and leading the school towards its targets.

Governors and heads have often asked for more specific advice about their respective roles and the guidance, *Roles of Governing Bodies and Headteachers*, broadly sets out who does what and areas where governing bodies may choose whether or not to delegate responsibilities.

The head is responsible for:
* managing the space, time, and staff at the disposal of the school to maximum effectiveness – the way in which the building and facilities are used day by day, the timetable, the assignment of teachers to classes and duties and their general guidance and management; complying with health and safety directions.
* Ensuring an appropriate curriculum for the school, that the National Curriculum is implemented, and a policy for the secular curriculum is drawn up and reviewed;
* creating an ordered atmosphere in which learning can take place, which means ensuring there are measures in place to deal with day-by-day breaches of the behaviour policy – including bullying.
* the quality of teachers' professional work and their professional development;
* informing and guiding governors on professional issues, since s/he is their chief professional adviser.

Governors are responsible for:
* promoting high standards of educational achievement (**S38 School Standards and Framework Act (SSFA)**) including target setting for pupils at the end of each key stage;
* approving the budget plan and broad management of the way in which the money is spent;
* staffing complements, gradings and pay; for performance management policy and teacher appraisal policy; staff selection and discipline.
* reviewing head's performance;
* agreeing, amending or rejecting the head's curriculum policy and monitoring its implementation; ensuring the school provides a broad and balanced curriculum and implements the National Curriculum requirements;
* setting up a complaints procedure under S39 SSFA (*see page 74*);
* ensuring religious education and worship is provided and a sex education policy drawn up;
* ensuring that special needs are identified and met;
* ensuring that parents receive all the information they are entitled to, and are able to exercise all their rights;
* (VA and foundations schools) admissions policy and admission arrangements;
* deciding and consulting with parents on a school behaviour policy;
* consulting parents on the home-school agreement and inviting them to sign it;
* the care and safety of the building and for its use outside school hours; asset management plans;
* a general catch-all responsibility for the conduct of the school and, more specifically, drawing up and reviewing a statement on behaviour after consultation with parents and the head;
* reviewing the use of exclusion in the school as well as deciding whether to confirm permanent

exclusions and some fixed period exclusions;
- ensuring pupils take advantage of dental and medical care available;
- ensuring free meals and, where requested, paid meals are provided where LEAs delegate the resources.

Governors' involvement is at a strategic level, not in the management of the school day-by-day. But recent proposals to confine governing bodies to a substantially back seat role have met hostility from many quarters – not only governors. While the need to simplify governors' work was not disputed, teachers, parents and governors themselves could foresee a danger of making it less real and less accountable. Also, incidentally less interesting - unless you happen to be addicted to writing mission-statements.

Problems may arise over territorial boundaries. But there has to be trust that these boundaries will be approached with care and rationally discussed. Often the grey areas relate to actions which in one sense are internal management but which have such broad repercussions in the community or among parents that a wise head would involve governors and a wise governing body would be ready to warn or advise. The best examples are those which relate to changes in age groupings (eg vertical grouping) or ability groups (eg mixed ability/setting), or in methods of teaching reading, or in traditional subject boundaries (eg separate to combined science). Parents often find these very disturbing and governors should for that reason be wary about them, even though they could be held to be management of staff, space and learning day-by-day. With goodwill most of these controversial issues can be steered away from the rocks. A good principle for heads is: when in doubt, at least consult. A good principle for governors: think hard before you act, but remember that you are in serious trouble if parents and community lose faith in your ability to watch their interests.

Further information

Heads in Partnership: working with your governors for a successful school, 2001, by Joan Sallis, Pearson Education, £16.
Managing Better with Governors: a practical guide to working together for school success, 1999, by Joan Sallis, Financial Times Management, 128 Long Acre, London WC2E 9AN, £69.
School Governors: a Plain Guide, 1999, by Joan Sallis, ACE, 1C Aberdeen Studios, 22, Highbury Grove, London N5 2DQ, £6.
Committees and Working Parties: guidance for governing bodies of schools, 1998, London Diocesan Board for Schools, 36 Causton Street, London SW1P 4AU.
Effective Governance: the evidence from Ofsted by Michael Creese, 1998, 22 Ashmere Grove, Ipswich IP4 2RE.
LEAs and Schools: a social partnership by John Bangs, 1998, The Education Network, 1-5 Bath Street, London EC1V 9QQ.
A Manual for Governing Bodies and their Clerks, 1999, ISCG, Avondale Park School, Sirdar Road, London W11

Index

Columns are identified as a and b after a page number.

Abbreviations used are-:

DfEE: Department of Education and Employment
GB: governing body
LEA: local education authority
SEN: special educational needs

Useful organisations

Department for Education and
Employment (DfEE)
Sanctuary Buildings
Great Smith Street
London SW1P 3BT
0870 000 2288
www.dfee.gov.uk
info@dfee.gov.uk

DfEE Publications Centre
PO Box 5050
Sherwood Park
Annesley
Nottinghamshire NG15 0DG
0845 602 2260
dfee@prolog.uk.com

Stationery Office Publications Centre
PO Box 29
St. Crispin's House
Duke Street
Norwich NR3 1GN
0870 600 5522
www.the-stationery-office.co.uk
esupport@theso.co.uk

National Assembly for Wales Training
and Education Department
Cathays Park
Cardiff CF1 3NQ
029 2082 5111
www.wales.gov.uk
education.training@wales.gsi.gov.uk

Ofsted – Office for Standards in
Education
Alexandra House
33 Kingsway
London
WC2B 6SE
020 7421 6800
Publications: 07002 637833
www.ofsted.gov.uk

Estyn - Her Majesty's Inspectorate for
Education & Training in Wales
Anchor Port
Keen Road
Cardiff CF24 5JW
029 2044 6446

Audit Commission
1 Vincent Square
London SW1P 2PN
020 7828 1212
www.audit-commission.gov.uk

Audit Commission Publications
Bookpoint Ltd
39 Milton Park
Abingdon
Oxon OX14 4TD
0800 502030

Social Exclusion Unit
Cabinet Office
35 Great Smith Street
London SW1P 3BQ
020 7276 2056
www.cabinet-office.gov.uk

Qualifications and Curriculum Authority
83 Piccadilly
London W1J 8QA
020 7509 5555
www.qca.org.uk

QCA Publications
PO Box 99
Sudbury
Suffolk CO10 6SN
01787 884444
QCA@Prologistics.co.uk

Awdurdod Cymwysterau, Cwricwlwm ac
Asesu Cymru/the Qualifications,
Curriculum and Assessment Authority
for Wales (ACCAC)
Castle Buildings
Womanby Street
Cardiff CF10 1SX
029 2034 3612
www.accac.org.uk
info@accac.org.uk

Local Government Association (LGA)
Local Government House
Smith Square
London SW1P 3HZ
020 7664 3000
www.lga.gov.uk
info@lga.gov.uk

Church of England Board of Education
Church House
Great Smith Street
London SW1P 3NZ
020 7898 1518

Jewish Education Bureau
8 Westcombe Avenue
Leeds LS8 2BS
0870 800 8532
jewishedbureau@easicom.com

Catholic Education Service
39 Eccleston Square
London SW1V 1BX
020 7828 7604
www.cesew.org.uk
general@cesew.org.uk

Muslim Education Trust
130 Stroud Green Road
London N4 3RZ
020 7272 8502

National Governors Council
Glebe House
Church Street
Crediton
Devon EX17 2AF
01363 774377
www.ngc.org.uk
ngc@ngc.org.uk

National Association of Governors and
Managers (NAGM)
Suite 1
4th Floor
Western House
Smallbrook Queensway
Birmingham B5 4HQ
0121 643 5787
www.nagm.org.uk
governorhq@hotmail.com

Information for School and College
Governors (ISCG)
Avondale School
Sirdar Road
London W11 4EE
020 7229 0200
www.governors.fsnet.co.uk
iscg@governors.fsnet.co.uk

Campaign for State Education (CASE)
158 Durham Road
London SW20 0DG
020 8944 8206
www.casenet.org.uk
tulloch-case@mcr1.poptel.org.uk

Advisory Centre for Education
1C Aberdeen Studios
22 Highbury Grove
London N5 2DQ
020 7354 8318 (business)
0808 8005793 (advice)
020 7704 9822 (exclusion info line)
www.ace-ed.org.uk
ace-ed@easynet.co.uk

How well is your school performing?

How can you do better?

'an endorsement of the school's hard work and commitment to raising standards for all the children'
Monica Haley, St John the Baptist Catholic Primary School

'an extremely good exercise in auditing the school's systems and achievements in basic skills'
Geoffrey Barham, St. Andrews and St. Marks C of E Junior School

'a very good management tool, it creates awareness of our strengths and weaknesses'
Mike Squire St. Philips C of E Primary School

'delivering our agenda of school improvement in a clear, focussed and celebratory way'
Mike Loncaster, Aldbrough Primary School

The Secondary Quality Mark: in a league of its own

The Basic Skills Agency

For more information on the Quality Mark for Secondary Schools contact:

Jane Martin at the Basic Skills Agency, Commonwealth House, 1-19 New Oxford Street, London WC1A 1NU.
Tel: 020 7405 4017. Fax: 020 7440 6626.
E-mail: janem@basic-skills.co.uk.

For up-to-date information about educational developments affecting school governors, subscribe to *Governors' Agenda*.

The aim of Governors' Agenda is to support school governors and those who train and work with them by providing information, comment and training ideas. The magazine is published five times a year. A single subscription costs £30.00. There are special rates for multiple copies.

Governors' Agenda is produced by CEDC, the national centre for community-based learning, which also offers the following services for those who work in school governance:

- Governors' Agenda Briefings for governor trainers and those who run governor support services
- Governors' Agenda Guides – summaries of information on major current issues affecting governors.

Governors' Agenda Briefings

These take place six times a year, with each Briefing being held both in London and in Coventry. Topics covered at recent Briefings include the Government's Consultation document on the role of governing bodies, the DfEE's national governor training strategy, and performance management. For information about costs and about the dates of forthcoming Briefings, please contact CEDC.

Governors' Agenda Guides

These Guides are produced in order to provide succinct information for governors on educational or organisational changes which will affect their work. Subscribing LEAs receive the Guides both as hard copy and on disk. They can then copy and distribute the Guide freely within their LEA. Topics covered in recent Guides include performance management, inspection and exclusions. The cost of this service depends on the size of your LEA and on whether you are a *Governors' Agenda* susbscriber. Details of the scale of charges are available from CEDC.

To subscribe to *Governors' Agenda*, or for further information about any of CEDC's services for governors, please photocopy and complete the form below.

Governors' Agenda

Name: _____ Job title: _____

Address: _____

☐ I wish to subscribe to Governors' Agenda. I enclose a cheque for £30, made out to CEDC.

Please send me information about:

☐ reduced rates for multiple copies of *Governors' Agenda*

☐ booking places at Governors' Agenda Briefings

☐ subscribing to Governors' Agenda Guides.

CEDC
Widening opportunities for learning

Registered Charity No 512702

Please return this form to Carolyn Sugden at CEDC, Unit C1, Grovelands Court, Grovelands Estate, Longford Road, Exhall, Coventry CV7 9NE.

Tel: 024 7658 8440 Fax: 024 7658 8441
E-mail: info@cedc.org.uk Website: www.cedc.org.uk

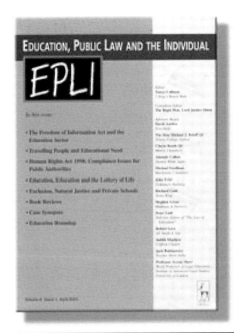

EDUCATION, PUBLIC LAW AND THE INDIVIDUAL

The one-stop, easy-to-read journal for the latest developments in education law

EDITOR
TANYA CALLMAN
Barrister
2 King's Bench Walk
Temple
London

E-mail:
Tanya@tcallman.freeserve.co.uk

CONSULTANT EDITOR
The Right Hon. Sir Philip Otton

EPLI provides a forum for debate on key issues facing those in education law and practice. Contemporary and easy to read, it is aimed at the busy professional wishing to absorb a large amount of information in a short time.

The coverage includes all levels of education. Discussion focuses on crucial areas where law meets education:
special educational needs, access to education, negligence actions, judicial review, further and higher education, school admissions/exclusions and religious education to name but a few.

EPLI includes

✓informed analysis in the form of short articles written by legal experts, teachers and other professionals involved in education
✓an Education Roundup section
✓news about legal developments in the form of case notes
✓literature update and book reviews

Contributors have included

Lord Nolan,
The Right Hon. Sir Philip Otton
Sir Ron Dearing

SOME OF THE TOPICS COVERED IN EPLI:

The Freedom of Information Act and the Education Sector

The Human Rights Act and education law: a game of two halves?

Travelling People and Educational Need

The Ofsted System inspected

Challenges facing independent schools in the millennium

Exclusions, truancy and accountability in education

Pupil mobility: policies on the move?

The Local Government Ombudsman explains his role in educational cases

Sport and the law in schools

Education Negligence Claims under the spotlight

Safe children, safe staff: physical interventions with children who have complex and challenging behaviours

Resources, rights and special educational needs

EPLI is read by

✓School teachers
✓School Governors
✓Lawyers
✓Special Needs Advisors
✓Voluntary Organisations
✓Academics
✓Local Authority Officers

ADVISORY CENTRE FOR EDUCATION

Keep up with ACE's work by subscribing to ACE Bulletin.

Each bi-monthly issue contains news and features on important topical issues of interest to parents, governors and education professionals.

Stay abreast of the law on education and the current debates on subjects as wide-ranging as drugs in schools to training for governors.

ACE's reputation for explaining complex legislation in clear, jargon-free language is evident in the Bulletin's regular features:

• Regular information sheets inside every issue concentrate on guiding parents and governors through subjects such as special needs, discipline and admissions
• Governor's Forum - a regular column from Joan Sallis, the well-known authority on parental involvement in schools
• Focus - facts and opinions on topical issues
• Digest - a comprehensive current awareness section giving information on a wide range of books, videos and other materials on educational issues.
• Case histories - compiled from calls taken on ACE advice lines.

For up-to-date subscription costs, write to;
Advisory Centre for Education (ACE) Ltd.
1c Aberdeen Studios, 22 Highbury Grove,
London N5 2DQ
Phone: 0207-354 8318 Fax 0207-354 9069
e-mail ace-ed@easynet.co.uk